Mrs. Troyer

ILLINOIS
OUR HOME

Gibbs Smith, Publisher
Salt Lake City

Much of the text in this book was adapted from *The Illinois Adventure* by Bill Stepien, Charnelle Lewis, and John Lewis.

CONTRIBUTING AUTHORS

Beverly Allen Taylor has been a classroom teacher for 20 years and currently works as a Differentiation Support Teacher to plan curriculum for varied student needs and interests. She has written curriculum for district social studies, math, science, and language arts for grades K-4. She presents lectures, workshops, and teacher training classes at local and state conferences. She has been awarded grants for a Van Gough Garden, Prairie Garden, and a World Environment Learning Laboratory that includes outdoor gardens in the shape of each continent. Mrs. Taylor received B.A. degrees in Child Development from Brigham Young University and in Elementary Education from Weber State University in Utah, and a M.S. in Instruction from Northeastern Illinois University. She is a verified instructor of gifted students.

Susan A. Myers has worked for 20 years as an author and editor of state history textbooks. She works with historians, reading specialists, authors, editors, and artists to develop engaging history textbooks for elementary and secondary students. She has produced 16 state history textbooks for schools across the country, including two for Illinois. Ms. Myers received a B.S. degree in Elementary Education and Art from Brigham Young University, Utah.

Gibbs Smith, Publisher
P.O. Box 667
Layton, UT 84041
800-748-5439
www.gibbs-smith.com/textbooks

Managing Editor: Susan A. Myers
Photo Editor: Janis J. Hansen
Cover: Alan Connell
Book Design: Alan Connell and John Vehar
Maps and Graphs: Alan Connell and John Vehar

Cover:
(top) James P. Rowan
(bottom) Panoramic Stock Images/National Geographic Image Collection

Printed and bound in China
ISBN 978-1-4236-0089-3

12 11 10 09 08 07   10 9 8 7 6 5 4 3 2 1

REVIEWERS

Kathie Bossier is the Director of Elementary and Middle School Education in Wheaton Warrenville School District 200. Prior to that she was a reading specialist for nine years in District 200. She has also taught at the middle school level and in second grade. She received both her B.S. in Elementary Education and her Masters in Curriculum and Instruction with an emphasis in Reading from Northern Illinois University.

David A. Joens is director of the Illinois State Archives. A lifelong resident of Illinois currently living in Springfield, Joens has a B.A. in History and Political Science from Northern Illinois University and Master's degrees in both History and Political Science from the University of Illinois at Springfield. He is currently a doctoral candidate in Illinois History at Southern Illinois University-Carbondale. Joens is the author of two books on Illinois history and government. He is a board member of the Illinois State Historical Society, the Abraham Lincoln Association, the Papers of Abraham Lincoln, the Illinois State Genealogical Society, and the Chicago Metro History in Education Center.

Mark W. Sorensen is vice-president of the Illinois Historical Society and recently retired after 24 years as assistant director of the Illinois State Archives in Springfield. He is an Adjunct Professor of History at Millikin University. He taught history classes at Richland Community College and social science for thirteen years in the Decatur public schools. Mr. Sorensen received a B.S. in Education from Eastern Illinois University, an M.A. in History from the University of Illinois Springfield, and an M.S. in Library and Information Science from the University of Illinois Champaign/Urbana. He has maintained the Illinois History Resource Website for ten years and is currently preparing to write a book about the Illinois State Capitol.

Evagelia Tiotis has been teaching for 10 years and is currently a third-grade teacher at Romona School in Wilmette, Illinois. She has written many curriculum materials that include hands-on activities, research-based activities, music, poetry, and math. Of special interest is a website she created of social studies objectives that students can access for information and help with homework. Ms. Tiotis has a B.A. in Elementary Education with a minor in History from the University of Illinois at Chicago and a M.A. in Special Education from Northeastern Illinois University.

Kevan H. Truman is in his 19th year of teaching third and fourth grade, including six years as a verified instructor of gifted students in Minnesota and Illinois. He is a winner of the coveted 2006 Golden Apple Award. Mr. Truman earned a B.A. degree in Education from Wittenberg University in Springfield, Ohio, and then a Juris Doctorate from the Hamline University School of Law in St. Paul, Minnesota. He now lives in Chicago.

Contents

Maps

Portraits

Illinois State Symbols

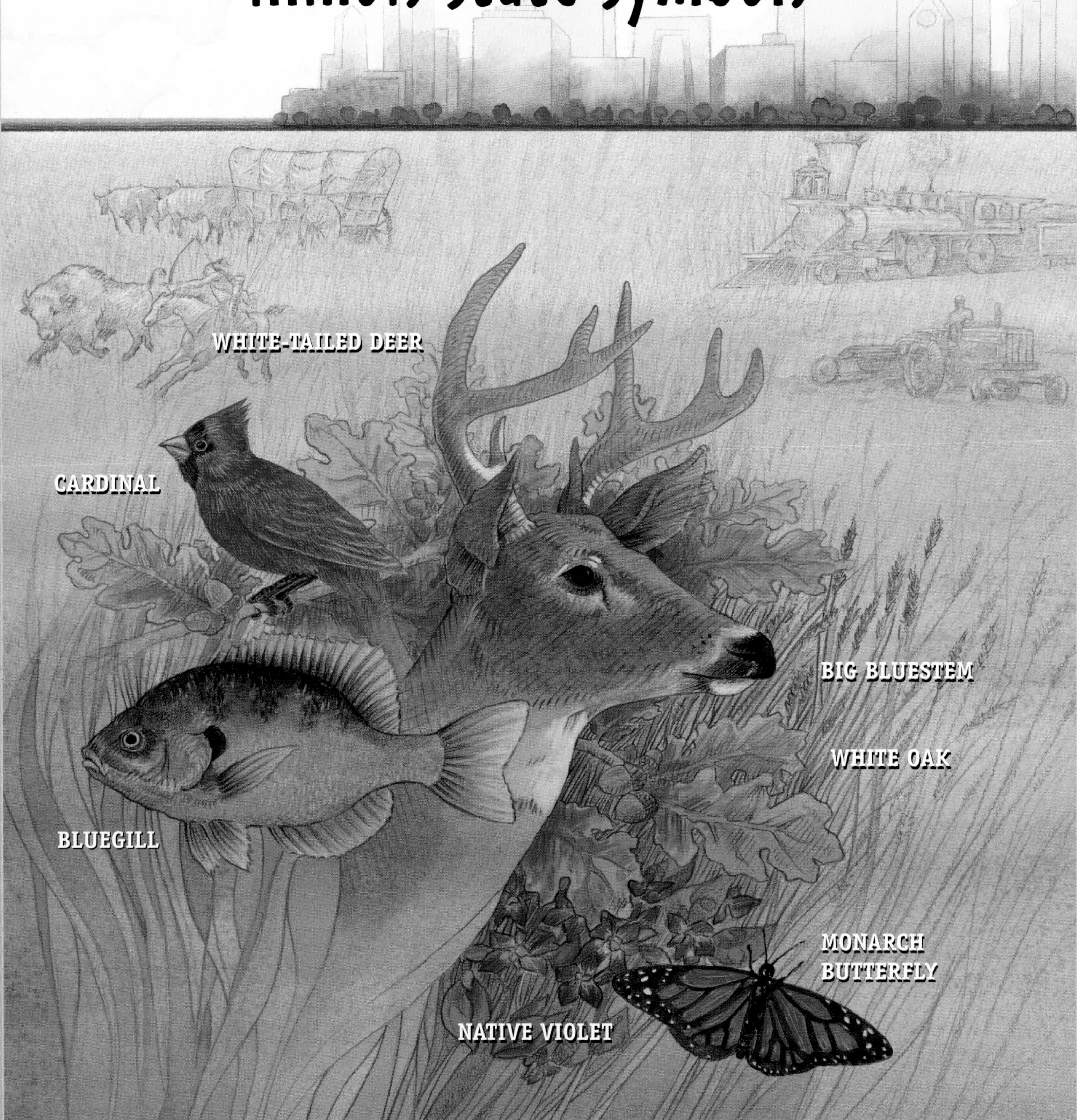

WHITE-TAILED DEER

CARDINAL

BIG BLUESTEM

WHITE OAK

BLUEGILL

MONARCH
BUTTERFLY

NATIVE VIOLET

The Illinois State Flag

The design for our state flag was decided in a contest. The winner was from Rockford. The flag was approved in 1915. Then, in 1969, the word Illinois was added to the flag. Today the state flag flies at the top of the State Capitol Building in Springfield.

The Illinois State Seal

Illinois' state seal has changed several times. The first seal was designed when Illinois became a state. Then the eagle and banner were added. On the banner was our state motto: "State Sovereignty, National Union." This means the state of Illinois has some of its own powers, but is also part of a larger country or union. After the Civil War, the banner was changed so the words "National Union" stood out more.

"The only thing new in the world is the history you don't know."
— Harry S Truman

"What is the use of a book," thought Alice, "without pictures or conversations?"
— Alice's Adventures in Wonderland

History Close to Home

Chapter 1

Learning about history is like going on a journey to the past. You can find new friends who lived long before you were born. You can gain courage by seeing how they did what was right even if they were shy or afraid. You can learn that people everywhere have had hard times and good times. What can you tell about any of the events in history these children are acting out?

WORDS TO UNDERSTAND

century
chronological order
decade
glossary
index
score
table of contents

Starting Your Adventure

Welcome to *Illinois, Our Home.* You live in a state with an amazing past. In this book you will learn that Illinois is part of our country and our world. You will learn how people in Illinois lived many years ago and how they live today. This book has some special parts that will help you learn about Illinois. Watch for them as you read.

Every chapter starts with a big picture. Pretend you can "step into" the picture. What do you see? What do you hear? What do you feel?

Timelines

At the first of each chapter you will see two timelines:

- **Anchor It!** When did the Pilgrims come to America? When did Abraham Lincoln live? These are events you already know about. They are "anchors" in history. When you learn about new events, try to anchor them to what you already know. A small colored bar near the Anchor It! timeline will help you make the connection.
- **Timeline of Events:** This timeline across the bottom of the opening pages shows exactly when events in the chapter happened.

Lessons

Each chapter is divided into lessons. Each lesson has some important lists.

- Can you read the names of the People to Know? They are people you will read about in the chapter.
- With your class, find the Places to Locate on a map. Are any of them near your city or town?
- Read the Words to Understand out loud with your class. Talk together about what the words mean. You can find each word in the Glossary in the back of the book.
- Use the lists before you read the chapter.

What Do You Think?

Many questions have no right or wrong answer. In this book, "What do you think?" questions help you think about what you would have done if you had been in the story.

Making Connections

Making a personal connection while you are reading this book will help you understand what you are reading. You probably know what it is like to have a mother or father read a story before you go to bed. By making that connection, you can better understand what it was like for a pioneer boy to listen to his father tell a story by candlelight. As you read in this book about early explorers, for example, the words or pictures might remind you of another book. Connecting both books will help you understand this book better. History means more to us when we connect it to our lives today.

Portraits

Our state's history was made by people who had both hard times and good times. They worked and made mistakes. They helped others. In this book, you will find short biographies called portraits. They tell a little bit about a person's life.

Memory Master

At the end of each lesson you will find a few questions about what you have read. Test your memory and review what you learned. Use the facts to solve a problem or analyze what happened.

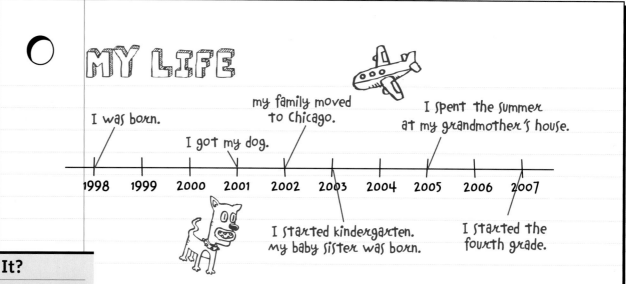

MY LIFE

I was born.

I got my dog.

my family moved to Chicago.

I spent the summer at my grandmother's house.

| 1998 | 1999 | 2000 | 2001 | 2002 | 2003 | 2004 | 2005 | 2006 | 2007 |

I started kindergarten. my baby sister was born.

I started the fourth grade.

What Century Is It?

Century	Years
18th	1700s
19th	1800s
20th	1900s
21st	2000s

Hint: To know the century, go up one number from the year.

For example,
1600s = 17th century.

Understand Dates and Timelines

Chronological Order

A timeline helps us see the order in which important events happened. This is called ***chronological order.*** The timeline above shows what happened first, next, and so on.

Events

What is an event? It is something that happens on an exact date in an exact place. The day you were born was a very important event. What day and year was it? Your birthday party is an event. Liking chocolate cake is not an event. Neither is growing older. Can you tell the difference?

Time Periods

Look at the timeline above. What year does it start? What year does it end? Timelines are divided into equal parts that stand for a certain number of years. Each part can represent 1 year, 10 years, or even 100 years or more. How many years does each part on the timeline stand for?

There are words, almost like shortcuts, that describe periods of time.

A **decade** is 10 years.

A **score** is 20 years.

A **century** is 100 years.

Activities

In this book, you will see many "Activities." They are not like going outside to play soccer or ride a bicycle. They are ways to learn about history. They are fun to do alone or with a friend. Sometimes you will pretend you lived long ago. Sometimes you will draw a picture, write a poem or a story, or make a model with twigs, dirt, and rocks. You will work, read, research, and report in different ways.

Activity

Use a Table of Contents, Glossary, and Index

There are other tools to help you on your journey through this book. At the beginning of the book there is a **Table of Contents.** It tells you what pages the chapters start on. It also tells you where the maps are. Go to the Table of Contents and read the title of each chapter.

At the end of the book, there is a Glossary and an Index. The **Glossary** explains the meaning of all the "Words to Understand" in the lesson. The words are listed in alphabetical order just like in a dictionary.

The **Index** lists the page numbers where you'll find important subjects, people, and places. Can you find the Glossary and Index pages?

1. Now look through this book and find two words under any "Words to Understand" list at the beginning of any lesson. Find them in the lesson. They will be highlighted in yellow. Write the two words on a piece of paper.

2. Now turn to the Glossary near the end of the book and find the same two words. What do they mean? Write down the meanings from the Glossary.

3. Turn to the Index near the end of the book. Find the people below and write down at least one of the pages after each name. Then turn to that page and find the information about that person. Why was he or she famous? Hint: names of people are listed with the last name first, like this:

Addams, Jane   **Deere, John**   **Lincoln, Abraham**

① MEMORY MASTER

1. How can timelines help you learn about the past?
2. Do questions always have right and wrong answers? Explain.
3. In this book, another word for a biography is a _____.
4. How can the Table of Contents help you use a book?
5. What can you learn from the Glossary and Index?

WORDS TO UNDERSTAND

artifact
document
expository
historian
narrative
oral history
primary source
reference books
secondary source

What Is History?

Look at a handful of coins. Which coin has the earliest date? Do you have a coin from the 1950s? The 1970s? Those coins were first carried by someone many years ago. Was she a student too? What was his school like? Have you heard your grandparents talk about life when they were young? All of these things have to do with the past.

History is the story of the past. It is the story of people and events. It is the story of what people thought, how they lived, and the choices they made.

For example, for many years women, Native Americans, and African Americans were not allowed to vote. Only some of the children went to school. Other children were not allowed in schools.

Then people made choices to change things because they believed there was a better way. Finally, people voted for leaders who changed the laws. Now almost all adults can vote. All children can go to school.

What Do You Think ?

What if leaders had made different choices? How would our lives be different?

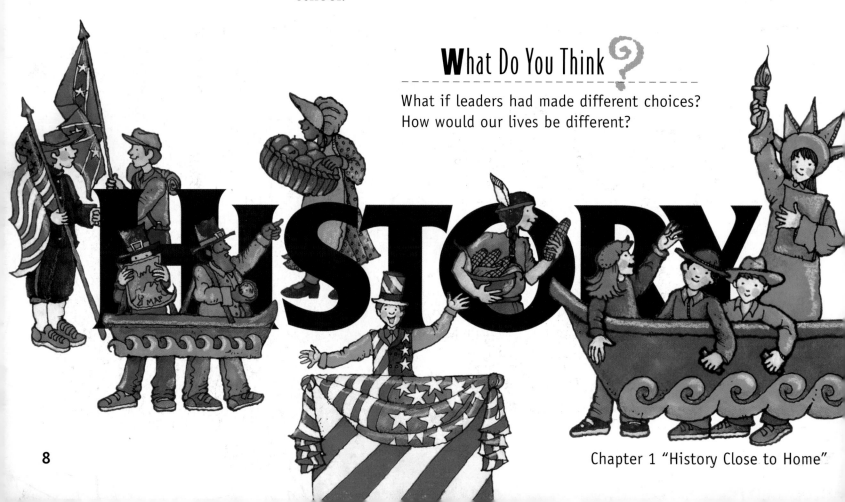

Learning from the Past

History was not always peaceful. Sometimes people worked well together to build homes and roads and make laws. Other times people fought over land, religion, and who should do the work. People often did not treat each other very well.

We can see what good things people did. We can also look back and see what mistakes people made. We can see how men and women were brave, honest, and worked very hard. We can see how they showed courage. By studying history, we begin to understand who we are.

Think Like a Historian!

People who study history are called *historians.* In many ways, historians are like detectives. A detective tries to figure out who committed a crime. A historian tries to figure out what happened in the past. You can be a history detective by asking questions such as:

- **What** happened?
- **Where** did it happen?
- **When** did it happen?
- **Who** took part in it?
- **Why** did it happen?
- **How** did it change things?

A historian uses clues to learn about the past.

What Do You Think?

- How can learning about the past help us today?
- What choices will you make today that might affect the future?

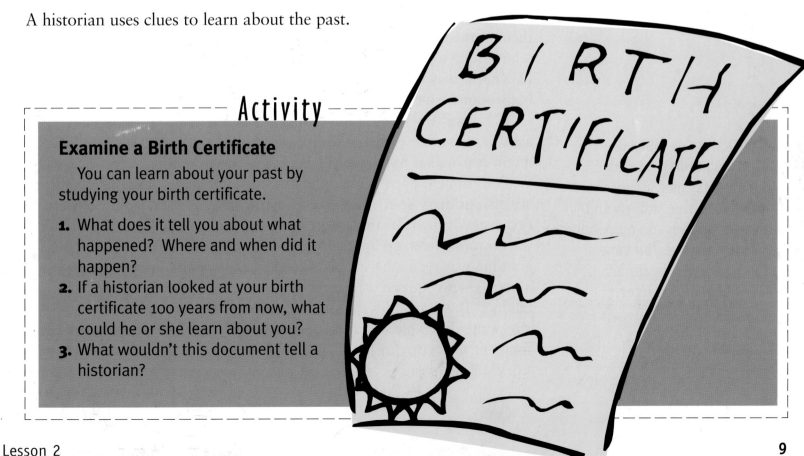

Activity

Examine a Birth Certificate

You can learn about your past by studying your birth certificate.

1. What does it tell you about what happened? Where and when did it happen?
2. If a historian looked at your birth certificate 100 years from now, what could he or she learn about you?
3. What wouldn't this document tell a historian?

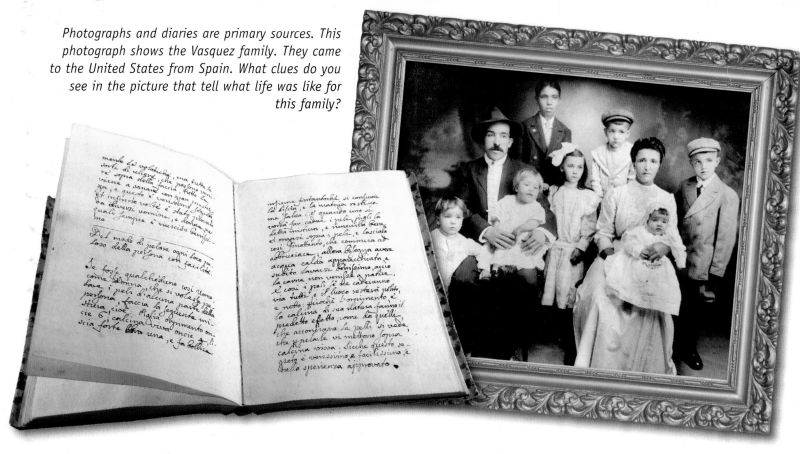

Photographs and diaries are primary sources. This photograph shows the Vasquez family. They came to the United States from Spain. What clues do you see in the picture that tell what life was like for this family?

Primary Sources

Historians use many kinds of clues to learn about the past. Some of the clues are *primary sources.* They were made by people who were there at the time. Pretend that your great–great–grandmother lived on a farm long ago. She wrote in a diary every day. Her diary would tell us what it was like to live in a time with no electricity and no indoor bathrooms. Her diary would be a primary source.

A Native American stone tool is an *artifact.* It was made long ago. It is another primary source. By looking at the stone tool, you might learn what materials the people found in nature.

Government papers and official forms are *documents.* Documents are also primary sources. A birth certificate is a document. So is the first copy of the Constitution.

Oral histories are other forms of primary sources. Suppose your grandpa was remembering a time when he was a young soldier in the army. Then you used a tape recorder to record his voice as he was talking. If you could write down the words fast enough, you could also write down his words as he said them. Oral history is history that someone tells you out loud. We can learn a lot by listening to people's stories of the past.

Diaries or journals, photographs, paintings, documents, maps, speeches, oral histories, songs, and artifacts were made by people who lived at the time. These items are all primary sources.

Chapter 1 "History Close to Home"

Activity

Artifacts Are Primary Sources

1. Do these items tell us anything about people of the past?

2. Choose one artifact. What was it used for? How does it compare to something similar today?

3. Look around your room. What items might be thought of as artifacts 200 years from now? Will people then know how the items were used?

Secondary Sources

A *secondary source* is something written, said, or made by someone who was NOT involved in the event at all. A historian uses information from an earlier time or place. He or she researches in books. The historian talks to people who know a lot about the subject. Then the historian, who was not even there at the time, writes a book or paints a picture about what happened.

For example, a book written today about steamboats in early Illinois is a secondary source. The author of the book gathers stories and pictures and puts them together in the book. But the author was not there to watch steamboats go up and down the river.

Stories are often secondary sources. So are textbooks. What can you learn from a secondary source?

Can You Tell the Difference?

Compare the two images below. Can you tell why the photograph of Lincoln is a primary source and the statue is a secondary source?

*This is a photo of Abraham Lincoln. It is a **primary source**.*

*This statue was made long after Lincoln died. An artist created it to honor Lincoln. The artist used pictures and paintings of Lincoln to make it look like him. It is a **secondary source**.*

Use Many Sources to Learn About the Past

It is important to look at many primary and secondary sources to learn what really happened.

Amber loves to read. She went to the library and checked out an exciting story of a pioneer boy who moved to Illinois. Then she visited a museum and saw an old covered wagon and a pioneer boy's faded shirt and straw hat.

Later, Amber's teacher showed her an old map of wagon roads. Then Amber's class read a diary of a red-haired 11-year-old boy who helped drive the oxen that pulled his family's wagon. The boy's father had drowned crossing a raging river.

Can you see how using many different sources helped Amber learn about pioneer children? What other primary and secondary sources could Amber have used?

Activity

Use Reference Materials

Before we study our state's history, it is good to know some basic facts. Where can you find them? You can look up facts in **reference books.** They have many kinds of useful information. You might use an atlas, encyclopedia, almanac, or books in the library. You can use a newspaper or magazine. You can also find information on the Internet.

- An **atlas** is a book of maps.

- An **encyclopedia** has information on many different topics. They are listed in alphabetical order so you can find facts quickly.

- An **almanac** is like a record book. It has all kinds of information, such as how many people live in a country, how much rain a city gets, or who the fifth president of our country was.

On a piece of paper, write your answers to the questions below. Choose which kind of reference book you would use to find the information.

1. If you wanted to learn about pioneers, you could look in a(n) _____.
2. If you looked under "S" in a(n) _____, you would find topics like snakes, stars, and John Smith.
3. If you wanted to find the countries next to Mexico, you would look in a(n) _____.
4. To find out how many days of rain people in Illinois get, you could look in a(n) _____.
5. What kind of reference materials would you use to learn how far it is from your town to Peoria? _____.

Fact or Opinion?

In history there are facts and there are opinions. A historian tries to learn the difference. What do these words mean?

A **fact** is something you can prove by studying primary sources. Here are some facts about Illinois:

- American Indians lived in today's Illinois before white settlers came.
- Pioneer children went to one-room schools.

An **opinion** is what someone believes but cannot prove. Here are opinions about Illinois:

- Indian boys wanted to learn how to hunt like their fathers did.
- Life was harder for pioneer children than for children today.
- Illinois is the best place to live.

Point of View

A point of view is how a person thinks about what happens. This affects their opinion of things. To understand this better, pretend that you and your friend go to the zoo. You really like silly little monkeys, and you think they are very fun to watch. But, your friend thinks monkeys are dumb. He wants to spend a long time looking at the grey elephants with large floppy ears. Who is right? Neither you nor your friend is right or wrong. It depends on your point of view. You each have a different opinion.

As you read about events in this book, try to think about them from the point of view of different people. For example, a long time ago, settlers built small log homes and started growing tall corn on land they got from the U.S. government. However, Indians did not want the settlers there. The land was their hunting ground. Each group had a different point of view about what was right.

The way you feel about animals at the zoo is your opinion, or point of view. What animals do you like the best? Do you think it is fair to wild animals to keep them in cages in a zoo?

What Do You Think ?

- How can different points of view help you better understand why people did what they did?
- Why is it important to consider another person's point of view?

What kind of books do you find in a library or media center? Are they fiction or non-fiction?

If you want to find a book about Illinois in a library, look for a book with the call number 977.3. Remember that the call number is always written on the spine of the book. Books are placed on the shelves in order of their call numbers.

Fiction and Non-Fiction

You can learn much about history by reading stories. Some stories are *narrative,* or fiction. The people and events may be partly true, but the author made up parts of the story. However, you can still learn a lot if the author did research for the book. You might learn about what type of clothes people wore and how they worked and played.

Other books are *expository* text, or non-fiction. Authors did a lot of research, studied primary sources, and tried to explain what really happened. Reference books are a type of non-fiction book.

Choose some books in your classroom and decide which are fiction and which are non-fiction. Can you tell if the author had a certain point of view? Was the author giving opinions or facts, or both? Was the writing expository or narrative?

2 MEMORY MASTER

1. What is history?
2. Give an example of a primary source and a secondary source.
3. What is the difference between a fact and an opinion?
4. Why is it important to consider point of view?

Chapter 1 Review

Activity

Primary Sources About You

On what day were you born? What has happened in your life so far? At home, find some primary sources that tell about you, and bring them to class. You could bring a baby picture, one of your favorite toys, or an award or trophy. Maybe you could bring a copy of your birth certificate or one of your report cards.

What do these primary sources tell about you?

Activity

Visit Historic Sites

Another great way to learn about history is to visit places where history happened. Some of these places might be right in your town or city. Others might be farther away.

An old home or fort, an ancient Indian village, and a pioneer town are historical sites. They have guides to tell you about what happened there long ago.   Visit a historical site and learn about history!

As you visit a site, ask these questions:

- What happened here?
- Who lived here, and when?

Write a story and draw a picture about what you learned at the site.

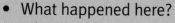

Have you ever visited these sites in Springfield? They help visitors learn about Abraham Lincoln.

"There seemed to be no edge to the land. The very weight of the sky made Addie duck her head a little. She felt so frightened and small! She turned around and around, but every way she looked the view was the same rolling prairie stretching for miles and miles."

— from Laurie Lawlor's
Addie Across the Prairie

A Place Called Illinois

Chapter 2

I am the Heartland,
Great and wide.
I sing of hope.
I sing of pride.

I am the Heartland,
On this soil
Live those who through the
seasons toil.

Welcome to America's
Heartland—a place where the
golden wheat waves in the
breeze, where great rivers
flow, and cornfields stretch
across the plains in glorious
patchwork quilts of greens
and yellows and browns.
Cattle graze in lush green
pastures, horses and sheep
fill the barns, and a newborn
calf stands damp and warm
in the sun. This is the
Heartland, where the farmer
is king—but over everything,
Nature reigns supreme.

—from Diane Siebert's
"Heartland"

absolute location
continent
country
geography
hemisphere
relative location

Planet
▼
Continent
▼
Country
▼
State
▼
County
▼
City or Town
▼

Neighborhood or Farm

The Place We Call Home

Illinois seems very large. Yet it is just one small part of the world. We live in Illinois, so it is important to us. It is our home. Millions of people all over the world live in different places that are important to them. Each place is someone's home.

Let's learn about Illinois by studying its *geography.* First we will study where Illinois is located in the world. Next we will learn about the relationship between the land, water, plants, and animals.

Why is it important to know about the geography of a place? Geography affects where we live and how we live. For example, if you live where it is warm all the time, you would dress differently from the people who live where it is cold. If you live in a green pine forest in the mountains, you might live differently than if you live next to the sunny seashore.

If you own a business that makes cereal or computers, you need to be near good roads, a railroad, or a shipping port. Why? You need to be able to get supplies. You might ship your cereal or computers to other places in the world.

Where in the World Is Illinois?

Let's take a closer look at where Illinois is. You know you live on planet Earth, but just where on the planet do you live? Illinois is located on one of the world's seven *continents.* Continents are the largest land areas. Illinois is on the continent of North America.

Within a continent are *countries.* A country is a land area under the control of one government. Our country is the United States of America. Canada is the country to the north of us, and Mexico is the country to the south of us.

Our country is divided into 50 **states.** Illinois is our state. Most states are divided into **counties.** What county do you live in? Within counties are communities called **cities** or **towns.** They may be large or small. The largest city in Illinois is Chicago. Our capital city is Springfield. In which county do you live? In what city or town do you live?

Where in the World Are We?

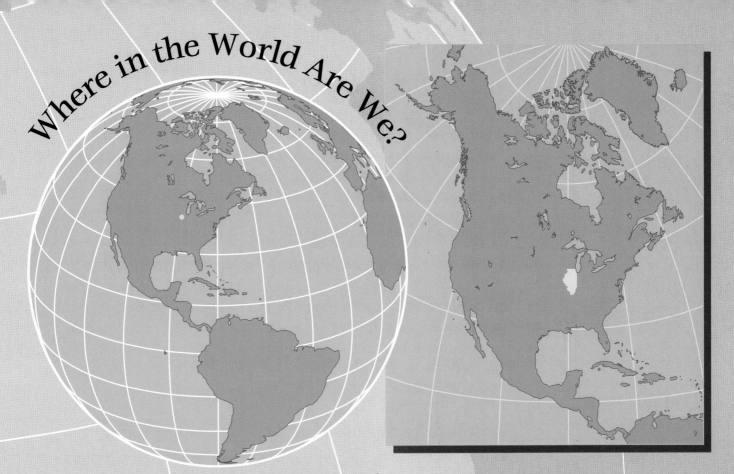

1. Our world is the **planet** Earth.

2. Our **continent** is North America.

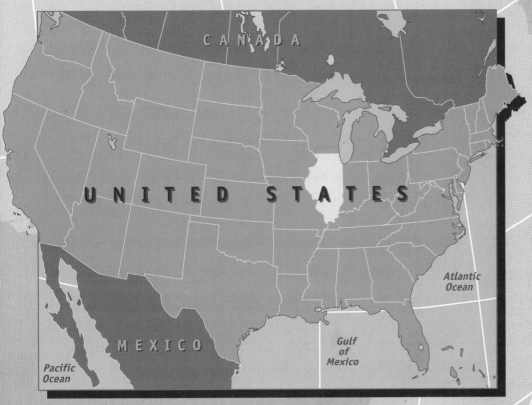

3. Our **country** is the United States of America.

4. Our **state** is Illinois.

Locating Places

Pretend you meet some friends from a different country and they want to visit your home. How would you tell them where to find it? There are two ways we can describe our location. They are *relative location* and *absolute location.*

Relative Location

Relative location tells us where a place is in relation to other places or things. For example, Illinois is between Missouri and Indiana. It is next to Iowa. You could also tell someone you live near Lake Michigan. Your house might be near a store, a park, or a bank. What is the relative location of your school?

You often hear the words north, south, east, and west. You might say you live in southern Illinois or north of Chicago or east of the Mississippi River. These would all be relative locations.

Absolute Location

Absolute location is the exact spot where a place is located. An address is an absolute location. No other house or apartment is in the very same place as yours. What is the address of your home or apartment?

Your city also has an absolute location. Every place on the earth has an absolute location.

Lines Around the World

Every place in the world has an exact location that is measured by **longitude** and **latitude** lines. You can find these lines on a map or a globe.

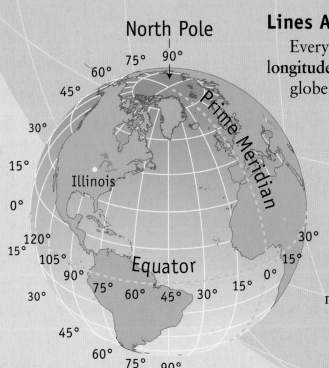

- Latitude lines run east and west (side to side on the map).
- Longitude lines run north and south (up and down on the map).

Along the lines you will find numbers. Each number has a tiny circle by it. This is a **symbol** for a **degree**. A degree is the unit we use to measure the parts of a circle or globe.

The **equator** is 0 degrees latitude. Find the line that is 0 degrees longitude. It is called the **prime meridian**. Find these lines on the globe. The degree numbers get larger as they move farther away from the equator and the prime meridian.

Hemispheres

There is another way we divide up the earth. We pretend that the earth is cut into two equal pieces. We call each half of the earth a *hemisphere.*

Look at these drawings of the earth. Find the equator. Find the hemisphere north of the equator. Find the hemisphere south of the equator. Since north is nearly always "up" on a map, it's not hard to guess that the hemisphere north of the equator is the Northern Hemisphere. What is the hemisphere south of the equator called?

Now, what if we decide to divide the earth another way? Geographers often divide it from the North Pole to the South Pole. The line runs through the Atlantic and Pacific Oceans. This drawing shows a Western Hemisphere and an Eastern Hemisphere.

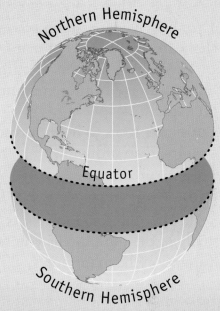

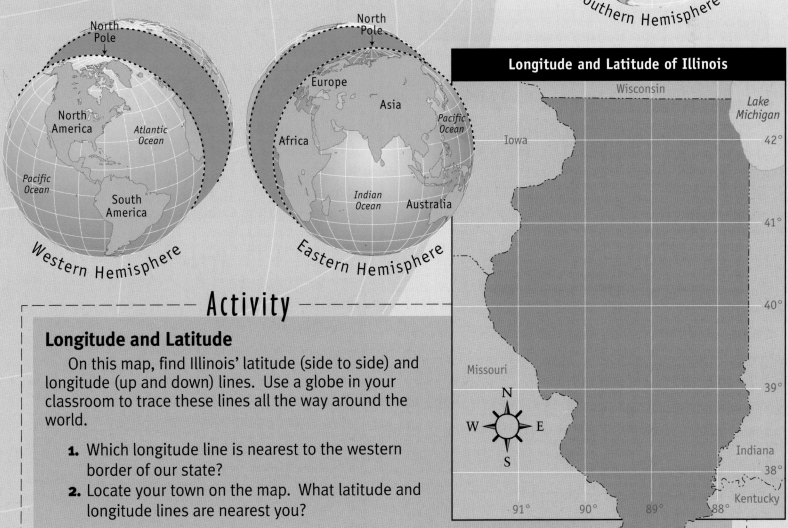

Longitude and Latitude of Illinois

Activity

Longitude and Latitude

On this map, find Illinois' latitude (side to side) and longitude (up and down) lines. Use a globe in your classroom to trace these lines all the way around the world.

1. Which longitude line is nearest to the western border of our state?

2. Locate your town on the map. What latitude and longitude lines are nearest you?

Read a Map of Illinois

Maps help locate places. Maps help us know where we are. They help us get where we want to go. They help us understand places better.

There are many kinds of maps. Can you think of some? Maybe you thought of a treasure map! Maybe you thought of the road maps your parents use on trips.

Maps have tools to help us read them. Find these tools on the map of Illinois.

Title:

The first thing to look for is the title. It is usually at the top. It tells you what kind of information the map shows.

Illinois Cities and Towns

Scale of Miles:

To show us how far apart things are, map makers use a scale of miles. This helps us measure the distance between places.

One inch on a map might stand for 50 miles on real land. Or one inch might mean 100 miles or even more.

Scale of Miles

Directions:

Maps show the directions north, south, east, and west. We call these *cardinal directions.* You will find them on a compass.

Halfway between north and east is northeast, or NE. Halfway between south and east is southeast, or SE. These are called *intermediate directions.*

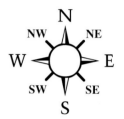

Legend or Key:

Map makers use symbols so they don't have to print words all over the map. The symbols stand for cities, rivers, and other things. The legend or key explains what the symbols mean.

Legend	
✪	Capital
◉	Major U.S. City
◎	Large City
○	Medium City
•	Small City or Town
〜	River

1 MEMORY MASTER

1. What is geography?
2. Describe two or three ways to find where a place is located.
3. In what hemisphere do you live?
4. What is the capital city of Illinois?

Activity

Illinois on the Map

Use the map to answer these questions:

1. What is the title of this map?
2. By using the legend, what do you know about East St. Louis, Decatur, and Joliet? What other cities belong to this group?
3. If you wanted to go from Springfield to Peoria, which direction would you go?
4. About how many miles is it from Galena to Freeport?

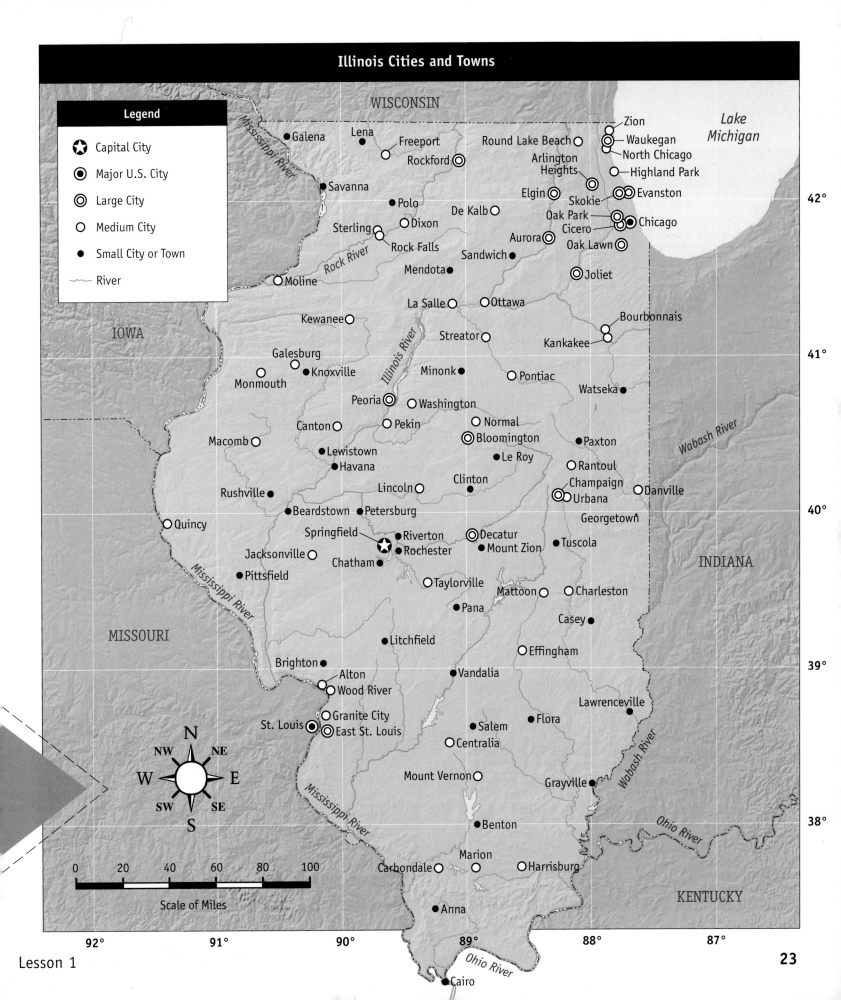

Illinois Cities and Towns

Legend

- ⭐ Capital City
- ◉ Major U.S. City
- ◎ Large City
- ○ Medium City
- ● Small City or Town
- 〜 River

WISCONSIN

Lake Michigan

Galena • Lena • Freeport

Rockford ◎

Round Lake Beach ○

Zion ◎
Waukegan ◎
North Chicago ◎
Arlington Heights ◎
Highland Park ○

Savanna •

Polo •

De Kalb ○

Elgin ◎
Skokie
Evanston ◎◎

Sterling
Dixon ○

Oak Park ◎ Chicago ◉
Cicero ◎

Rock Falls

Aurora ◎
Oak Lawn ◎

IOWA

Moline ○

Mendota •

Sandwich •

Joliet ◎

42°

La Salle ○ Ottawa ○

Kewanee ○

Streator ○

Bourbonnais ◎
Kankakee ◎

41°

Galesburg ◎
Knoxville •

Minonk •

Pontiac ○

Watseka ○

Monmouth ○

Peoria ◉ Washington ○

Canton ○ Pekin ○

Normal ○
Bloomington ◉

Paxton •

Wabash River

Macomb ○

Lewistown •
Havana •

Le Roy •

Rantoul ○
Champaign ◎
Urbana ◎

Danville ○

Rushville •

Lincoln ○

Clinton ○

40°

Quincy ○

Beardstown • Petersburg •

Georgetown •

Springfield ⭐ Riverton •
Rochester •

Decatur ◎
Mount Zion •

Tuscola •

INDIANA

Jacksonville ○

Chatham •

Pittsfield •

Taylorville ○

Mattoon ○ Charleston ○

Pana •

Casey •

MISSOURI

Litchfield •

Brighton •

Effingham ○

39°

Alton ○
Wood River ○

Vandalia ○

Lawrenceville ○

Granite City ◎
St. Louis ◉ East St. Louis ◎

Flora •

Salem •

Centralia ○

Mount Vernon ○

Grayville •

Wabash River

N
NW NE
W E
SW SE
S

Benton •

38°

0 20 40 60 80 100

Scale of Miles

Marion ○
Carbondale ○ Harrisburg ○

KENTUCKY

Mississippi River

Ohio River

Anna •

Cairo •

92°   91°   90°   89°   88°   87°

How are climate and weather different? **Weather** is what it is like outside each hour or each day. It might be sunny or rainy. It might be hot or cool. **Climate** is the weather pattern year after year.

Climate

Can you imagine living in a place that is the same temperature all year long? What if it never rained or snowed, or was rainy most of the time?

Where a place is located has a lot to do with its climate. Find Illinois on a globe. It is in the middle of North America. It is not close to the equator, where it is warm all year long. It is not close to either the North or South Poles, where it is cold all year long. This means that Illinois has a *moderate climate* with four seasons: spring, summer, fall, and winter.

In spring, the grass begins to grow again, and green buds pop out on trees. Summers can be very hot and *humid.* This means there is a lot of water in the air. Humid air feels hotter and more uncomfortable than dry air.

In the fall the air cools, and the leaves on trees turn brilliant gold, orange, and red. In winter, our towns and farms are covered in a beautiful blanket of snow. You need to wear a warm coat, hat, and gloves while you wait for the school bus.

What Causes Our Climate?

Our climate is different in different parts of the state. There are several reasons for this.

One is the distance from large bodies of water. Large bodies of water help keep nearby places cooler in the summer and warmer in the

| Spring | Summer | Fall | Winter |

winter. That is why communities near Lake Michigan are not as hot in the summer as other regions of Illinois.

Large bodies of water also affect how much rain and snow the land gets. Water that falls in the form of rain, snow, sleet, or hail is called *precipitation*. During the spring and summer, the land near the Great Lakes gets about 32 inches of precipitation each year. Southern Illinois, far from the lakes, gets about 48 inches. The moist air moves north from the Gulf of Mexico.

The opposite is true in the winter, when areas near the Great Lakes get 36 inches of snow, but southern Illinois gets less than 10 inches.

Wind can make quick changes in the weather. A strong wind from the south can quickly bring warm, moist air into Illinois. A wind from the north can bring cold, dry air. That is why we get tornadoes.

Illinois Temperatures:

- **Highest:** 117° in East St. Louis on July 14, 1954
- **Lowest:** -36° in Congerville on January 5, 1999

Making Connections

Have you gone sledding down a snowy hill during the winter? Was it so cold you could see your breath? Have you splashed in the cool water during a hot summer? Have you picked apples or pumpkins in the fall? Which season do you like the most?

Tornado Alley

Illinois sits in a region called Tornado Alley, where warm and cold air meet. When this happens, the warm air rises, forms a spiral, and spins. The air around the spiral moves it over the ground.

Most tornadoes move at 10 to 20 miles per hour, but they can reach 300 miles per hour! Some have so much force they pick up cars or houses and whirl them down several miles away.

Whenever there is a tornado warning it is important to follow safety rules, tune into a radio for information, and get to a safe place quickly!

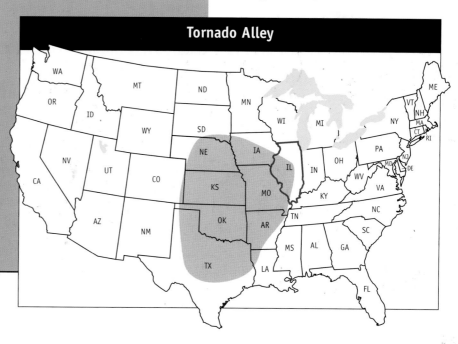

Tornado Alley

Strong, cold winds blew across the flat land next to the glaciers. Only low plants could survive; there were no trees. However, woolly mammoths, mastodons, deer, giant sloths, bison, saber-toothed cats, huge beavers, and other large animals roamed the land during the Ice Age.

Ice Age Glaciers

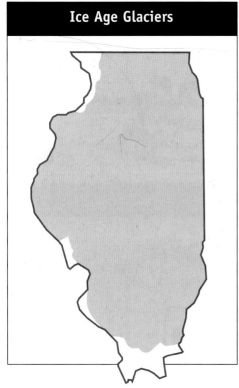

At least four times, glaciers spread across most of Illinois. The ice sheets covered the land for thousands of years.

Long, Long Ago

Illinois' flat land did not always look like it does today. How did it get to be this way? To answer this we must go back millions of years. Long ago, a shallow sea called the Silurian Sea covered the land. We know the sea was here because layers of tiny shells are found under the ground today.

Millions of years passed, and the climate changed. The sea dried up, leaving warm, swampy lowland. Many kinds of trees and plants grew in the region that used to be covered by the sea.

Over time, the swampy lowland became a hot, moist forest that was perfect for amphibians and reptiles. However, no people lived anywhere.

More time passed, and the climate became colder. The forest plants died. The animals had to *adapt* to the cold or die.

Glaciers Shaped the Land

No one really knows why the climate changed. But year after year, the climate grew colder. The snow from winter didn't melt. It piled up, winter after winter. We call this time the Ice Age.

As the snow piled up, it became so heavy that the top snow pressed the bottom snow into sheets of ice. These huge sheets of ice are called *glaciers.* The glaciers became so heavy that they started to move. Very slowly, they moved like giant blankets of ice scraping over the land. Sand, gravel, larger rocks, and boulders as big as a house stuck in the glaciers as they moved over the land. The movement flattened the land underneath.

Glaciers, like this one in Alaska, flow downhill, carrying soil and rocks. There are no glaciers in Illinois anymore.

Changing Illinois

Silurian Sea
▼
Swampy Lowlands
▼
Tropical Rainforest
▼
Glaciers of Ice

Flat, Fertile Prairie

Making Connections

Have you ever been in a huge snowstorm? How high was the snow? Imagine what it would have been like during the Ice Age when glaciers were a mile high! Are there still glaciers on the earth? Where are they?

Forming the Prairie, Lakes, and Rivers

Finally, about 10,000 to 15,000 years ago, the climate began to warm up. Glaciers started to melt and break apart. As they melted, they dropped off large amounts of sand, rich soil, rocks, and boulders that filled in the central region of Illinois. The land became a fertile prairie that was a perfect place for grasses and other plants to grow.

As the ice melted, water ran into low places and formed lakes and rivers. The Great Lakes were formed. Melting glaciers also formed the Mississippi River.

2 MEMORY MASTER

1. If the weather report said, "Today it will be sunny, with a high of 85°, would it be describing the weather or the climate?
2. What evidence do we have that Illinois was once covered by water?
3. What change in the climate caused the glaciers to form?
4. How did melting glaciers change the land?

WORDS TO UNDERSTAND

ecosystem
environment
habitat
human feature
natural feature
prairie
tributaries

Natural and Human Features

All places have certain features that make them alike or different from other places. Some of these are natural to the environment, such as soil, rivers, lakes, some plants, and some animals. These are all *natural features* of Illinois.

Places also have *human features.* There are farmhouses with silos. There are tall city buildings. People made these. Freeways, shopping malls, and homes are also examples of human features. So are fields of corn or wheat, because people planted the crops.

Places are usually a mix of natural and human features. The next time you drive away from your home, see what natural features and human features you see. The farther away you get from a city or town, the more natural features you will find.

All Around the State

Our state has wonderful natural and human features from north to south, west to east. Look at the photos and read about these great places. Which places are more natural, and which have been built or made by humans? Which places would you like to visit?

Adler Planetarium, Chicago

A planetarium is a place to learn about the planets. Located along the shore of Lake Michigan, this was the first planetarium in the United States. You can see exhibits on the solar system, the Milky Way, and the history of astronomy.

Capitol Building, Springfield

Our state government offices are in this building. It is also an interesting place to visit. You can see paintings and statues that tell the story of Illinois.

Lincoln Trail State Park, Marshall

When Abraham Lincoln was a young boy, his family followed this trail as they moved from Indiana into Illinois. Native American groups once lived at the site. Today, visitors enjoy the woods and wildflowers. They go boating, camping, fishing, and hiking around Lincoln Trail Lake.

Illinois Beach State Park

Stretching for six miles along the sandy shore of Lake Michigan, the park offers swimming, boating, picnicking, hiking, fishing, camping, and just enjoying nature. The park has dunes and marshes, oak forests, and many kinds of animals and plants.

The Field Museum of Natural History, Chicago

If you walk through the huge museum you can learn about African, Eskimo, and Native American cultures. You can see bird habitats, sea mammals, gems, fossils, and everyone's favorite—Sue, the world's largest Tyrannosaurus Rex.

Trail of Tears State Forest

The forest is part of the Ozark Hills, one of the most rugged places in Illinois. Watch out for snakes! Poisonous rattlesnakes and copperheads hide under cool rocks. Chipmunks, flying squirrels, opossums, skunks, and raccoons live next to larger deer, foxes, coyotes, and bobcats.

Ridges *are long narrow chains of hills or mountains.*

Plateaus *are high, wide, flat areas that often end with steep cliffs. They look like tables or wide steps many miles across.*

Bluffs *are steep cliffs or riverbanks.*

Plains *are wide level areas of land without many trees.*

Land Regions

Central Lowland

Ozark Plateau

Interior Low Plateaus

Gulf Coastal Plain

Landforms

A landform is a feature of the earth's surface. Several kinds of landforms are found in Illinois. They are plains, plateaus, bluffs, and ridges. All of these are the result of powerful forces moving inside the earth. They are also the result of wind and water wearing away the earth's surface. This wearing away is called erosion.

Land Regions

Regions are places that have common features. For example, you might live in a region where there are many farms, and you can watch the corn grow taller than you are. You might live in a busy city region of tall buildings and a lot of traffic. There are mining regions where salt and coal are dug from the earth.

Our state is divided into four land regions. Although each region may have cities and towns, roads and farms, the landforms are about the same throughout the region.

- The **Central Lowland** is our largest region.
- The hilly **Ozark Plateau** is part of the Ozark Mountains.
- The **Interior Low Plateaus** has high ridges and hills.
- The **Gulf Coastal Plain** covers the tip of our state.

Chapter 2 "A Place Called Illinois"

Central Lowland

The Central Lowland covers almost all of Illinois. Most of this region is a flat or slightly rolling plain with low ridges and broad river valleys. Thousands of years ago the land was smoothed out by moving glaciers. The glaciers left rich soil that we use for farms.

Ozark Plateau

The Ozark Plateau is a small section of hilly land. This region also has rocky forests, so not much farming is done here. There is a rock called limestone under the region. Limestone is an important building stone. It is also used to make cement.

Interior Low Plateaus

Glaciers never covered this region, so it has high ridges, bluffs, and hills. You can stand on a high ridge and look out over the lowlands. It is a great view!

Gulf Coastal Plain

The moving water of the Mississippi and Ohio Rivers have left rich soil at the southern tip of our state. Some of the land is swampy and wet all the time.

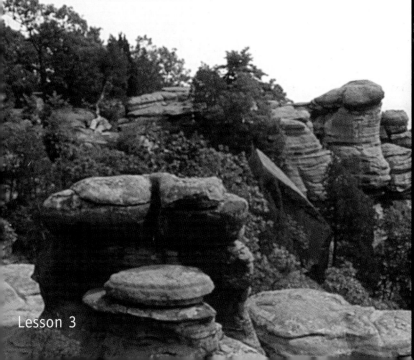

The Prairie

Illinois is nicknamed the "Prairie State." A *prairie* is a wide, level, grassy land with few trees. Illinois prairies are in the Central Lowland region.

When European settlers first came to Illinois, over half of the land was covered with tall grass. Many settlers moved on when they came to these grassy lands. They thought that trees did not grow here because the soil was too poor. There was little wood to build their houses.

Later settlers plowed the grasslands and changed them into farm fields. They learned that the prairie soils were deep and rich. They had found some of the best farmland in North America.

The settlers lived through hot, humid summers with biting insects and prairie fires. The winters were cold and windy. But there was great beauty. In early summer the wildflowers formed a sea of color that waved in the wind.

The settlers called their wagons "prairie schooners." A schooner is a sailing ship. The wagons were given this name because they looked like ships sailing on a sea of grass.

Each plant and animal plays a special role in prairie life.

The term "prairie" comes from a French word meaning "meadow."

At one time, elk, buffalo, wolves, black bears, and deer grazed on the tall prairie grass. Then, as more and more land was used for farming, those animals had to move to other places.

Today, animals such as ground squirrels, skunks, raccoons, snapping turtles, toads, gophers, red fox, deer mice, coyotes, cottontail rabbits, and white-tailed deer live on the prairie. Birds such as hawks and meadowlarks also make their homes there.

Hundreds of types of plants grow naturally on the prairie. The four most common prairie grasses in Illinois are:

• Big Bluestem   • Indian Grass   • Little Bluestem   • Switch Grass

Farms and growing cities took over much of the prairie. Today, most of the original prairie is gone.

Ecosystems

The prairies are one of the five natural *ecosystems* found in Illinois. An ecosystem is a natural community of plants and animals, soil, water, and air. Each does its own special job. Some animals hunt smaller animals. Some animals eat only plants. Plants make food for animals and give oxygen to the air. Water keeps everything moving and growing.

When plants and animals die, they become part of the soil and make it richer. Then new plants grow and some are eaten by animals. The cycle repeats over and over. In this way nature keeps things in balance.

Each ecosystem contains many kinds of life. For example, a prairie is more than just tall grass. There are insects, birds, and animals. Each does its own special job.

Making Connections

How would your life be different if you lived near a different ecosystem? What if you lived in a forest or on the banks of a river?

Illinois Has Five Natural Ecosystems

Prairie

The small animals eat prairie grasses and flowers. Then larger animals eat the smaller animals. When plants and animals die, their bodies return important nutrients to the soil.

Forest

At one time forests covered more of Illinois than they do today. Much of the wildlife in our state lives in the forests.

River and Stream

Rivers are important for water, transportation, and beauty. They are a home for fish. When people build dams, pollute the water, or bring in animals and plants from other regions, they can harm the river ecosystem.

Wetland

Wetlands are good for Illinois. They help keep water levels steady when there is heavy rain or melting snow. By absorbing the water, they prevent flooding. The wetlands are home to many rare animals.

Lake

You know that rivers are important in Illinois, but did you know that lakes and reservoirs are also very important? Most of our drinking water comes from lakes and reservoirs. Fish from lakes are an important source of food.

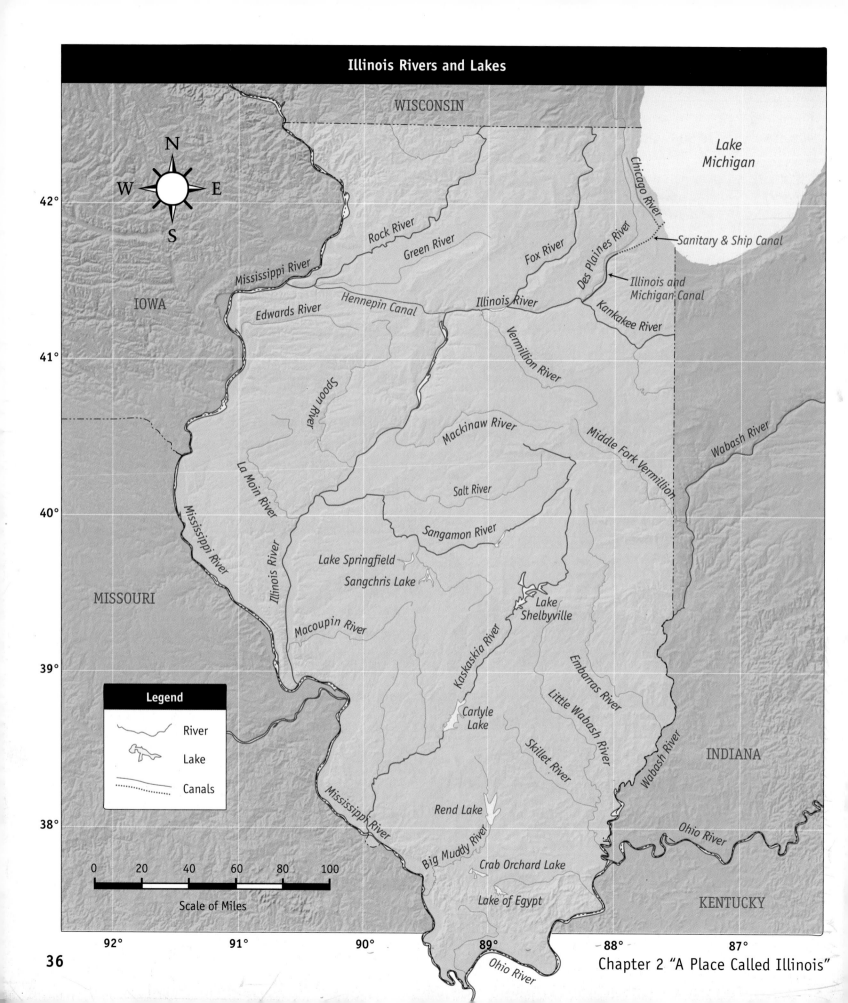

Illinois Rivers and Lakes

WISCONSIN

Lake Michigan

IOWA

42°

41°

40°

39°

38°

MISSOURI

INDIANA

KENTUCKY

Rock River

Green River

Fox River

Chicago River

Sanitary & Ship Canal

Des Plaines River

Illinois and Michigan Canal

Mississippi River

Edwards River

Hennepin Canal

Illinois River

Kankakee River

Vermillion River

Spoon River

Mackinaw River

Middle Fork Vermillion

Wabash River

La Moin River

Salt River

Illinois River

Sangamon River

Lake Springfield

Sangchris Lake

Lake Shelbyville

Macoupin River

Kaskaskia River

Embarras River

Little Wabash River

Wabash River

Carlyle Lake

Skillet River

Rend Lake

Big Muddy River

Crab Orchard Lake

Ohio River

Lake of Egypt

Mississippi River

Ohio River

Legend

~~~ River

Lake

Canals

Scale of Miles
0   20   40   60   80   100

92°   91°   90°   89°   88°   87°

N
W   E
S

Chapter 2 "A Place Called Illinois"

Our Wonderful Rivers and Lakes

The lake and river ecosystems provide *habitats* for many animals. Rivers and lakes provide water for animals, humans, and farms. Fish live in our rivers and lakes. Rivers and lakes add interest and beauty to the land.

We use waterways for travel. People have built canals to link rivers together. Now river systems are used like highways to ship goods to and from cities and countries around the world.

Mississippi River

People of all time periods have used the wide Mississippi River. American Indians lived beside the river, fished in it, used it to travel to other villages, and even gave it its name. Later, French explorers used the river like a giant highway.

After the pioneers came west, steamboats paddled up and down the Mississippi. They carried people and goods to new towns along the river.

Along its course, the Mississippi River is joined by many *tributaries*. A tributary is a smaller river that flows into a larger one. The Illinois River and the Ohio River are two long tributaries.

Animals of the River

Ducks, geese, swans, warblers, woodpeckers, herons, and egrets are some of the birds that live along the Mississippi River. The land near the river is home to muskrats, minks, beavers, otters, raccoons, skunks, weasels, foxes, squirrels, rabbits, and deer. Over 200 kinds of fish live in the river.

3 MEMORY MASTER

1. Give examples of both natural and human features.
2. What are some of the landforms found in Illinois?
3. What is a prairie?
4. What is an ecosystem?
5. Give several reasons why lakes and rivers are valuable to Illinois.

WORDS TO UNDERSTAND

agribusiness
agriculture
livestock
natural resources
recycle
refuges
reservoir

Our Natural Resources

Illinois is rich in **natural resources.** They are found in nature. They are useful to people. In fact, we couldn't survive without them!

You have already read about our state's sun and rain, land and water, and plants and animals. These are all part of our natural resources. Our rich soil, rock, and minerals, are other important resources.

Raising Crops and Animals

Our Illinois climate is just right for growing grains and vegetables. Our state has rich soil for growing crops. Most of Illinois is flat land. These things make Illinois a great place for **agriculture,** or raising crops and animals to sell.

Agribusiness is simply agriculture and business put together. Farmers figure out the best way to raise, ship, and sell their crops and animals. Our state's leading crops are corn, soybeans, and wheat. **Livestock** such as hogs and cattle are also important.

What Is Dirt Worth?

Nobody likes dirty hands, dirty clothes, or dirty floors. But dirt in the right place is very important! Plants need good dirt, or soil, to grow. Soil protects seeds in the ground. Soil holds heat and water. Soil provides minerals for plants.

Farmers need soil to grow their crops. But not all soils are good for plants. Some soils are better for other things, like making bricks or building roads.

Can you think of some things people get from soil? How much do you think dirt is worth?

What Grows in Our Soil?

Soybeans

People use soybeans for animal feed. People can also cook soybeans or eat them raw.

Some of the liquid in soybeans is called soy milk. It can be used like cows' milk. Soybeans are made into oil that is used to cook food. Maybe you've used soy sauce on Chinese food.

Soy is often found in health foods. You can find soy in food like meatless burgers.

Soy isn't just used in foods. It is also used to make ink, fuel, paint, crayons, shampoo, soap, glue, medicine, and much more.

Grasses

Many kinds of native grasses grow in our state. Cattle, horses, sheep, and other livestock graze on these grasses. When grass is used this way, it is called a pasture. Sometimes the grasses are cut and baled or stacked as prairie hay.

Sometimes other grasses are planted for hay. Alfalfa is a green plant that looks like tall thick clover. Alfalfa hay can be dried into pellets for animal feed.

Wheat

Bread, cereal, and wheat crackers—all of these things and other foods are made from wheat. What wheat foods do you like to eat?

Wheat has many uses. The dried stalks of the plant are straw. Straw can be fed to livestock, but most straw is used in barns as bedding for horses, cattle, and hogs.

Corn

The next time you eat popcorn at the movies, think about where the corn came from. Illinois corn is sold all over the world.

Many kinds of corn grow in our state. One kind is sweet corn. People eat it right off the cob. Field corn is fed to pigs, cattle, and chickens.

Corn syrup is a sweetener used in soda pop and many foods. People use cornstarch to thicken sauces and soups.

Corn is also used to make things you don't eat, such as paint, soap, and some paper. People are finding ways to make plastic-like products from corn. You may even use fuel made from corn, called ethanol, in your family car.

Minerals

Coal is an important natural resource that is found under almost two-thirds of Illinois. It has been very important to the growth of industry. Long ago, people built factories in places where there was plenty of coal for fuel and rivers for transportation.

Oil and limestone are also found in Illinois. At one time, iron and lead were mined in our state. A mineral called fluorite is found in southern Illinois. Throughout the state, sand and gravel are taken from the land and used to make buildings and roads.

Flourite is our state mineral. It forms beautiful blue-black, cube-shaped crystals. Fluorite is used in producing steel and in making an acid used in making pottery, plastics, glass, and cookware.

Gravel and tar make asphalt used in paving roads. This man is repairing a hole in the road.

Coal is carried by train to provide energy for factories.

Chapter 2 "A Place Called Illinois"

COAL

1. Millions of years ago, the land was a swamp with large plants. When the plants died, they were slowly covered by layers of sand and mud.

2. Pressure and heat from the layers turned the plants into coal.

3. Miners dug the coal from its "bed." Then they covered the mine with soil and planted seeds so new plants would grow.

4. We use some of the coal right here but . . .

5. Much of it is moved by train, truck, or ship to places around the world.

6. Most of the coal is used to make electricity. The coal is cleaned before it is burned so it won't pollute the air as much.

7. Coal will continue to be an important source of energy in the future.

How Do People Use and Change the Land?

Throughout history, people have used and changed the land. People have always cut down trees and gathered rocks and earth to build homes. They built their homes near a river or lake. They gathered nuts and berries.

People today cut trees for wood and use it to build houses and make other products. They make bricks out of clay. They take oil, coal, and other minerals from the ground. People build cities and freeways, bridges and dams. Rivers back up behind the dams and form new lakes. People plant trees and fields of corn. When adults drive cars and trucks, put fertilizer on crops, and produce goods in factories, they change the air, water, and soil.

Taking Care of the Land

If people and industries are not careful, they can harm the environment. Some people think we will never use up all the grass, trees, coal, and other natural resources. They think there will always be plenty of fresh air and clean water. But if Illinois is to remain a healthy and beautiful place, we must take care of our natural resources.

People have made laws that protect the environment from pollution. Workers in factories and mines have to be careful to keep our land and water clean and safe. People who drive cars, trucks, and buses have to make sure they do not put too many harmful fumes into the air.

Making Connections

Can you think of ways your neighborhood has changed over time? Are there any new buildings or roads?

Boats dry along Lake Michigan. In this picture, find ways people use and change the land and water.

Our state has special places that protect plants and animals.
- Wildlife *refuges* are places where wild animals can live without being hunted.
- Rare plants and many kinds of trees grow in protected forests.
- State and national parks are other places where our state's scenery and resources are protected.

Recycling

One thing we can do to help save our resources is recycle. That means using things again and again. Paper and cardboard are made from trees. If we recycle paper, we won't have to cut down as many trees. See how it works? If your family doesn't already recycle, ask them to start!

Making Connections

What does your school or community do to help people recycle or reuse materials?

Renewable Resources

Some natural resources are **renewable.** This means that even if they are used up, they can come back. Forests are a good example. If all the trees in a forest are cut down, seeds already in the ground will grow more trees. However, a forest takes many, many years to grow back. Is wind a renewable resource? What others can you think of?

Other resources are **non-renewable.** This means that after they are used up, they will never come back. Coal and oil are non-renewable resources. Since they took millions of years to form under the ground, we will never have more of them than we have right now.

4 MEMORY MASTER

1. What is agriculture?
2. List three important Illinois crops.
3. What are some ways people change the land?
4. What is the difference between a renewable and non-renewable resource?

You Can Help

It is up to everyone to help protect the environment. What can you do?

- You can stop littering and remind others not to litter.
- You can recycle cans and paper.
- You can turn off lights and the TV when you aren't using them.

Chapter **2** Review

Activity

Make an Advertisement for Illinois

   Pretend you work at an office that tells people about Illinois so they will want to visit. How would you describe our climate? Create an ad that might be placed in a tourist magazine. Write the words and include some pictures. Can you think of a clever saying that will make people want to come to Illinois?

Activity

Create a Quadrarama of Four Seasons

   A quadrarama is made up of 4 triaramas that show our four seasons. You will need four pieces of 9"x 9" square paper. Follow these steps for each triarama:

1. Fold the top right corner of one square down to the lower left corner. Open the paper and repeat with the top left corner. Open the square to see four triangles.
2. Cut along one fold line to the center of the square.
3. Draw a background scene on the half of the square that does not have the cut.
4. Overlap the two bottom triangles so one completely covers the other, and glue.
5. Place small objects or glue cut-out people, trees, etc., so they stand up on the bottom of each triarama.
6. Create four triaramas and glue or tape them all together back to back.

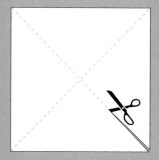
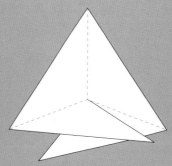

Illinois' Boundaries

Each state in our country has boundary lines. However, these lines are only on a map. You won't find them if you walk across the land.

Natural features such as rivers and a lake form some of Illinois' boundaries. People decided where other boundary lines would be.

Use the map if you need help to complete the answers.

1. What lake forms one of our borders?
2. What three rivers form part of our border?
3. How many other states border Illinois?
4. What are they?

Mental Map

Can you close your eyes and draw a map of Illinois on a piece of paper?

Can you label the rivers and lakes that form some of our state's boundaries?

Make a Natural Resources Collage

1. Cut out pictures from magazines that represent the natural resources found in our state. Remember to include the animals, plants, minerals, and rich soil.
2. Use a glue stick to make a collage that completely covers a sheet of paper.
3. Once the paper has dried, carefully trace the shape of our state over the pictures. (Use a map your teacher will give you.)
4. Carefully cut out the shape and glue it on a piece of colored paper.
5. Add a title to your picture.

12,000 B.C.
First people in North America

1400S
Columbus discovers America.

1500S
America first appears on
the map.

1600S
Pilgrims arrive.

1700S
Declaration of Independence
George Washington

1800S
Abraham Lincoln
Pioneers go west.

1900S
Martin Luther King
Your parents were born.

2000S
A New Century
9/11 Terrorists attack the U.S.

Timeline of Events

12,000 B.C.
Paleo Indians live all over
North America. They are
also the first people in the
Illinois region.

8000 B.C.–**500** B.C.
Archaic Indians live in
North and South
America.

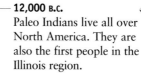 12,000 B.C. 8000 B.C. 500 B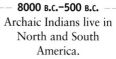

American Indians

Native Americans lived in this country long ago. On the plains, the native people made their own trails. They hunted animals, like buffalo, elk, and deer, for food and clothing. The people built homes from earth or from buffalo hides. The native people kept alive a rich culture with many traditions.

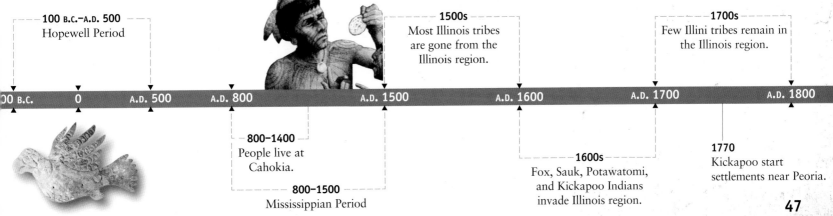

100 B.C.–A.D. 500
Hopewell Period

1500s
Most Illinois tribes are gone from the Illinois region.

1700s
Few Illini tribes remain in the Illinois region.

OO B.C. 0 A.D. 500 A.D. 800 A.D. 1500 A.D. 1600 A.D. 1700 A.D. 1800

800–1400
People live at Cahokia.

800–1500
Mississippian Period

1600s
Fox, Sauk, Potawatomi, and Kickapoo Indians invade Illinois region.

1770
Kickapoo start settlements near Peoria.

47

WORDS TO UNDERSTAND

archaeologist
barter

PEOPLE TO KNOW

M.C. Hopewell

PLACES TO LOCATE

Cahokia
Dickson Mounds

Paleo Indians

Who first lived near where you live today? What did they look like? What did they eat when they got up in the morning? What kinds of homes did they live in? How did the boys and girls learn what they needed to know? Did they play with friends? Did their parents tell them stories at night?

The word "paleo" means ancient, or very old. The first people to live in North America and what we now call Illinois were probably following herds of wild animals. It was the end of the Ice Age and large mammoths and bison roamed the land. The men hunted the animals for food and to get the thick fur.

The people used materials they found in nature to make tools such as spear points, knives, and scrapers. In modern times, mammoths have been found with spear points in their fur. Men had tried to kill the huge beasts.

For many years the people hunted large mammoths by thrusting spears into them. Later, the climate changed and the mammoths became extinct.

48

Men, women, and children also gathered wild berries, nuts, and roots to eat. We call this way of getting food "hunting and gathering."

The people must have been pleased with the land of quiet prairies and gentle streams. They lived among wooded hills, grassy plains, and high bluffs. The rich soil made Illinois a good home. Plants grew very well.

Because they moved so often, the people did not live in the same homes all the time. They lived in caves and in very small shelters made of brush and rocks.

Making Connections

Have you moved to a new home? Did you like moving to a new place, or would you rather have stayed in the same place for a long time? Why?

Archaic Indians

Over time, the people learned new skills. They made better tools and started weaving baskets to carry food. We call these people Archaic Indians.

They made a tool called an *atlatl* (at·LAT·l). The *atlatl* helped them throw a spear farther and with great force. This was important because small, fasterer animals such as deer and antelope were hunted instead of mammoths.

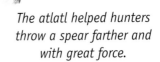

The atlatl helped hunters throw a spear farther and with great force.

The people still made baskets, but they also learned how to make clay pots and bake them until they were hard. They used the pots to carry water. They also filled pots with dried corn, berries, and nuts. Then they dug holes in the ground and put the pots down in the holes to keep them cool and safe from insects and squirrels who might want to steal a snack!

Over time, the people learned how to farm. They planted crops in fields near rivers or streams. Growing crops near home meant they did not have to travel far to get food. As time went on, the people still hunted, but they grew more and more of their own food. This meant they did not have to move so often. People started to live near each other in small villages. They built larger homes to last longer.

The Hopewell People

After thousands of years, the way people lived had changed. We call one of these large groups the Hopewell people. They had enough food to stay in one place all year. They built rectangular houses in groups near the rivers. Most of their food came from wild plants and animals, but they also planted a few crops. They stored the food for the winter.

Living in one place made the Hopewell people different from those who had to move from place to place to find food. For example, the Hopewell took special care in the way they buried their dead. They formed large hills over the graves of their loved ones. Each hill contained many graves. Before, when people moved around all the time, they had to bury their dead along the way. Archaeologists have dug up many mounds that held bones of people who died long ago.

What Do You Think?

Should people be allowed to dig up the remains of those buried long ago? Why or why not?

The Hopewell people made beautiful works of art. They pressed a thin sheet of copper onto a clay figure to make this bird.

This carved stone figurine was found at a Hopewell site. It is much smaller than it looks here.

Trade and Barter

The people traded, or ***bartered,*** with people in faraway places. They traded what they had for what other people had. A child who lived along the coast might wear a copper bracelet made in a faraway place. A child who lived a long way from the ocean might wear a necklace of shells.

In Hopewell mounds, archaeologists have found shells from the Gulf of Mexico that were used for jewelry. They have found a mineral called mica and items made of copper. Mica is a soft rock that can be peeled off in thin layers. It is found near the Appalachian Mountains. The copper probably came from the land around Lake Superior. The people bartered for new supplies to make tools, weapons, and jewelry.

The Hopewell people were probably the first to use a kind of money. They chipped pieces of hard, dark rock called flint into flat round shapes. This money made trading easier.

Mr. M.C. Hopewell was plowing when he found his farm was an ancient burial site.

Making Connections

How do you get the things you want? Does money make trading easier?

A Farmer Discovers Hopewell Mounds

A farmer is plowing his field. His tractor goes back and forth. In the middle of his field is a great hill of earth. It must have been there a long time, for big trees and bushes are growing on it. The farmer has never plowed across the hill before.

M.C. Hopewell was that farmer. He had more than 30 small hills, or mounds, on his farm. He called in people to study the bones, broken pottery, and metal he found buried under the mounds of earth. The Hopewell people were named after the man who found the curious mounds on his farm.

ARCHAEOLOGISTS & *Artifacts*

How do we know about the ways the early people lived? They left no written records of their lives. However, they did leave clues called **artifacts**. An artifact is something made or used by people and left behind. The people left spear points and other tools made from stone and bone. They left shells and bones from the food they ate. They left ashes from cooking fires.

Archaeologists are scientists who study artifacts to learn how people lived in the past. Many of these clues are buried in the earth. Archaeologists dig carefully to find bones, fire pits, burial sites, and trash piles. Each artifact gives a clue about the people who used them. Archaeologists put these clues together to tell a story.

Making Connections

What might the things in your house and your town tell about you in the future? Look at all the things in your desk. Do you have an old pencil, marker, or broken crayon? What books and papers are there? If they were found buried in the ground, what could they tell future archaeologists about you?

What Do You Think ?

- What can archaeologists learn about people just by studying artifacts and ruins?
- What things about life long ago might the artifacts not tell?

Chapter 3 "American Indians"

Mississippian Mound Builders

The Mississippian people lived after the Hopewell people. They lived in valleys all along the Mississippi River. Like other people before them, they hunted and fished for food. They searched the rivers for mussels and steamed them over the fire. They also gathered wild rice, seeds, and nuts. Farmers grew maize (a kind of corn), beans, and squash. Maize became their most important crop.

The Mississippians also traded with other Indian groups. Scientists believe they traveled all the way from the Gulf of Mexico to Lake Superior, and from the Appalachian Mountains to the Rocky Mountains.

The Mississippians built larger mounds than the Hopewell did. That is why they are called "mound builders." Mounds were built by hand. Day after day, week after week, people filled baskets with dirt and carried them to the mound, going higher and higher.

The shape of each mound was important to the people. They built them in the shapes of cones, pyramids, and animals. Sometimes they shaped the mounds to look like birds, snakes, lizards, or even people.

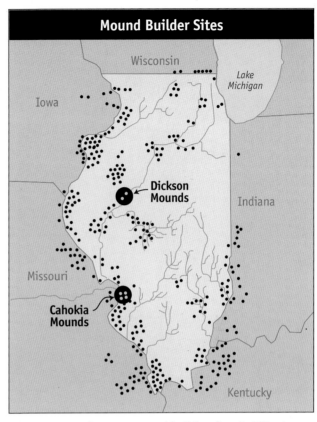

Mound Builder Sites

The two most famous mound builder sites in Illinois are Dickson and Cahokia. Each dot on the map shows other mound sites. Notice that the people built mounds along rivers. They needed the rivers for water and for transportation.

Let's Play!

The Mississippians loved to play games. What is our most popular game today? Baseball? Football? Soccer?

For the Mississippians, it was a game called chunkey. Two players threw spears in front of a round, rolling stone called a chunkey stone. Each player tried to get his spear to land closest to where the stone would stop rolling. Chunkey was played by all ages, from children to adults.

Cahokia

The largest early community of mound builders was Cahokia. Cahokia was a huge ciy. Over 100 mounds have been found there. It is believed that at one time from 10,000 to 20,000 people lived there.

Most of the mounds were rectangular and had flat tops. Leaders lived in homes on top of the mounds. Ceremonies were also held there. Other mounds were shaped like cones. They were built to bury important people and their servants.

Most of the people lived in smaller homes on the ground and on small farms that were spread around the large city. At one time there was a strong log wall around the center of the city. The wall protected the people from attack and kept the wealthy people, who lived in the center of the city, separate from the workers who lived farther out.

Cahokia

Monks Mound

Monks Mound, at the center of Cahokia, is the largest mound in North America. It covers 14 acres and rises to an amazing height of 100 feet—about as high as an eight-story building. A huge building once stood on the top of the mound. It was probably the home of the leader. The mound was not built all at once, but in stages. It may have taken as long as 300 years to build the mound.

Where Did They Go?

No one knows what became of the mound builders. After about 400 years, their great city was left silent. The people may have used up all the natural resources. Perhaps changes in the climate hurt their crops and animals. Disease could have ended their way of life. Many could have been killed in battle with other Indian groups. Or, the whole group could have moved to another place. It might have been a combination of these things.

1 MEMORY MASTER

1. What were some of the different reasons mounds were built?
2. How do we know that the people bartered with other groups?
3. What is the main difference between the Hopewell people and the Mississippians?

alliance
edible

The Illini

Long after the Mississippian mound builders disappeared, a group of tribes who called themselves "Illiniwek" or "Illini" (ih·LIE·NI) moved into the region. About 12 tribes made up the Illini Nation. Among them were the Cahokia, Peoria, Kaskaskia (kas·KAS·kee·uh), Tamaroa (tam·ah·ROW·ah), and Michigamea (mih·shi·GAH·mee·ah) tribes.

The Illini made their homes in the prairies and woods. The way they lived depended on where they lived. Illini tribes in the north and south lived differently.

The tribes agreed to share their hunting grounds, follow certain rules, and help protect one another. They believed that by joining together, each tribe would benefit. This agreement is called an *alliance.*

What Do You Think

Do you think it was a good idea for the Illini tribes to form an alliance? Why or why not?

The Five Largest Tribes of the Illini Nation

Lake Michigan

Kaskaskia

Peoria

Cahokia

Tamaroa

Michigamea

Which Illini tribes lives closest to where you live now? Can you imagine the time when these people lived and worked there?

Clans, Villages, Tribes, and Nations

The Illini had families, just like people do today. Some of them lived with larger family groups called "clans." Several clans lived near each other in a village. Each village had a name. Each village was part of a larger group that we call a "tribe."

Members of a tribe had about the same lifestyle and language. Sometimes these tribes joined together in larger groups called "nations."

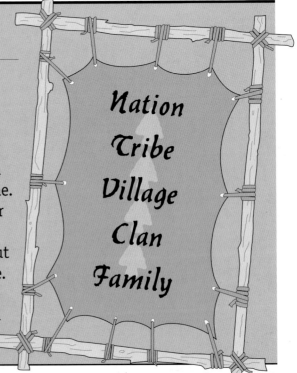

Nation
Tribe
Village
Clan
Family

Homes of Trees and Bark

The people built their own homes from the materials they found all around them. Smaller homes, called **wigwams,** were made from a frame of thin young trees that were bent over so the wigwam had a rounded shape. Then the frame was covered with more small branches and grasses or thin pieces of tree bark. Sometimes the women wove mats from reeds and covered the outside of the wigwam with the mats instead of bark.

Much larger homes, called **longhouses,** were built with a sturdy frame of thick wooden poles. Then the frame was covered with wooden planks and pieces of bark or mats. Longhouses had high roofs. Inside, they had built-in platforms that were covered with thick fur and used for beds. Each family had a place to sleep and to store tools and clothing. Each family had a fire pit. The smoke escaped through holes in the roof.

If you lived in a longhouse, your grandparents, aunts, uncles, and cousins might all live with you. A longhouse was large enough for five to ten families.

Northern Illini Groups

In the north, people depended more on foods that grew wild than on farming. Day after day, the children and their mothers looked for *edible* plants, seeds, and nuts. If they did plant small gardens, they moved after the harvest.

In the summer, the families of men, women, and children of all ages lived in large groups near rivers and lakes so the men could fish and hunt. They hunted deer, bears, turkeys, ducks, pigeons, and other wild birds.

Near the end of summer, the families got ready to move again. Everyone had to help. Each family rolled up the bark cover on its wigwam so it could be used again. The women carried the rolls of bark to rebuild their homes in the new place. When it was time to move, large dogs helped pull supplies along the ground with a travois (tra·VOI).

During the winter, each family lived alone or with one or two other families. They moved from place to place, hunting buffalo or deer. They walked or traveled in birch bark canoes. They used dogs to help carry supplies. The families were careful to stay within their own tribe's hunting grounds.

Dogs and Travois

Many groups of American Indians had strong dogs to carry supplies or firewood. Women went into the trees to gather firewood. Then they tied bundles of sticks on the dogs' backs. The women also carried a large load of sticks. Together they walked back to their village or campground.

Dogs could carry even more on a travois. It was a simple way of moving supplies. The people did not have any kind of wagon or cart on wheels, so dogs and travois solved the problem. The travois had two long, thin poles about 8 feet long attached to a platform of crossed sticks. The poles were strapped on each side of the dog so he could pull the travois along the ground. For really heavy loads, or for carrying children or a person who was too sick to walk, two or more dogs pulled the travois.

In the winter, the dogs were even more useful. It was easier for them to pull loads over the snow than on the ground. They could travel a long way with a heavy load. Years later, after the Indians got horses, they attached the travois to the horses. Then they could pull even more.

Southern Illini Groups

Farther south, most Indians lived in villages along the rivers. The villages were made up of longhouses that held four or five families. Some villages were large, with more than a hundred longhouses.

Farming was important to these people. They planted crops in fields outside the villages. The women grew tall green cornstalks, climbing plants that grew heavy with bean pods, and fat orange and yellow squash and pumpkins on long vines.

In warm weather the men wore only a loincloth and deerskin moccasins. The women wore a skirt. In the cold months they all added fur robes and leggings to keep warm. On special occasions both men and women wore jewelry, painted their bodies, and decorated their hair.

Making Connections

You live in Illinois, where you have to dress warmly in winter and heat your house. If you lived in Florida, you could wear shorts in the winter. Instead of heating your house, you would try to keep it cool.

The Three Sisters

Corn was planted first. When the corn started to grow, the women planted beans that grew up around the cornstalks. Later, the women planted pumpkins and other types of squash. The vines from the plants covered the ground between the cornstalks. The vines helped keep weeds away. Corn, beans, and squash growing together were sometimes called the "three sisters."

Sharing the Work

The men and women of the tribes shared the work. The men hunted, built the wigwams, and made the weapons. They used wood and stone to make knives and bows and arrows. They made canoes out of tree trunks. Both men and women made pottery for carrying water or food.

The women planted gardens and gathered wild food. They dried corn, berries, fish, and meat for the winter.

If a woman had a baby, she carried it on her back on a cradleboard and went about her chores. In the winter she wrapped the baby in moss and fur and set it in the cradleboard.

Women wove baskets, mats, and belts from strips of tree bark and plant fibers. They also made all the clothes for the tribe.

Children's Work

If you were an Illini child, you were expected to help the tribe. If you were a boy, you learned all about the woods and rivers. You learned how to tell rabbit tracks from turkey tracks. You and the other boys sharpened arrows and practiced your aim. You often thought of the day when you would be old enough to go on a buffalo hunt with the men.

If you were a girl, you learned about working in the garden. You also learned which wild plants you could pick to eat. You learned to cook over the fire. You helped to take care of the younger children. When you were old enough, you learned to make clothes. On warm days you might join the boys and dig for clay to make pots.

Making Clothing

Fall was a time for the women to make new clothes from the hides they dried during the summer buffalo hunt. They used soft hides to sew moccasins, shirts, skirts, and pants.

First, a woman had to prepare the animal skins. To do this, she scraped off the fur. Then she soaked the skins to make them soft. She stretched them so they would be smooth and tight.

Young girls also learned how to sew. They had to practice before they could make clothing of their own. They might learn how to make a pillow by sewing together animal skins. Then they stuffed it with grass.

Making Connections

What are some of the chores you do? Do any of them help you prepare for life as an adult? How?

Indian men and boys played a game similar to lacrosse. (Painting by George Catlin)

Games and Celebrations

There was a lot of work to do, but the people also played games. They held races and contests to test their speed and strength.

Boys practiced shooting their arrows. The games were fun, and they helped to sharpen hunting skills. For example, in the hoop and pole game, the "hunter" tried to throw a pole through a moving hoop. This helped him to hit a moving target.

Girls played with dolls. They laughed and talked with their friends. They also did beadwork.

Music and dancing were important as well. People sang songs and played drums or rattles. They danced for fun as well as to please the spirits or to celebrate a good harvest. They danced to bring the deer or buffalo near and to get the corn to grow.

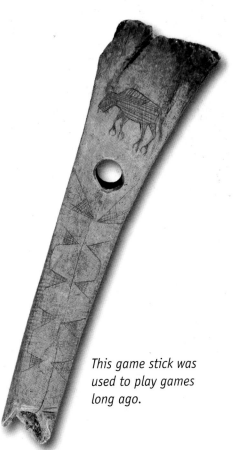

This game stick was used to play games long ago.

2 MEMORY MASTER

1. How do we know the Illini were skilled farmers?
2. Summarize how life changed from season to season.
3. Describe the work of men, women, and children.

starve

New Tribes Move to Illinois Lands

Word of the rich hunting grounds in the place we now call Illinois spread all the way to the East Coast. The mighty Iroquois (ir·a·KOI) had lived in the East for many years. Then people from Europe started moving onto Iroquois lands, building homes, and farming. The Iroquois left their lands and traveled west. They wanted to live on the rich land where the Illini were already living.

As the Iroquois moved west, they took over lands where other tribes were living. The Sauk, Fox, Potawatomi (pot·ah·WAH·toe·mee), and Miami tribes also had to move. They also wanted Illini lands. They moved into the Illini region and killed many of the Illini people.

As a result, the Illini split into smaller groups and moved in different directions. Their groups became smaller and weaker.

The Fox and Sauk

The Fox Indians lived near the Fox River. However, after years of fighting other tribes, there were few Fox people left. They formed an alliance with the Sauk so they would be stronger against their enemies.

This is how an englishman described a Sauk village:

"This is the largest and best built Indian town I ever saw. It contains about 90 houses, each large enough for several families. These are built of . . . planks neatly joined, and covered with bark . . . to keep out the . . . rains. Before the doors are . . . comfortable sheds, in which the [people] sit, when the weather will permit, and smoke their pipes.

The land near the town is very good. In their [gardens], which lie next to their houses, they raise . . . Indian corn, beans, melons, . . . so that this place is . . . the best market for traders to furnish themselves with provisions [supplies], of any within 800 miles of it."

Compare the two maps. You will see that the Illini lost much of their land to other tribes.

Shrinking Illini Lands

1675   1765

Illini

Miami
Illini
Kickapoo
Potawatomi
Fox and Sauk

Potawatomi

The Potawatomi tribe took over much of Illinois. Their lands stretched all around the lower part of Lake Michigan, and then they moved all over central Illinois. They wore clothes made from animal skins. After they met the French trappers, they wore cotton clothes. Women decorated their skirts with colorful ribbons.

The Kickapoo

About 100 years after the Illini first came into Illinois, a group called the Kickapoo (kik·uh·POO) moved into a region near today's Peoria. Like the other groups, they got food by hunting, gathering, and farming corn, beans, and squash.

Starved Rock

After the new groups came into Illinois, the Illini Alliance lost much of its power. A small group of Illini escaped to the top of a rock. They knew they could defend themselves easily from the enemy tribe below. The rock stood high above the river and could only be reached from one side. On the other three sides there was a drop of more than 150 feet to the river below.

To get water, the people on the rock used long vines to lower their pots to the Illinois River. But their plan did not work. Some of their enemies hid near the base of the rock. They cut the vines each time the Illini tried to get water from the river.

After a while, there was no more water. The people ran out of food and *starved* to death. They chose to die rather than give themselves up to their enemies.

Today, you can visit Starved Rock State Park along the Illinois River. Inside the park is a high, flat rock called Starved Rock. Now you know how the rock got its name.

Starved Rock
State Park

3 MEMORY MASTER

1. Why did new tribes move onto the lands of the Illini?
2. How did Starved Rock get its name?

Starved Rock

WORDS TO UNDERSTAND

legend
shaman

A Spiritual People

Throughout time, all cultures have had belief systems that give meaning to their lives and explain how our world and the people and animals came to be. The belief system of American Indians was an important part of life. The people believed all living things had a spirit. They held ceremonies with dancing and music to ask the spirits for a good hunt or success in war.

Sick people went to special religious men called **shamans.** A shaman was a leader and a healer who tried to get special help from the spirit world. He also knew which plants could cure a bad infection or heal a wound.

The Illini worshiped one god above all others. They called him *Kitchesmanetoa* (Kitch·es·man·e·TOH·a). He was the maker of all things. The people also honored the sun and thunder.

Making Connections

When was the last time you were sick? What did you do to get better? How does this compare to the ways the Illini children got help when they were sick?

Close to Nature

American Indians lived close to nature. They knew all about the land. The ground under their feet was more than just grass, rock, and dirt. The sun in the sky was more than just a ball of fire. They wanted to see and feel and touch the earth every day.

The people made almost everything they used from the natural resources around them. The wood, rock, water, soil, plants, and animals were part of everyday life.

Sharing was important. They said that all land people farmed and hunted on and all rivers and lakes they fished in belonged to everyone in the group. They believed that the land was made for the good of all the people.

Respect for Animals

American Indians shared the land with animals. They did not step on a snake's tracks or disturb the fox's den. Trees, flowers, squirrels, and insects all had the same value. They said the land belonged to the spider and the ant and the deer the same as it does to people. When they killed an animal for food, they used every part of it. Nothing was wasted.

Making Connections

Today, we also enjoy the outdoors. We delight in the beauty of a sunset or the sound of a running river. What are ways we show respect for nature today?

Using the Buffalo

At one time over 40 million buffalo, or bison, roamed North America. The large, shaggy animal was sacred to the Indian people. It provided food, shelter, and clothing. The Indians used all parts of the buffalo.

Buffalo Parts and Uses

1. **Meat** was eaten.
2. **Skins** were made into blankets, drums, shields, saddles, and clothing.
3. **Hair** was used to make rope.
4. **Horns** were used for spoons, bowls, and cups.
5. **Bones** were made into tools, knives, and needles.
6. **Fat** was made into soap.
7. **Tongues** were made into hairbrushes.

Learning from Legends

Especially during the winter months, people gathered together by a warm fire and told stories. Children learned about their world by listening to **legends.** Legends are stories that tell about the past. Storytelling was a time for sharing and for being close. It was a time for telling about the good things people had done. It was a time of laughing and listening.

Some stories told the history of the people so that it would not be forgotten. Some stories explained things, like why the stars were in the sky or why the wolf howled at the moon. These kinds of stories are called *pourquois* (por·KWA). They explain why things are the way they are in nature. Through legends, children learned important lessons. They learned to treat all living things with respect.

What Do You Think?

Storytelling was fun, and it was also like school. Children learned many things from the stories they heard. Do you think we can learn things from stories today?

The Creation of the Owl and the Rabbit

The Great Maker was busy creating different animals. He was working on Rabbit. Rabbit was saying, "I want nice long legs and long ears like Deer. I want sharp fangs and claws like Panther."

"I will make you the way you want to be," said the Great Maker. "I will give you what you ask for." He went on working on Rabbit's hind legs, making them long the way Rabbit asked.

Owl was sitting in a nearby tree, waiting for his turn. He was saying, "Whoo, whoo. I want a nice long neck like Swan's and beautiful feathers like Cardinal's. I want you to make me into the most beautiful, the fastest, and the most wonderful of all the birds."

The Maker said, "Be quiet. Turn around and look in another direction. Even better, close your eyes. I don't allow anyone to watch me work!" The Maker was just then working on Rabbit's ears. He was making them very long, the way Rabbit had asked.

Owl refused to do what the Great Maker said. "Nobody can forbid me to watch!" Owl said. "Nobody can order me to close my eyes! I like watching, and watch I will!"

The Great Maker became very angry. He grabbed Owl, and pulled him down from his branch. He stuffed his head deep into his body, shaking him until his eyes grew big with fright. He pulled at his ears until they were sticking up on both sides of his head.

"There," said the Maker, "that will teach you! Now you won't be able to turn your neck so far to watch things you shouldn't watch. Now you have big ears to listen when someone tells you what not to do. Now you have big eyes, but you will not be able to watch me because you will only be awake at night. And your feathers won't be red like Cardinal's but they will be gray."

Owl flew off, crying, "Whoo, whoo, whoo..."

The Great Maker turned back to finish Rabbit. But Rabbit had been so afraid at the Maker's anger that he had run off half done. That is why only Rabbit's hind legs are long. He has to hop about instead of walking and running. Rabbit is afraid of most everything because he never got the claws and fangs he asked for.

As for Owl, he remains as the Maker shaped him—with big eyes, a short neck, and ears sticking up on the sides of his head. He has to sleep during the day and come out only at night.

A Vision Quest

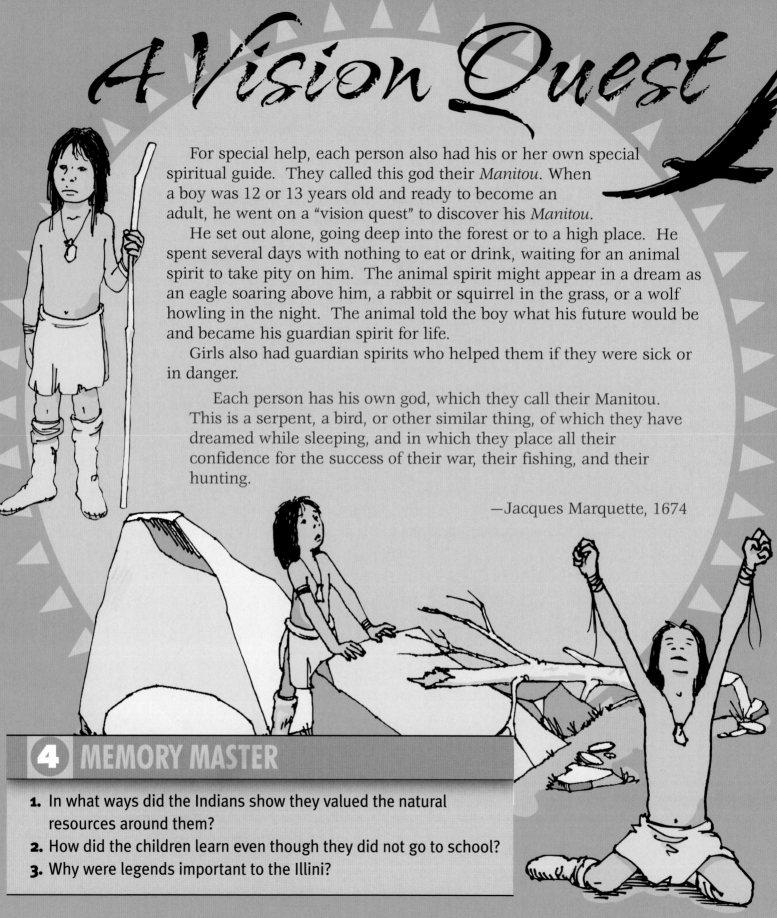

For special help, each person also had his or her own special spiritual guide. They called this god their *Manitou*. When a boy was 12 or 13 years old and ready to become an adult, he went on a "vision quest" to discover his *Manitou*.

He set out alone, going deep into the forest or to a high place. He spent several days with nothing to eat or drink, waiting for an animal spirit to take pity on him. The animal spirit might appear in a dream as an eagle soaring above him, a rabbit or squirrel in the grass, or a wolf howling in the night. The animal told the boy what his future would be and became his guardian spirit for life.

Girls also had guardian spirits who helped them if they were sick or in danger.

Each person has his own god, which they call their Manitou. This is a serpent, a bird, or other similar thing, of which they have dreamed while sleeping, and in which they place all their confidence for the success of their war, their fishing, and their hunting.

—Jacques Marquette, 1674

④ MEMORY MASTER

1. In what ways did the Indians show they valued the natural resources around them?
2. How did the children learn even though they did not go to school?
3. Why were legends important to the Illini?

Chapter 3 "American Indians"

Chapter 3 Review

Activity

Saving Our Resources

The Indians respected the land and did not waste resources. Brainstorm to make a list of all the possible ways to use something you might normally throw away. For example, what are some ways you could use a worn-out shoe, an old garden hose, or a flat football?

Activity

An Interview with the Illini

Write an interview that might take place between you and a member of the Illini Alliance. Choose a partner to help you think of questions and answers. Use the information in this chapter to help you answer questions about what life was like in the 1600s. Then act out the interview for your class.

Activity

Find Out More

Choose an Indian tribe you want to know more about. Make a list of questions you have about the tribe. Use the Internet or books from the library to find the answers. Present the information to your class with a poster, song, or model.

Activity

Write a Legend

Why does the chipmunk have black stripes? Why does the fawn lose its white spots as it grows older? Write a legend to answer these questions or another question about nature. Then tell your legend to a friend out loud. That is the way Indian legends were passed from one person to another.

Illinois Changes Hands

Anchor It!

12,000 B.C.
First people in North America

1400s
Columbus discovers America.

1500s
America first appears on
the map.

1600s
Pilgrims arrive.

1700s
Declaration of Independence
George Washington

1800s
Abraham Lincoln
Pioneers go west.

1900s
Martin Luther King
Your parents were born.

2000s
A New Century
9/11 Terrorists attack the U.S.

Timeline of Events

1673
Marquette and Jolliet explore
the Mississippi River.

1699
The French set up a
permanent settlement at
Cahokia.

1670   1680   1690   1700

1675
Marquette dies.

1680
La Salle and Tonti
build Crevecoeur near
present-day Peoria.

1682
La Salle reaches the Gulf of Mexico
and claims the entire Mississippi River
for France. He builds Fort
St. Louis near Starved Rock.

1703
Kaskaskia is
first settled.

Chapter 4

For a very long time our prairie land was a place of mystery to everyone except the American Indians. Then explorers, fur traders, and missionaries came.

Louis Jolliet and Father Marquette traveled the upper Mississippi River in birch bark canoes. Can you imagine what they saw along the shore?

1719
Fort de Chartres is built near present-day Prairie du Rocher.

1754-1763
French and Indian War

1763-1765
Pontiac's War

1710   1720   1750   1760   1770

1720
African slaves are first brought to Illinois region.

1763
Proclamation Line of 1763

PEOPLE TO KNOW

Louis Jolliet
Jacques Marquette
La Salle
Henri de Tonti

PLACES TO LOCATE

Canada
England
France
Ottawa
Peoria

WORDS TO UNDERSTAND

ambitious
portage
rival
voyageur

Europe is a continent across the Atlantic Ocean. There are many countries in Europe. The people who live there are called Europeans.

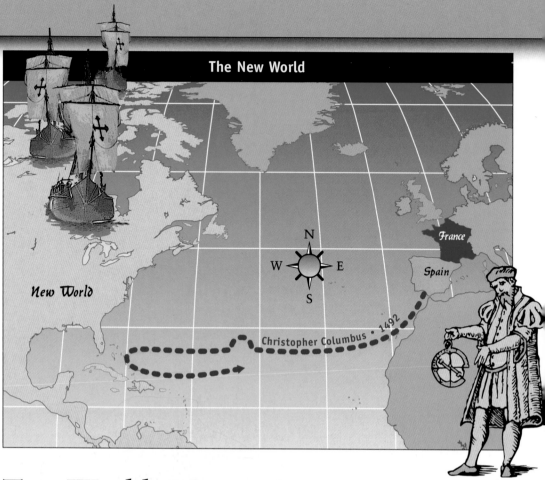

The New World

New World

France

Spain

Christopher Columbus · 1492

Two Worlds Meet

In fourteen hundred ninety-two
Columbus sailed the ocean blue.

You have probably heard this little verse about the year Columbus and his crew landed on a small island in North America. When he returned to Spain, everyone started talking about the new land across the Atlantic Ocean. They told each other stories of the beautiful land that was good for farming. They thought there was a lot of gold in the New World. They wanted to trade with the Indians for thick animal furs. They also wanted to bring their Christian religion to the Indians.

Fur traders and Catholic priests sailed in small wooden ships to North America. The first meetings between these Europeans and the Native Americans brought great changes to the lives of the Indians.

In this chapter you will read that the Europeans brought some things that were good for the Indian people. They brought metal weapons and pots. The Indians liked the glass beads and mirrors they had never seen before. Europeans brought horses that helped Indians travel faster. Indian people started wearing clothes made from European cloth.

New Problems

Soon, however, there were problems between the Indians and the white men. They had different spiritual beliefs. They each had their own ways of thinking about how the earth was made and how to ask for blessings from a god or gods.

The American Indians and people from Europe also had different ideas about owning land. The Indians didn't believe land was something that could be owned by one person. Like air, it was to be shared by the whole group. The white explorers wanted to claim the land for their own country. Later, white settlers wanted to own land, fence it, and farm it. They did not want the Indians on their land. This caused problems for both groups.

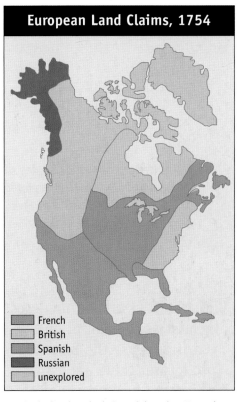

European Land Claims, 1754

French
British
Spanish
Russian
unexplored

Find the land claimed by the French. Was today's Illinois part of this region? What other countries claimed land in North America? Why do you think the people in Europe claimed land where American Indians had lived for centuries?

Disease Kills Native Americans

Another problem was disease or sickness brought to the Indians by traders and settlers. Smallpox, whooping cough, and measles spread quickly from person to person across the country.

The Indians had lived here for thousands of years. They had never had smallpox or measles before, so their bodies could not fight off the illness. The old and the young had the hardest time. Many Indians got well, but thousands died. In some places, entire villages died.

Native Americans served as guides to Marquette and Joliet as they explored the Mississippi River.

France Enters the New World

After Columbus visited North America, European countries sometimes sent men to explore and settle parts of the new land. Over 200 years later, much of North America was claimed by three countries—England, France, and Spain. Kings and queens in Europe claimed the land, but hardly any European people lived in the land of the American Indians.

Jolliet and Marquette

The land we call Illinois was part of the very large French claim in North America. So were parts of Canada. France knew it must stop its old **rival,** England, from becoming too powerful. England already had colonies along the Atlantic Coast. So France made plans to explore the land it claimed.

The French governor in Canada sent Louis Jolliet (joh·le·ET), an expert mapmaker, to find out where the Mississippi River went. They hoped it would go to the Pacific Ocean.

Father Jacques Marquette (mar·KET), a Catholic priest, was asked to go along on the trip. He had lived in Canada for seven years and had learned to speak many Indian languages. Father Marquette would teach the Indian people about the Catholic religion.

Christianity is a belief in Jesus Christ as the Son of God. Christians use the Bible as scripture. There are many different Christian churches today. The Catholic Church is one of them.

Since Catholic priests wore long black robes, Indians called the priests "black robes." Father Marquette promised the Indians that other "black robes" would come and teach them more about Christianity.

Jolliet and Marquette paddled across Lake Michigan into Green Bay in two birch bark canoes. With the help of other boatmen, they followed smaller rivers that flowed into the Mississippi River. They traveled on the Mississippi all the way to the Arkansas River, and then they turned back. By then they realized that the river did not flow into the Pacific Ocean, but probably went to the Gulf of Mexico instead. They had learned from Indians that if they kept going, they would run into land claimed by Spain and unfriendly Indians.

On their trip, Jolliet and Marquette visited American Indian villages near today's cities of Peoria and Ottawa. Father Marquette promised the Indians at a Kaskaskia village that he would return to teach them more about Jesus.

The return trip against the current of the river was very hard. Again, Indian guides helped. They suggested that the men return on the Illinois River when they got to it, instead of on the Mississippi.

Marquette and Jolliet traveled a very long way back to Canada with exciting news. The soil was rich. The land was flat. Trees did not have to be cleared before houses could be built.

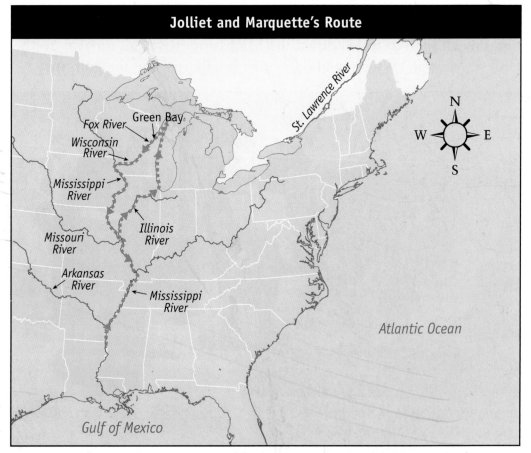

Jolliet and Marquette's Route

The men traveled down the Mississippi River to the Arkansas River. On their return trip, they went up the Illinois River.

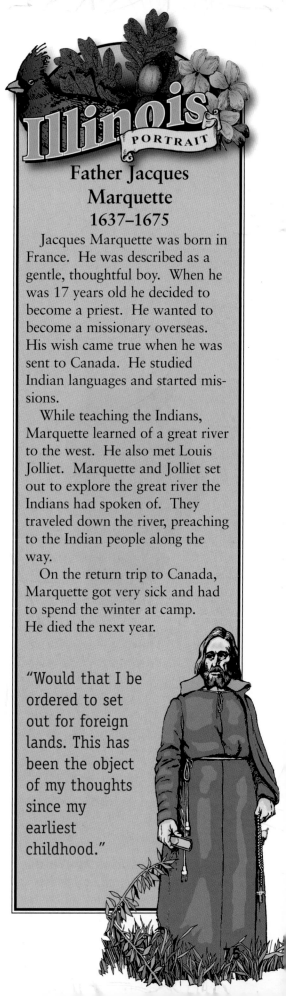

Illinois PORTRAIT

Father Jacques Marquette
1637–1675

Jacques Marquette was born in France. He was described as a gentle, thoughtful boy. When he was 17 years old he decided to become a priest. He wanted to become a missionary overseas. His wish came true when he was sent to Canada. He studied Indian languages and started missions.

While teaching the Indians, Marquette learned of a great river to the west. He also met Louis Jolliet. Marquette and Jolliet set out to explore the great river the Indians had spoken of. They traveled down the river, preaching to the Indian people along the way.

On the return trip to Canada, Marquette got very sick and had to spend the winter at camp. He died the next year.

"Would that I be ordered to set out for foreign lands. This has been the object of my thoughts since my earliest childhood."

La Salle and Tonti

René-Robert Cavelier (kav·uhl·YAY), a wealthy Frenchman, had the title Sieur de La Salle. A *sieur* is a French knight or lord, so his title was similar to "Lord of La Salle." We call him La Salle for short.

La Salle was **ambitious.** Excited by the news of Marquette and Jolliet's trip, he made plans to start a fur trading company. He hoped the Indians in America would trade only with the French. Then he would build a chain of forts from the St. Lawrence River all along the Mississippi River.

The king of France was pleased. He gave La Salle land in Canada and put him in charge of the fur trade south of the Great Lakes.

LaSalle Meets Tonti

During his travels La Salle met an Italian man named Henri de Tonti. Tonti had lost a hand in battle, so he wore an iron hook. La Salle and Tonti became partners. In a boat Tonti had made himself, they led a group of men into Illinois. The men cut down logs, dug holes to set them in, and built Fort Crevecoeur (krev·KUR).

La Salle wanted to do more than build forts. He wanted to be the first French man to travel down the Mississippi River all the way to the Gulf of Mexico. When he and his men finally reached the gulf, they

Fort Crevecoeur

La Salle traveled down the Mississippi River all the way to the Gulf of Mexico. He claimed the river and all the land next to it for France.

This painting shows La Salle's second trip to the New World. His men are probably unloading supplies. What can you learn about the people on the trip by the ways the artist painted their clothes and their hair?

held a ceremony. La Salle put a flag in the ground and claimed the land on both sides of the river for France. He named it Louisiana, after King Louis of France.

Then the travelers went back to Illinois. On top of Starved Rock, La Salle and his men built Fort St. Louis. Many Illini Indians built their homes near the fort for protection against other tribes. La Salle left Tonti in charge of Fort St. Louis and returned to France.

La Salle Runs into Trouble

La Salle left with a new idea to share with the king of France. He told the king he would start a colony where the Mississippi River flowed into the Gulf of Mexico. The king gave La Salle four ships and a crew of about 200 men. They left France for the Gulf of Mexico, but there was trouble right from the start.

The Spanish captured one ship near Florida. The other ships made it to the Gulf of Mexico, but they missed the Mississippi River. They sailed right by and went ashore on the coast of Texas. La Salle's crew was angry. They had been on the ship for many months, were out of supplies, and wanted to go home. The captain and some of the crew sailed back to France.

La Salle kept trying to reach the Mississippi River. Each time something tragic happened. The ships crashed and some men drowned. The rest tried to find their way by land to the river. Finally the weary men had had enough. They shot and killed La Salle.

What Do You Think ?

Why do you think the Illini felt safer near the French forts? How could the fort protect both the Indians and the settlers?

Tonti Takes Over

Tonti, who was still in Illinois country, took over La Salle's work there. He built a larger fort called Fort St. Louis and tried to get people from France to come across the ocean and settle there. However, he could not get many French people to make their homes in Illinois.

It wasn't until Fort de Chartres was built that French settlers came in larger numbers. The stone walls of the fort helped farmers, trappers, and traders feel safer from unfriendly Indians.

Indian Life Changed

The French changed the way the Indian people lived. The Indians no longer hunted animals only for their own food and clothes. They hunted for furs to trade at the French trading posts. They traded the furs for goods such as metal knives and pots, cloth, blankets, and sugar.

The French gave Illinois its name. They added the French suffix "ois" to the name of the local Indians and came up with "Illinois." The French would pronounce it "Il in wah."

At a frontier trading post, Native Americans traded furs for guns, food, blankets, metal tools, and other things the white people had.

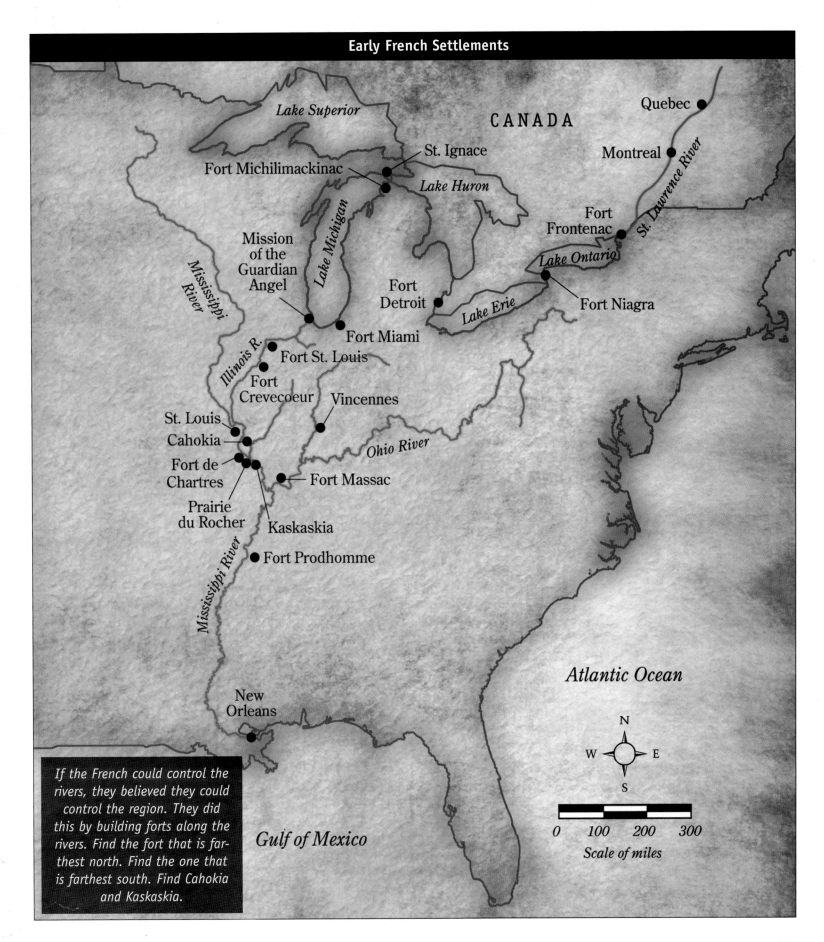

Early French Settlements

Lake Superior

CANADA

Quebec

St. Ignace

Fort Michilimackinac

Montreal

St. Lawrence River

Lake Huron

Fort Frontenac

Mississippi River

Mission of the Guardian Angel

Lake Michigan

Lake Ontario

Fort Detroit

Lake Erie

Fort Niagra

Illinois R.

Fort Miami

Fort St. Louis

Fort Crevecoeur

Vincennes

St. Louis

Cahokia

Ohio River

Fort de Chartres

Fort Massac

Prairie du Rocher

Kaskaskia

Mississippi River

Fort Prodhomme

Atlantic Ocean

New Orleans

N
W   E
S

Gulf of Mexico

0   100   200   300
Scale of miles

If the French could control the rivers, they believed they could control the region. They did this by building forts along the rivers. Find the fort that is farthest north. Find the one that is farthest south. Find Cahokia and Kaskaskia.

The Amazing Voyagers

French merchants wanted furs they could sell in Europe. They wanted the soft, thick furs of foxes, bears, otters, wolves, and beavers—especially beavers. There were many beavers in Canada and the Illinois region.

At trading posts and forts, merchants and Indians bartered for furs. The traders offered a metal cooking pot for a tall stack of furs. When a fair trade was agreed upon, the items were exchanged. The furs were put into bundles that weighed 90 pounds. The bundles were then stored until a group of men called *voyageurs* came to collect them and take them to larger trading posts or shipping ports.

Voyageurs spent months on rivers and lakes. To help pass the time they sang songs. Often the songs helped the men paddle faster or with the same rhythm. Mostly, their songs helped them through long hours of hard work.

Voyageurs traveled on rivers in Canada. They also worked on the Mississippi River and along the major rivers in Illinois. Voyageurs used the rivers as highways for moving furs.

Often eight men spent 15 hours a day paddling a canoe that was 20 to 40 feet long and 6 feet wide.

Portages

Sometimes the rivers or lakes did not connect with one another. There was land in between that needed to be crossed. This land was called a *portage.* When it was time to move the canoes and furs over land, the men had to unpack everything from their canoe. Then they carried the furs on their backs and shoulders. Somehow, they also had

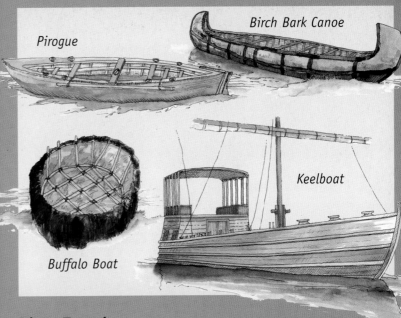

River Travel

The Indians taught the French how to make birch bark canoes and buffalo boats. A buffalo boat was a round willow frame covered by buffalo skins.

The French also built *pirogues*. A *pirogue* was a hollowed-out log that looked a lot like a long birch bark canoe. Planks were added across the sides of the boat to use as seats.

For large shipments of fur, the trappers used keelboats. A keelboat had a wooden wedge called a "keel" along the bottom of the boat and a sail that pushed the boat along in the wind. The trip upriver was very hard. Men on the boat stuck long poles down into the river and pushed the boat upstream. Sometimes men on the bank pulled ropes tied to the boat to force it upstream, inches at a time.

to carry the canoe. Some of the portages were five miles long. When the men reached the next body of water, they had to repack the canoe. To avoid making too many trips back and forth, the voyageurs carried more than one bundle of furs on their back. Sometimes they carried several at a time. Remember, each bundle weighed 90 pounds. It was a heavy load.

Who Could Be a Voyageur?

Fur trading companies looked for special men to be voyageurs. First, they had to be strong. Because of the heavy lifting and long hours of rowing boats, voyageurs needed strong muscles.

The fur companies also looked for men with pride. Each voyageur felt he did something better than anyone else. Some showed how strong they

were by carrying more than one bundle on a portage. The men who paddled in the front and rear of the canoe took pride in their ability to miss rocks as they raced through rapids.

All the men showed their pride by decorating themselves and their canoes with bright colors and feathers. A voyageur canoe could be quite a sight. Picture it in your mind: a brightly painted boat, feathers front and back, and eight men singing at the tops of their lungs as they steer left and right to miss dangerous rocks in a roaring river.

Voyaguers carried bundles of furs to trading posts a long way away. From there the furs were shipped to the American colonies and across the Atlantic Ocean to Europe.

Chapter 4 "Illinois Changes Hands"

High Fashion

The beaver hat was the reason our land was explored so much by the trappers. For over 100 years, they were the fashion for European men. Hat makers could hardly keep up with all the hats people wanted. People wanted fur for other reasons, too. It became popular for both men and women to wear fox, otter, and other animal fur on coat collars, sleeves, gloves, and boots.

The trappers in Europe had killed all the beavers there. When they learned that the land around Illinois had rivers full of beavers, they came here to trap them.

Activity

Study a Primary Source

This price list from 1703 shows what English goods were worth in beaver skins. Use the list to answer the questions. Notice that the letter "s" looks like an "f."

1. List three things you could get if you had one beaver skin to trade.
2. How many fox furs would equal one beaver fur? Why was beaver fur worth more than fox fur?

One yard Broad Cloth, *three* Beaver skins, *in season.*
One yard & half Gingerline, *one* Beaver skin, *in season*
One yard Red or Blew Kersey, *two* Beaver skins, *in season.*
One yard good Duffels, *one* Beaver skin, *in season.*
One yard & half broad fine Cotton, *one* Beaver skin, *in season*
Two yards of Cotton, *one* Beaver skin, *in season.*
One yard & half of half thicks, *one* Beaver skin, *in se*
Five Pecks Indian Corn, *one* Beaver skin
Four Pecks Pease, *one* Beaver skin, *in season.*
Two Pints of Powder, *one* Beaver skin, *in season.*
One Pint of Shot, *one* Beaver skin, *in season.*
Six Fathom of Tobacco, *one* Beaver skin, *in season.*
Forty Biskets, *one* Beaver skin, *in season.*
Ten Pound of Pork, *one* Beaver skin, *in season.*
Six Knives, *one* Beaver skin, *in season.*
Six Combes, *one* Beaver skin, *in season.*
Twenty Scaines Thread, *one* Beaver skin, *in season.*
One Hat, *two* Beaver skins, *in season.*
One Hat with Hatband, *three* Beaver skins, *in season.*
Two Pound of large Kettles, *one* Beaver skin, *in season*
One Pound & half of small Kettles, *one* Beaver skin, *in season*
One Shirt, *one* Beaver skin, *in season.*
One Shirt with Ruffels, *two* Beaver skins, *in season.*
Two Small Axes, *one* Beaver skin, *in season.*
Two Small Hoes, *one* Beaver skin, *in season.*
Three Dozen middling Hooks, *one* Beaver skin, *in season.*
Blade, *one* & *half* Beaver skin, *in season.*

What shall be accounted in Value equal
One Beaver in season : *Viz.*
One Otter skin in season, is one Beaver
One Bear skin in season, is one Beaver,
Two Half skins in season, is one Beaver
Two Foxes in season, is one Beaver.
Two Woodchocks in season, is one Beaver.
Four Martins in season, is one Beaver.
Eight Mincks in season, is one Beaver.
Five Pounds of Feathers, is one Beaver.
Four Raccoones in season, is one Beaver.
Four Seil skins large, is one Beaver.
One Moose Hide, is two Beavers.
One Pound of Castorum, is one Beaver.

1 MEMORY MASTER

1. How did the life of a voyageur compare to that of explorers such as Marquette and Jolliet?
2. What qualities did a man have to have to be a voyageur?
3. What did France hope to gain by developing the fur trade?

PEOPLE TO KNOW

Philippe Renault

PLACES TO LOCATE

Africa
West Indies
Cahokia
Kaskaskia

WORDS TO UNDERSTAND

surplus

Life in French Villages

Soon more people came to the Illinois region from France. Some were trappers who searched the rivers for beavers, so they could sell the furs in Europe. Others were priests and farmers.

The French at Cahokia and Kaskaskia set up the first two permanent European settlements in the region. Other small villages, such as Prairie du Rocher, grew up around French forts.

French villages in Illinois were made up of small houses along narrow streets or paths. The houses were built close together for safety. A church stood at the center of most villages. The Catholic Church was very important to the people. Often the priest served as the schoolteacher for the children in the village.

Land and Houses

In the village, the small houses were usually made of heavy logs with white plaster on the outside. Plaster gave the houses a fresh, clean look. The houses often had a living area, a bedroom, and a fireplace in between. Most houses were one story with a steep roof.

Each house had a large porch that sometimes went around all four sides of the house. The porch was called a "gallery." It protected the

This drawing of a French home in Kaskaskia appeared in a French magzine in 1826. Why do you think the home was built up on stilts? Why would a porch that went all around the house be a good idea?

family inside from sun and rain. It also allowed the house to be opened up in the summer to take in cool breezes. People could sit and work outside on the porch and stay up off the dirt. Porches were a good place for children to play.

Farming and Food

Outside the village were large fields. Here the common people collected firewood and let their pigs and cattle roam. There was also a field where the village raised their crops of wheat, oats, and barley. The field was called the "grand champ," or "great field."

The French king gave every family one long strip of land reaching to the riverbank. This allowed every family access to the river. They used the river for water and transportation.

Families also had a small garden next to their home. They grew fresh potatoes, pumpkins, corn, cabbages, carrots, and melons. They grew apple, peach, and plum trees. They grew grapes to make into wine.

The people also ate meat—mostly pork or dried beef. They got the meat by hunting and fishing. Rather than frying or roasting meats over the fire, as English or American settlers did, the French spent hours slowly cooking their meat in rich gravy. A favorite food was buffalo tongue!

Because the land was so good for farming, a family often had leftover crops to sell. This is called a *surplus.* Wheat, oats, and tobacco grew well in the rich soil. The surplus crops were sent to New Orleans along with bacon, buffalo hides, and furs. There they were sold or traded for sugar, rice, furniture, tools, and clothing.

Everyone was busy during the planting and harvesting seasons, but between seasons the men went on long hunting trips and trapped animals for fur companies. Some men worked on boats going up and down the Mississippi River.

Making Connections

Have you ever planted carrots or melons in a garden? Have you ever eaten an apple picked right off a tree?

French Clothes

The French settlers dressed in colorful clothes. They combined European-style clothes with other styles from the Indians.

The women made clothing for the family. They bought colored cotton cloth from boats that came once a year from France.

A man might wear a bright cotton shirt with buckskin (leather) pants and moccasins. Women wore long calico skirts and blouses. Both men and women tied colorful red or blue cloths over their hair. In the winter, all the people wore warm capes, jackets, hats, and mittens made of fur or wool.

For special days the people wore nicer clothes made of special silk and satin from France. The women decorated their clothes with ribbons and lace.

French men and women danced to the tune of a fiddle. This celebration was in a French village near Kaskaskia. What do you think the Indian man is thinking?

The French at Play

The people visited each other on Sundays after church. Everyone, young and old, sang folksongs and danced. They had many parties and feasts, especially on holidays.

Most of the time, the French people got along well with the Illini. Together they fished, hunted, trapped, and explored. Some Indians had been taught by the French missionaries and went to French churches.

Slavery

At this same time, thousands of people from Africa were being brought to the villages as slaves. They were bought and sold as if they were property. They were forced to work for the rest of their lives for a master. Family members were often separated from each other. Sadly, many people saw slavery as an easy way to get strong workers.

Work in the Mines

Philippe Renault (fil·EEP·ren·OH) brought slaves to Illinois. Renault planned to open mines where there might be gold or other valuable minerals.

Renault stopped in the West Indies and bought black slaves on his way to Illinois. He planned to use the slaves for the hard work in his mines. He would also use them to farm his land and grow food for the miners.

Galena

Chapter 4 "Illinois Changes Hands"

Renault, his slaves, and other miners started to mine lead at the mouth of the Galena River. The demand for lead was great. It was used to make water pipes, tools, and bullets.

Before Renault returned to France, he sold his slaves to French villagers. For the next 100 years, some people in Illinois owned slaves.

Black slaves were first brought to the American colonies in sailing ships. Some were taken to mine lead in Galena.

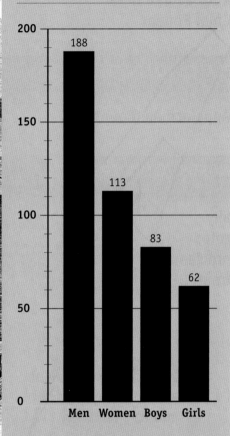

African Slaves in Illinois, 1752

Men — 188
Women — 113
Boys — 83
Girls — 62

1. What year is shown on the graph? 1752
2. Which was higher, the number of African men or women? Men
3. Were there more boys or more girls? Boys
4. Why do you think there were more male slaves?
5. How many slaves were in Illinois in 1752? This was about 32 years after the first slaves arrived. 346

② MEMORY MASTER

1. Describe the relationship between the French and the Indians at this time.
2. How were the villagers able to earn extra money to buy things that came on boats from France?
3. Why were slaves brought to the Illinois region?

PEOPLE TO KNOW

King George III
Chief Pontiac

PLACES TO LOCATE

Appalachian Mountains

WORDS TO UNDERSTAND

ally
colony
proclamation
treaty

A **colony** is a settlement or land ruled by another country far away.

An **ally** is a person or group who is on your side and tries to help you. In war, countries choose sides and become allies of each other.

Weapons during the French and Indian War were quite different from today's weapons.

The French and Indian War

While the French were starting new settlements in North America, the English also had their eye on the rich land. Both France and England were trying to build the largest empire. Both countries believed new colonies would make them rich and powerful. The natural resources here were valuable. The two countries went to war over control of this land. Native Americans had been living peaceably with the French and trapping furs for them. The Indians did not want to see the English take their lands, so they became allies with the French.

Because many Native Americans supported the French, the war is known as the French and Indian War. Other Indians, however, fought on the side of the English.

The English Rule Illinois

For nine years the two countries fought. The war finally ended when English soldiers captured French cities in Canada. A peace *treaty* was signed. England took control of Canada and all the land from the Atlantic Ocean to the Mississippi River. The place called Illinois was now in English hands.

Many French people were not willing to live under English rule. Some left North America and went back to France. Some moved south to New Orleans. The French who stayed wondered what would happen to them.

The Proclamation Line of 1763

In the treaty, Indian lands had been given to the English. But this was land the Indian people lived and hunted on. To settle the quarrels over Indian lands, England's King George III issued a *proclamation.* It stated that no English settlements could be made west of the Appalachian Mountains.

Think of an imaginary line down the Appalachian Mountains. The government said that white settlers would not be allowed to cross west over the line. For the moment, Indian land was protected.

However, the colonists were bitter about the line. Some had gone to war and fought for the right to trap and settle on that land. Many colonists didn't think the Indians deserved to have all of the land. Fur trappers ignored the line and moved west onto Indian lands anyway. So did many other people.

What Do You Think?

Indian tribes did not think the land, the rivers, or the animals could be owned. It was for the whole tribe and their allies to use. France and England thought differently. They wanted to own land. They took it, traded for it, or bought and sold it. What do you think is the best way to use the land?

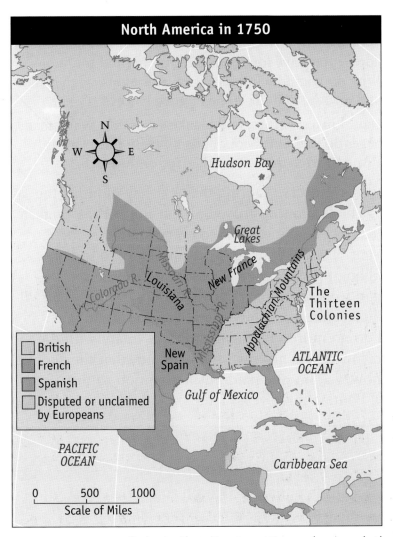

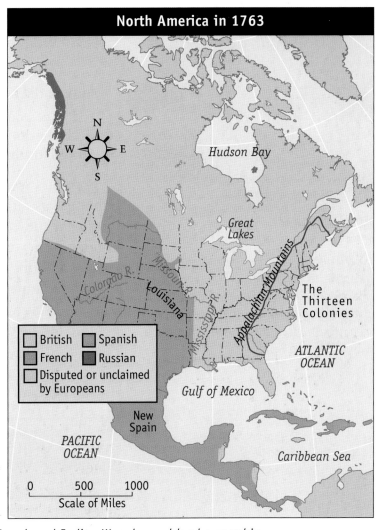

Compare these two maps to see how much the French and Indian War changed land ownership in North America. How did the change affect Illinois?

Pontiac's War

A chief of the Ottawa tribe was part of the Illini group. The English called him Chief Pontiac. Pontiac believed the Indians should take their land back. He believed in the words of an Indian prophet who had warned the people to keep the French and English settlers off their land. He claimed the Great Spirit was angry with all Indians.

Indians from tribes all around the Great Lakes gathered on the shores of Lake Erie. At the meeting, Chief Pontiac stood up. He was tall. He was strong. He had many tattoos and wore beaded earrings and silver bracelets on each arm. His face was covered with war paint. A collar of white feather plumes was around his neck. He was ready for war.

Standing before the other chiefs, Pontiac told them about the words of the Great Spirit:

> I am the Maker of heaven and earth, the trees, lakes, rivers, and all things else. . . . The land on which you live I have made for you, and not for others. . . . My children, you have forgotten the customs and traditions of your forefathers. Why do you not clothe yourselves in skins, as they did, and use the bows and arrows, and the stone-pointed lances?

> You have bought guns, knives, kettles, and blankets from the white man, until you can no longer do without them. Fling all these things away. And as for the English . . . wipe them from the face of the earth.

Pontiac's speech was a war cry. During the next few months, the fighting was terrible. The Indians destroyed all but four of the English forts near the Great Lakes. The English tried everything to stop Pontiac. They even sent blankets infected with smallpox to Indian villages in hopes of killing their people. It was a terrible time.

Pontiac's men began to desert him. They left to go back to their villages and stay with their families. After several years of fighting, Pontiac felt he could do no more. He signed a peace treaty with the English. It said the colonists did not own the land, but that they could use it. Once again, however, no one paid much attention to the treaty. An Illini Indian killed Pontiac three years later.

Chief Pontiac held a wampum belt when he spoke to his people. A wampum belt was made of tiny white and purple shells strung together. Holding the belt meant he wanted the people to know he was telling the truth.

③ MEMORY MASTER

1. Who fought on each side during the French and Indian War?
2. What was the purpose of the Proclamation Line of 1763?
3. What did Chief Pontiac want his people to do?

Chapter 4 Review

An Indian Leader

Imagine you are the chief of a tribe. You might watch your people make deals with fur traders. You watch your people smile as they try on new jewelry. You watch the men take their guns to the edge of the village to practice shooting. You know some are accepting the new religion brought by the priests.

How do you feel about the future of your tribe? Do you welcome the changes, or do you worry about what is happening to your way of life? As the leader, what can you do?

Make up a speech or skit and present it to your class.

Activity

Charting Causes and Effects

A cause is something that happened. The effects are the results, or what happened because of the cause. In the chart below, the cause is in the center bubble. Think of some effects for the empty bubbles.

Activity

Write a Journal Entry

Put yourself in the place of Marquette and Jolliet. What was it like exploring the Mississippi River in a canoe? Write a journal entry that might have been written after a long day of travel. Describe what you might have seen. Describe how you might have felt. Let the reader know what you're thinking.

Life on the Frontier

Anchor It!

12,000 B.C.
First people in North America

1400s
Columbus discovers America.

1500s
America first appears on
the map.

1600s
Pilgrims arrive.

1700s
Declaration of Independence
George Washington

1800s
Abraham Lincoln
Pioneers go west.

1900s
Martin Luther King
Your parents were born.

2000s
A New Century
9/11 Terrorists attack the U.S.

Chapter 5

"Pushed from crowded cities and worn-out farms, pioneers trekked toward the sunset and opportunity."
—*Ray Allen Billington*

Settlers followed trails called "traces" through the mountains and hills to start a new life on the prairie. What would their new homes be like? Could they grow enough food to survive? How would the land and the weather be different from their own town? These are questions the pioneers asked each other.

PLACES TO LOCATE

Europe
Appalachian Mountains

WORDS TO UNDERSTAND

canvas
frontier
merchant
pioneer
settler

Moving West

A *pioneer* is a person who is one of the first to do something. Illinois pioneers were some of the first to travel across the country and start farms and towns. They wanted the chance to own their own land. They wanted adventure and a fresh start. While most were farmers, there were also blacksmiths, teachers, *merchants,* and doctors.

The first wave of pioneers settled in the southern part of what would later become the state of Illinois. There were woods and hills here. At first, they stayed away from the prairie. They were not familiar with prairie soil, and they did not think it would be good for growing crops.

Pioneers left their homes behind and moved beyond towns and farms to the wild lands of the *frontier.*

Pioneers are also called *settlers* because they built homes and settled down in the new place.

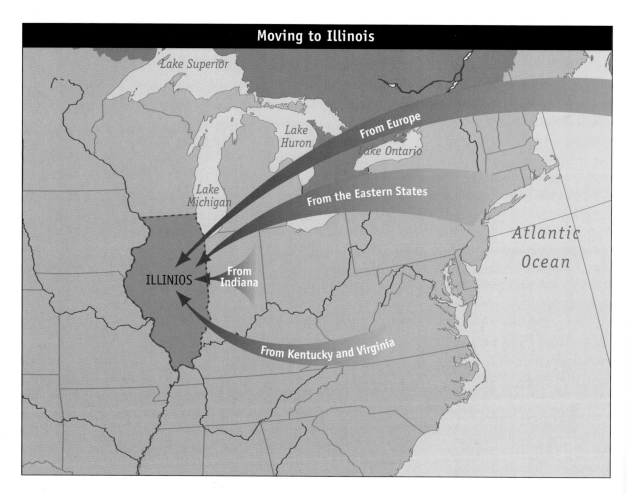

Moving to Illinois

Lake Superior
Lake Huron
Lake Ontario
Lake Michigan
From Europe
From the Eastern States
From Indiana
From Kentucky and Virginia
ILLINIOS
Atlantic Ocean

Where did the pioneers move from?

The next wave of pioneers came from eastern states. Since the land along the rivers was already dotted with new farms, they began to settle on the land between the rivers. They found out that the prairie had very rich soil indeed.

Pioneers also came from European countries. They had to first cross the Atlantic Ocean on a ship. Then they had the long trek west. We will read more about these people in another chapter.

Activity

Reading a Graph

Graphs help us to "see" information. If you can read a graph you can learn the facts quickly. It is always important to understand just what kind of information a graph is showing. The title and labels are good clues to the kind of information a graph contains. Study the graph. On a separate piece of paper, write down yes or no if the facts below could be learned from the graph.

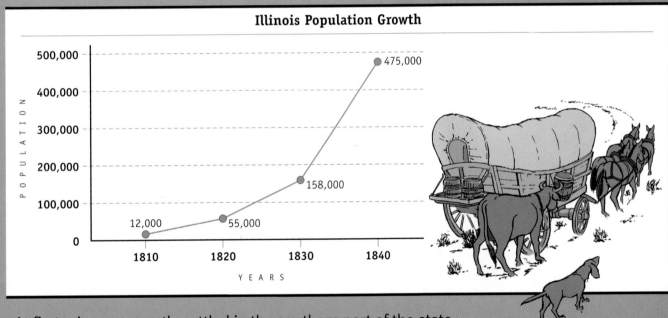

Illinois Population Growth

1. At first, pioneers mostly settled in the southern part of the state.
2. Between 1810 and 1820 the population of Illinois grew by 43,000.
3. After Illinois became a state (in 1818), the population grew.
4. There were many more settlers than Indians in Illinois by 1860.
5. In 1840, the population of Illinois was less than one-fourth of the population of the United States.
6. The population of Illinois more than doubled from 1820 to 1830.

Traveling By Land

People came to Illinois on the rivers or across the land, or both. If they came by land, they walked, rode horses, or came in covered wagons pulled by horses, mules, or oxen. The wagon was usually a wooden wagon made of hickory, maple, or oak. The front wheels of the wagon were smaller than the back wheels. This helped the wagon turn. Underneath the back wheels there was a bucket full of grease. This was used to make the wheels run smoothly.

The wagon box had long wooden hoops, called bows, bent over to form the top of the wagon. Heavy *canvas* cloth was put across the hoops to keep out the rain and dust. Men rubbed oil on the canvas to make it waterproof. Inside the wagon there were many hooks that hung from the wooden hoops. A family could hang clothes, bags of flour, milk cans, and anything there was room for.

Since the family carried all their belongings with them, it was very crowded inside the wagon. There were trunks, wooden boxes, oil lamps, bags of grain, a spinning wheel, and perhaps a butter churn. Some families tried to set up a bed and take other furniture, but most of it had to be dumped along the trail because it was just too heavy.

What Do You Think?

What do you think the children in the wagons were thinking? Were they excited? Nervous? Scared? Homesick? How would you feel?

Traveling in a wagon was not an easy trip. The ride was very uncomfortable and bumpy. Anyone old enough to walk usually walked beside the wagon.

Dirt Roads

Early roads were only dirt trails and tramped-down grass. Most were old Indian trails. They were rocky and bumpy. Often there were large holes in the way. The path was very muddy when it rained. Sometimes a horse's hoof or a wagon wheel got stuck in the mud.

Travel was very slow. Often a family covered only 12 miles a day. It might take them three months or more to get to the end of their journey. Sometimes bushes, trees, or large rocks were in the way, and travelers had to stop, get out of the wagon, and clear the trail. This could take hours.

What Do You Think

Which animals would you have chosen to pull your wagon? Why?

Horses, Mules, or Oxen?

People on the trails used three kinds of animals to pull their wagons: horses, mules, or oxen. Horses and mules moved the fastest, but they were the most expensive. They needed better food and better care to keep them going. Mules were cheaper. They could eat tougher, drier grasses. They could pull more than horses. But, they could also be very stubborn.

Oxen were the cheapest to buy. They moved much slower than horses or mules, but they could pull a heavier load. Oxen were not picky eaters, either. They could eat almost any grass along the trail.

Making Connections

When traveling in a car today, you usually go more than 35 miles per hour. If you travel by plane you go hundreds of miles per hour. Think of the last time you went to visit a friend or relative out of town. How long would it have taken if you had traveled in a covered wagon?

Mountain Passes

Pioneers faced another problem—mountains. Pushing and pulling heavy wagons over the slippery mountain rocks of the Appalachians was hard. Sometimes the horses were frightened and would not go down steep canyons. Sometimes wagons tipped over.

"A dozen yoke of oxen were hitched to one wagon, and with hard pulling they reached the top. After all the wagons were over, we took lunch on top of the mountains, and then prepared to go down . . . . The mountain was very steep. One yoke of oxen was hitched to a wagon, and one at a time went down. Heavy chains were fastened on behind the wagon and as many men as could catch hold of the chain did so, and when the wagon started they pulled back to keep the wagon from running down the mountain and killing the oxen."

—Mary Ackley

Activity

Packing Up

Pioneers had to be well prepared for the trip. They had to make sure they had enough food and supplies. One pioneer said that travelers should bring these things:

flour	butter	medicine	rope	water bucket
cornmeal	lard	salt for animals	shovel	soap
sugar	vegetables	rifle	axe	clothing
fruit	bacon	pots and kettles	hammer	extra bedding
				grease for wheels

If you had to leave your home, what things would you need? Make a list of at least ten things you would take with you.

Then compare your list to the pioneer's list. Share your list with a small group. Discuss how you decided what things you needed and what things you just really wanted.

Chapter 5 "Life on the Frontier"

Traveling by Water

Whenever they could, the pioneers used the rivers as highways. Traveling by boat was easier than traveling across land when there were no good roads.

Some pioneers floated down the rivers on wide, flat-bottomed boats called **flatboats.** A family loaded all their food, clothes, tools, seeds, and even animals on the boat. When they got to the end of their journey, they broke their flatboats apart and used the wood to build other things.

Other boats were called **keelboats.** They were the same kinds of boats some of the early explorers used. They had a long pole that a man stuck down into the water to help push a boat upstream against the current of the river. Sometimes men tied a strong rope to the front of the boat. Then a crew of strong men or mules walked along the shore and pulled the boat up the river.

The pioneers could only travel so far on the rivers. Then they had to find a way to get to a place where they could build a home and start a farm. What kind of boat is this group using?

1 MEMORY MASTER

1. Which part of Illinois was settled first? Why?
2. List some of the reasons why travel was slow.
3. Why did families have to limit the things they took with them in wagons?
4. Why did some families travel to Illinois on rivers?

sod

Making Connections

What materials were used to build your home? How is your home different from homes built by early pioneers? How is it similar?

The First Homes

Pretend you and your family have come to make a new life for yourselves. There is so much to do. You need to build a home. There is land to clear and crops to plant. There is furniture to make. Just about everything you use has to be made by hand.

First your parents find a good clear stream or river. It's important to build your house near water. You will need water for drinking, cooking, and cleaning. If you decide to live away from a stream, you will have to dig a well to get water.

If you can, your family picks a spot near some trees because you need wood to build your house, furniture, and fences. You also need trees for firewood. You'll keep a fire burning almost all the time for cooking, heating the cabin in winter, and warming water for your weekly baths.

No plumbing in your cabin means no running water. You must carry water in from the stream or from a well, if you dig one. Of course, no running water also means no toilet. So the next thing you build is an outhouse.

How to Build a Log Home

To build a log home, men first needed to clear the land. They cut away brush and chopped down trees. The men stacked heavy logs on top of each other to make walls. They laid them across the top to make a roof. Then they put clay or a mixture of mud and straw between the logs. When it dried, it sealed the cracks and kept out the wind and rain. A rock fireplace along one wall kept the cabin warm in the winter and gave the settlers a place to cook.

Log houses could be built quickly but they were not fancy. Many had only dirt floors, but later, wood was cut into flat planks to make a wooden floor.

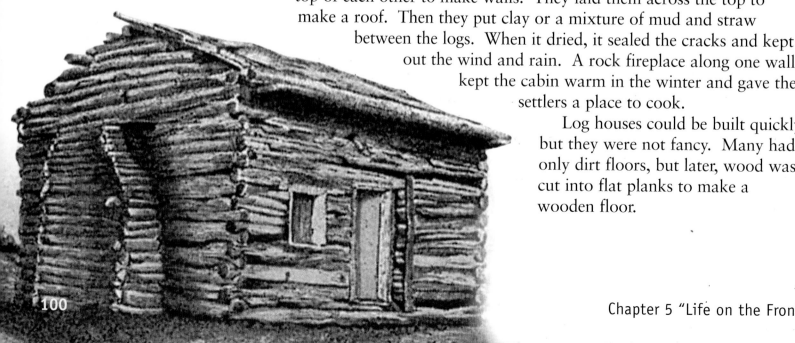

Chapter 5 "Life on the Frontier"

Glass cost a lot of money and had to be brought from other places, so settlers used greased paper for windows. They could cover them with wooden shutters if they needed to.

Most cabins were only one room, but they often had a loft. The loft was used for storage, but it was also where the children slept. They climbed a ladder to get to the loft and then went to sleep as the fire crackled in the fireplace below.

When the house was finished, the family made simple beds, tables, and benches. There might be a few chairs and a cradle for the baby. Sometimes they used wood from their wagon to make furniture. Can you imagine how nice it was for the children to finally get to sleep in a real bed after camping along the trail for many months?

After a while, families added more rooms to the cabin. They might build a larger, more permanent home of wood, stone, or brick. The cabin then became a barn for animals or a storage shed for tools and food.

"Our cabin . . . had one room. Trees of the same size were notched, as to bring them as near together as possible. The cracks were 'chinked' [filled in with mud] to keep the wind from whistling through."

—Jeanette Pigsley Mitchell

Sod Homes

Some settlers moved onto the prairie, where there were few trees. They built homes out of prairie **sod.** Sod was a thick, heavy piece of earth with a lot of grass roots still in it. The roots held the dirt together.

A home built of sod was called a "soddie." The best part about using sod blocks to build a house was that there was plenty of it. It was also free. The worst part was that the sod was very hard to dig up from the ground. If you were going to live in a sod house, your father spent days in the hot sun cutting through the tough prairie grasses. The roots of the grasses sometimes grew down six to ten feet.

First your father and the older boys cut the sod into rectangular slabs and pulled them up from the ground. The most common size was 12 inches by 24 inches. These blocks made walls two feet thick.

The men lifted the heavy slabs of sod onto a wagon and the family horse or mule pulled it to the home site. They laid the sod with the grass side down. The first layer was placed right on the ground. The others were then stacked up just like a brick wall. When the walls were high enough, logs were placed across the top. Then sod pieces were put on top. The grass kept growing, and a family had a living roof!

A sod house needed a stone fireplace for cooking and winter heat. Sod houses were dark inside because there were only a few windows. The floor was usually hard dirt. Because the walls were so thick, a sod house was warm in winter and very cool in summer. Prairie fires could not burn them, but rain often dripped through the roof.

Making Connections

You have probably seen rolls of sod ready to be laid out on someone's front yard. In a few weeks the family would have a beautiful new lawn. How does that sod differ from wild prairie sod?

Sod homes were built standing alone or as the front part of a dugout home that was cut into a hill. Sod homes were very common in the Midwest, but very few were built in Illinois. This soddie was built in Nebraska.

Chapter 5 "Life on the Frontier"

Point of View in Pictures

Not all people shared the same view of life on the prairie. Be a detective and see what you can learn by carefully looking at both pictures below. One is a painting and one is a photograph. Can you tell which is which? Discuss these questions with your class:

1. How is the painting different than the photograph?
2. Does one picture tell you more about the real life of the pioneers?
3. Does the painting change the way you feel about prairie life?
4. Which picture would you use to convince someone to settle on the prairie?

2 MEMORY MASTER

1. Why was it important to build a home near a river or stream?
2. Why did some pioneers build log homes and others build sod homes?
3. Compare and contrast the two kinds of homes.

calico
infested
linen

Corn and More Corn

Corn was delicious roasted and eaten on the cob. Most of it, however, was dried and then ground into cornmeal. It lasted all winter without going bad. The cornmeal was used to make cornbread, Johnny cakes, or mush. Frontier families ate corn nearly every day. They even fed corn to their animals. Farmers also used corn to make whiskey.

Families made use of the entire corn plant. They used corn husks for the bottoms of chairs, mats, brooms, or mattress stuffing. The dry cobs were burned for fuel.

Work, Work, Work

Everyone in a pioneer family had to work hard. Men worked outside building the home, furniture, and tools. The farmland had to be cleared, plowed, and planted. It took weeks to walk behind a strong animal and plow a large field of corn or wheat. Caring for the crops and farm animals also took a lot of time.

Men did the hunting and fishing. They might search all day to find a deer or wild turkey. Then they had to get it home, skin and clean it, and cut up the meat. They dried, smoked, or salted it so it would last longer.

It is easy to see that life on the frontier was very hard work. Work for mothers and daughters was never done. They took care of the babies and children. They swept the dirt floor and washed the dishes in a pan of water. They prepared the meals. They made the clothing. They sewed quilts. They also helped work in the gardens and fields. They milked the cows and made butter and cheese. They dried corn, vegetables, and fruit so it could be used during the long winters.

Food for the Family

Most of the food the family ate was grown on their small farm. They could not go to a store to buy what they needed.

Growing food began with plowing the soil. Plowing the land for the first time was very hard. Some farmers burned sections of the prairie grass. A prairie burn was helpful in getting rid of the tall prairie grass. However, the roots of prairie grasses went deep into the soil. Farmers used wooden or iron plows pulled by a mule or an ox. After plowing the land, seeds could be planted.

Farm families grew large fields of corn. They ate it and fed it to their animals. Sometimes they also grew wheat. They ground the wheat into flour and used the flour to make bread. Next to the house, the mother kept a garden with pumpkins, squash, beans, potatoes, and other vegetables and herbs.

Livestock was another food source. Cows provided milk, butter, and meat. Hogs provided pork and fat called lard. Chickens provided eggs. Many families let their cattle and hogs roam free though the woods. They marked the ears of the animals with a family mark. This helped identify their animals later. Men and boys hunted deer, wild turkeys, squirrels, and rabbits to provide meat for the family. They fished along the river for blue gill, catfish, and pike.

Cooking the Food

Growing crops or hunting wild animals for food was only the beginning. It took hours to prepare a meal. Everything had to be done by hand. Early cabins had no stoves. The women cooked in large pots over an open fire in the fireplace. When they finished cleaning up after one meal, it was often time to begin another meal. In later years, some people bought metal stoves that made cooking easier. However, the stoves still had to be fed wood or coal to keep the fire going.

Making Connections

How many nights a week does your family sit down to dinner at home? Who does most of the cooking?

What can you learn about pioneer life from this picture? How did the family heat their home and cook their food? Where did food come from? What animals lived on the farm?

Women wove cloth on large wooden looms. This woman is working outside on her front porch, where it was probably cooler than inside the cabin.

The stems of the flax plant were soaked, dried, beaten, and separated. The short fibers were used to stuff mattresses and to make string, rope, and candle wicks. The long fibers were woven into a light-colored cloth.

Making Connections

How often do you change your clothes? Would you like to wear the same clothes every day?

Making Clothes

Just as frontier settlers had to produce all of their own food, they also had to make their own clothing. Sheep provided wool to be woven into wool cloth or knitted into wool socks or sweaters. Warm pants, coats, and winter dresses were made of wool.

Flax was a plant grown on the prairie to be used to make sewing thread and cloth called **linen.** Linen was a softer, lighter cloth than wool, so it was better for summer shirts and dresses.

The mother of the family spent hours and hours making clothing. First she washed wool. Then she "carded" or brushed it to make all the fibers go one way. Next, she spun the wool into thread or yarn on a spinning wheel. Sometimes she boiled wild plants to make colored dye and soaked the yarn in the die until it was just the right color.

The mother and older girls used a loom to weave the thread into cloth. Then they used a paper pattern and cut the cloth. Each piece had to be sewn together by hand with a needle and thread to make shirts, pants, or dresses.

In later years, after there were better roads and railroads, people bought some cotton cloth that had been made in factories in the East. Cotton cloth was called **calico.** It was cooler to wear and came in many colors and patterns.

You can see why people owned only a few pieces of clothing. A boy wore the same pants week after week. He might have two shirts. A girl wore the same dress for many days. She might have one better dress for church on Sunday and one everyday dress for the rest of the week.

Washing the Clothes

To make soap, the mother saved ashes from the fireplace. She kept the ashes in a barrel. When the barrel was full, she poured water over the ashes. The liquid that oozed out the bottom of the barrel was called lye. She put the lye in a big kettle, added animal fat, and cooked the mixture over the fire. This was usually done outside. After it cooled, she molded the gooey liquid into soap "cakes." The soap was strong and smelly. It was used to wash dishes, clothes, and even the children.

Washing the clothes was a big job, especially if there were a lot of children in the family. Babies all wore cloth diapers that had to be washed. In the summer, the women washed the clothes outside. They carried the dirty clothes down to the creek and scrubbed them against rocks. Some families used washtubs, washboards, and hot water they heated on a stove or fire. Then the clothing had to be laid out over rocks or hung out to dry on a tree branch or a long rope.

Do you wonder how ashes and animal fat could help you keep clean?

Cloth scraps were not wasted. The women cut them into small pieces and sewed them into beautiful quilts. Scraps too small for anything else were used for stuffing cushions or even toy animals and dolls.

Lighting the Darkness

There were no electric lights like we have today, so candles and oil lamps were a way to produce light when it got dark. Women made candles from beeswax or animal fat. The people could not afford to waste candles, so when it was dark they sat around the fireplace and then went to bed.

Don't Get Sick!

Families were often large. It was not unusual to have six, eight, or even ten or more children in a family. There were plenty of brothers and sisters to play with.

Sadly, however, babies and small children often died of diseases. Measles, smallpox, diphtheria, and cholera sometimes killed several children in a family all in the same week. Those were very hard times.

One reason people got sick was because they did not understand what caused most diseases. They also did not know how disease was spread from one person to another. They had a hard time keeping food cool so it would not spoil. It was even hard to keep themselves and their homes clean.

Early Illinois was an unhealthy place. It was *infested* with insects. There were millions of mosquitoes in the swampy land around rivers. Fevers and a disease called the "ague" were very common. Ague was a form of malaria caused by mosquito bites. The sick person had chills and burning, shaking, headaches, and backaches. People with ague had to stay in bed for weeks. Many died.

There were usually no doctors nearby to help a family when they were sick. However, there were many home cures for the ague. One was to swallow pills made from cobwebs.

A corn husking in a large barn was a time to work and play at the same time. Families lived far apart from each other, so when they got together a few times a year they stayed all day.

Young men and women might play a game where if a man husked an ear that had red kernels, he got to kiss the girl of his choice!

Working Together

Families who didn't live too far apart sometimes worked together to get work done faster and to enjoy each other's company. "You help me and I'll help you" was the way people worked on the frontier. If a cabin or barn needed to be built, families came together for a "raising."

Sometimes women got together at a home or at the church and made quilts together. They could talk and sew while small children ran around or played under the quilt. Older children played games outside.

When the corn crop was ready, people took turns having "husking bees." Families from other farms came and joined in. Husking bees were part work, part party. Husking the corn meant taking the husks off of the ears. As everyone worked they laughed, told stories, and sang. Someone might bring a fiddle so they could dance.

Making Connections

How do neighbors on your street help each other?

③ MEMORY MASTER

1. How did a man and woman provide food for their family?
2. Describe three steps in making clothes.
3. Compare the way the settlers washed clothes to how your clothes are cleaned today.

memorize
recite

What kinds of work and play are going on in this drawing?

Making Connections

How are the chores divided in your house? What jobs do you do?

Frontier Children

Living on a farm meant everyone had to work together. Children were expected to work hard. Parents were strict, and chores were not an option.

Girls helped their mother prepare meals, sew, wash the clothes, and work in the garden. Boys helped their fathers tend crops, feed the animals, chop wood, and hunt and fish. Older children had to help take care of the smaller children. That could be a lot of work!

Having Fun

Just because work was hard does not mean frontier families never had fun. After a hard day on the farm, the family might relax by singing folksongs passed down from generation to generation. They might also play fiddles, banjos, or flutes.

Dancing was the way people had a good time when they had a celebration on a holiday. Someone played the fiddle, and everyone danced, even the children. Small babies slept off in a corner where they could be watched. The dances went on late into the night.

Children loved living out on the prairie next to streams and rivers. They could watch wild animals, go fishing, and make secret forts in the tall grass. They could ride a horse or even a goat! They could watch clouds make pictures in the wide-open sky.

Child's Play

When children were finished with their chores, they might have time to play. They played with toys like dolls, marbles, or dominoes. They also made up their own games. They played group games like Button, Button. This is how it worked:

The children sat in a circle. Everyone held the palms of their hands together. One child was "It." She held a button between the palms of her hands. Then she went from one player to another and passed her hands between their hands. She left the button in one of the children's hands. She tried to do this secretly, so that the other children would not know where the button was. Then she said, " Button, button, who has the button?" All the children took a guess, and the one who got it right was "It" next time.

Now it is your turn. As a class, play Button, Button. After you finish playing, answer these questions:

1. What do you like to do for fun? Make a list of five activities.
2. Of those five activities, which ones could settler children have played?

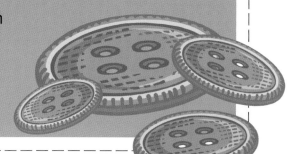

Storytelling

Families also liked to tell stories. They told stories from the Bible, or they might tell ghost stories or folktales. The folktales could be funny or they could be about people who lived through hard times. Without movies, television, or radio, storytelling was a favorite form of entertainment. Children loved to hear their parents and grandparents tell stories.

Going to Church

Religion was very important to many of the settlers. They often prayed and read the Bible together. As soon as several families settled a place, small churches were built. Children went to church with their parents. To get to church, families walked or rode in a wagon behind a horse. It was fun to be around other families to share news from the week. Sometimes families shared a picnic lunch after their meetings were over.

The people looked forward to Sunday. It was the only day of the week that they stopped working and rested. Sunday was a day of rest, when all businesses closed.

Making Connections

If you are lucky, you might be able to listen to your parents or grandparents tell stories about what life was like when they were children. Are there any family stories you listen to over and over?

Pioneer Schools

As more and more pioneers moved into an area, they needed a school for the children. They built a one-room schoolhouse and hired a teacher. All the children learned together in one room, no matter what grade they were in. Brothers and sisters were in class together. The younger children sat in front. Children usually walked to school or rode a horse. They took their lunch in a pail.

The outside of the school was usually made of logs. Inside, the floor was sometimes just hard dirt. Later, schools had wooden floors. Children sat on long wooden benches. A stove in the middle of the room burned coal or wood. This was the only source of heat. Sometimes the children took turns bringing in wood to burn.

Teachers were usually men. They were paid a little money, and they got free room and board. This meant that the families with children at the school took turns having the teacher live with them for a while. In later years, more young women started teaching school.

Reading, Writing, and Arithmetic

Students learned their ABC's from the Bible or from a hornbook. A hornbook was a wooden paddle with letters and sentences written on it. Children were expected to learn the basics of reading, writing, and arithmetic. Paper was very rare. Children wrote with chalk on small blackboards called slates. Sometimes they wrote on tree bark or even scratched out letters in the dirt.

Learning meant *memorizing*. The teacher read a lesson to the students. Then the class repeated it over and over and over. One by one, the students stood up and *recited* the lesson from memory. If the child missed a word, or did not stand perfectly still while reciting, he had to do it over again until he got it just right. Most of the school day was spent memorizing and reciting.

Mind Your Manners

Pioneer schools were strict. Students had to sit up straight, be quiet, and always have their lessons ready. Students who did not pay attention or caused trouble had to stand in a corner. Another common punishment was writing the same sentence hundreds of times on a blackboard.

This hornbook is very old. Would you like to learn to read from a hornbook?

Chapter 5 "Life on the Frontier"

Summer Vacation

It was fun to get away from the hard work on the farm and be around other children at school. Just like today, most children loved learning to read, write, spell, recite poems, sing songs, and do arithmetic. They liked to play outside games during recess.

However, school usually lasted only the few months of the year in the winter, when children were not needed to plant or harvest crops at home. Some children lived too far away from a school and didn't go at all. If they were lucky, their parents taught them at home.

Making Connections

Even though you probably don't have to work on a farm all summer, you still get out of school. Why? Now you know how the tradition of not having school in June, July, and August began.

Boys and girls stood up in front of the teacher to recite their lessons. Would you like to be in a school like this one?

4 MEMORY MASTER

1. What kinds of work did pioneer children do to help their families?
2. How did the children have fun?
3. Describe a pioneer school.

Activity

Measure Up!

The settlers had to live in small spaces until they could build a larger home. Their covered wagons looked large, but not when you think about how much they had to carry to a new home. Read what some pioneers said about their homes and wagons:

"The wagon was 4 feet wide and 10-to-12 feet long. With the cover, a wagon stood about 10 feet tall, and its wheels were over 5 feet wide."

"Most log cabins had a single room, about 12-to-16 feet on each side. There was one door, and usually no windows."

"I found a place about 10 feet by 12 feet with sod walls, dirt floor, and a shingled roof that slanted to the south. We had two windows, which I could only reach by the aid of a chair."

Now see how large (or small!) these places really were. On the floor or out on the playground, measure out a wagon, log house, and soddy. As you measure, stick masking tape or rope down on the ground. Now multiply the length times the width to figure out the square feet of space in each.

Are you surprised by the size of your wagon? Have four or more friends stand with you in the rectangle. What if you added your backpacks and desks to represent supplies? Imagine where you might fit a butter churn, bedding, and bags of wheat and corn.

Now stand with six people in the log home or soddy. Where would you put the fireplace? Where would you sleep and eat?

At home, measure your family car and your house or apartment. Figure out the area (square feet). How do these measurements compare to those of the pioneer wagon and house?

Shake and Pass the Butter

Pioneers made their own butter from the cream they got from their cow's milk. The cream separated from the milk and floated to the top of the milk bucket. Then someone scooped the cream off the milk and put the cream into a wooden butter churn. They had to push and pull a tall paddle up and down to churn the cream into butter.

Pioneers often cooled small tubs of butter in cold water, then wrapped the tubs in wet burlap. They kept them in a hole in the ground to keep cool.

To make your own butter, you will need:

- one small glass jar with a tight lid
- one-half pint (one cup) of heavy cream

Pour the cream into the jar and screw on the lid. Sit in a circle with your classmates. Hold the jar sideways, with one hand on each end of the jar. Shake the jar up and down. Keep shaking the jar as you count to ten, then pass the jar along to the next student. In a few minutes you will be able to see small globs of butter. Keep shaking until there is a larger glob of butter.

Open the jar and pour off the liquid. This is buttermilk. Put the lid on again and keep shaking until almost all the liquid is separated from the ball of butter. Spread the butter on crackers.

Geography Tie-In

Natural Resources and Pioneers

Check back to Chapter 2 and review the information about the landforms, natural resources, and weather in Illinois.

1. Which of these things would have been helpful to the pioneers as they traveled, and which would have made the trip even harder?
2. When was the best time of year for pioneers to set out for the trip to Illinois? Why?
3. How did the people use the land once they got to the prairie? How did they change the land?

12,000 B.C.
First people in North America

1400s
Columbus discovers America.

1500s
America first appears on the map.

1600s
Pilgrims arrive.

1700s
Declaration of Independence
George Washington

1800s
Abraham Lincoln
Pioneers go west.

1900s
Martin Luther King
Your parents were born.

2000s
A New Century
9/11 Terrorists attack the U.S.

Journey to Statehood

Timeline of Events

1775-1783
The American Revolution

1776
American colonies declare
independence from Great Britain.

1784
Virginia turns
Illinois over to the
U.S. government.

1775   1780   1785   1790

1778
George Rogers Clark
takes Kaskaskia.

1779
Clark captures Vincennes.
Du Sable starts a farm and trading
post that later becomes Chicago.

1787
The Northwest
Territory is created.

116

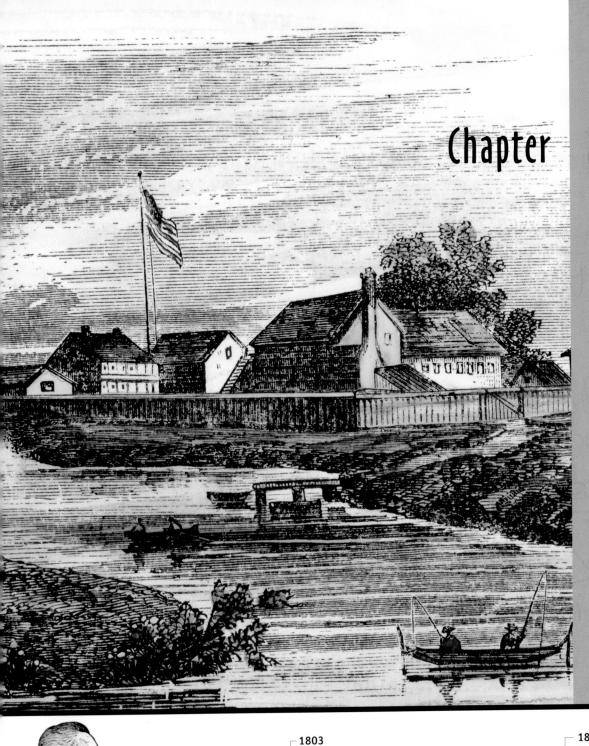

Chapter 6

Illinois wasn't always a state, and the United States of America wasn't always a country. In this chapter you will read about how our country started and how it grew. You will also read about how Illinois grew and became a state.

This drawing shows du Sable's Trading Post and Fort Dearborn. These places were built when our country grew and settlers started to move west. The post and fort were built along the Chicago River, and the place we now call Chicago started growing into a real town.

1803
Fort Dearborn is built across the river from du Sable's trading post.

1809
The Illinois Territory is created.

1812
Fort Dearborn Massacre

1818
Illinois becomes the 21st state. Kaskaskia becomes the first state capital.

| 1795 | 1800 | 1805 | 1810 | 1815 | 1832 |

1800
Illinois becomes part of the Indiana Territory. Du Sable sells his farm and trading post and moves away.

1812-1815
The War of 1812 is fought with Great Britain.

1832
Black Hawk War

PEOPLE TO KNOW

George Rogers Clark
Thomas Jefferson
George Washington

PLACES TO LOCATE

Kentucky
Virginia
Kaskaskia, Illinois
Vincennes, Indiana

WORDS TO UNDERSTAND

independence
revolution
surveyor

The War for Independence

While French settlers were still living in today's Illinois, England claimed land along the East Coast and set up small communities called colonies. The colonies were settlements ruled by England. Other countries also sent people to live in new colonies, but these colonies were later taken over by England.

The colonists argued with English tax collectors.

After a while, the people in the 13 colonies became angry. England made them pay taxes they didn't want to pay. The colonists did not feel like they had a voice in their government. They thought they should pay taxes only if they could help make the tax laws. Even though they were far away from the king and queen of England, the colonists were still under English rule.

The colonists became more and more upset. People started to fight, and soon a war was raging. More than a year after the war started, Americans demanded *independence,* or freedom from English rule.

English or British?
England is part of a large island in Europe called Great Britain. That is why the English are often called "British." What other countries are also a part of Great Britain?

The Declaration of Independence

Thomas Jefferson wrote a document called the Declaration of Independence. It said that because the colonists had been treated unfairly, they were cutting all ties with England. It also stated that the colonists had certain rights.

One of the reasons the colonists wanted to break away from England was the Proclamation of 1763. You read about this in an earlier chapter of this book. It said no colonists could live on the west side of the Appalachian Mountains. That land was only for Indians.

However, colonists kept moving west anyway, so England sent soldiers to stop the people from crossing the mountains. The writers of the Declaration of Independence did not feel this was fair. They added it to their list of reasons for becoming their own country. Then they could make their own laws. On July 4, 1776, leaders of the colonies declared their independence from England.

The colonial leaders signed a document declaring their independence from England.

Making Connections

Do you and your family watch fireworks on the Fourth of July? Can you think of any groups of people who are fighting for independence today?

Americans fought to become a free country.

A Long War

Although the colonists were on their way to becoming a new and united country, it was not going to be easy. The American Revolution would last about eight years. George Washington led the colonists in the war against England. Today, the war is also called the War of Independence or the Revolutionary War.

Most of the battles were fought within the 13 colonies. Some fighting, however, stretched west of the Appalachian Mountains. One battle took place in Illinois.

George Washington led the colonists in the war against England.

A **revolution** is when one government is overthrown and replaced with another government. The American Revolution was a time when the people in the American Colonies fought against the British.

George Rogers Clark

Clark was a young man, only 24 years old. Clark was worried about his home in Kentucky. Would Indians or British soldiers attack his friends and family? What could he do to keep them safe? The British held forts at Kaskaskia and Vincennes. Their Indian allies were already raiding American settlements.

Clark asked for help from the governor of Virginia. At that time, Virginia claimed Indiana and Illinois. But the governor told Clark that no help would be coming. He said all his men and supplies were needed to fight the English soldiers in Virginia.

Clark was angry. He wrote a letter back to the governor. In it he said, "If a country is not worth protecting, it is not worth claiming." The governor thought about the problem again. This time he sent gunpowder to Clark. He also told him to form an army.

Unfortunately, fewer than 200 men were willing to join Clark. Even so, the tiny army set out for the forts controlled by the English. The men left Kentucky and floated down the Ohio River by boat. About 100 miles from Kaskaskia they left their boats and went on foot. After walking for six days, they could finally see the fort, surrounded by cabins of French settlers.

The small army hid deep in the forest until dark. By dawn, Clark's men had the town surrounded. When the people in the town woke up, they found their streets guarded by fierce-looking bearded men. They locked themselves in their cabins.

Clark saw a chance for victory without bloodshed. He went from cabin to cabin to talk to the people. He told them he and his army had come as friends. Slowly, people left their cabins to join the soldiers in the streets. By the end of the day, the people of Kaskaskia and the soldiers from Kentucky were celebrating together. Not a shot had been fired.

Another Clark

The American government asked George Rodgers Clark to explore the land west of the Mississippi River. At the time, only Native Americans knew what was between the United States and the Pacific Ocean. Clark turned down the job.

Twenty years later his younger brother, William, took the job. He became part of the famous Lewis and Clark team that explored the west.

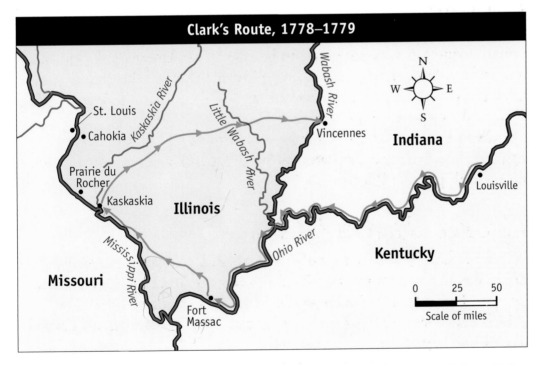

Clark's Route, 1778–1779

Clark and his men started their long march in Louisville, Kentucky. Trace their route to Kaskaskia. What happened there? Read the next page to see what happened when the men went to Vincennes.

War or Peace?

Clark and his men soon faced another problem. Almost half of his men had signed up to be in the army for only a few months. It was time for them to go home. After they left, the Indian allies of the English outnumbered Clark and his soldiers. Clark decided to bluff his way to safety. He invited the Indians to a meeting. At the meeting he offered them a choice. They could pick war or peace. Impressed by his courage, they agreed to peace. Again, not a shot was fired.

Clark was still worried. Surely the English at Vincennes would attack when the weather improved. Many of his soldiers were now gone. The rest of his men would never be able to hold off an attack. He would have to attack first. No one would expect him to march to Vincennes during the winter. He would surprise the English.

A Long March

Clark was able to enlist 200 new men. However, almost half of them were French settlers who had never been soldiers. In early February, the little army set out on foot toward Vincennes. The trip took almost three weeks. They waded through mud and water

George Rogers Clark leads his men to Vincennes. At the time, the only way to cross rivers was by wading, swimming, or boating across the icy water.

Chapter 6 "Journey to Statehood"

sometimes a foot or two deep, sometimes up to their necks. They had to be careful not to be seen by the enemy or unfriendly Indians. That meant camping with no fires to dry and warm them. Clark had to work day and night to keep up the men's spirits. With a week of marching left, they ran out of food. They went five days with only one deer to eat.

Making Connections

When you are hungry, cold, and tired, what keeps you going? Why do you think Clark's men did not give up?

Surprise Attack

Finally, the weary army reached Vincennes. They attacked the fort. The British were not prepared. They could not believe they had been attacked in the middle of winter. They turned the fort over to Clark the next afternoon.

By taking Vincennes, Clark won the Illinois region for the Americans. The new United States of America now stretched all the way from the Atlantic Ocean to the Mississippi River.

The Illinois region was part of the new country. But Illinois was not yet a state. The state of Virginia still claimed it owned the land called Illinois.

What Do You Think ?

What kind of a leader was Clark? How did he take over two forts without fighting?

1 MEMORY MASTER

1. Why is the American Revolution also called the War of Independence?
2. Where were most of the battles of the American Revolution fought?
3. How did Clark help win the land that is now Illinois for the United States?

Illinois PORTRAIT

George Rogers Clark
1752–1818

As a boy, red-headed George Rogers Clark rarely went to school. He got most of his education at home. Like other boys, he also learned to plant, trap, hunt, ride, and wrestle. As a young man, he worked as a *surveyor,* measuring the land.

During the war, Clark convinced the government to give him supplies to fight the English. His wise plans and the Long March helped the United States claim the huge region where Illinois, Ohio, Michigan, Indiana, and Wisconsin are today.

When he got older, Clark moved to Clarksville, Indiana, built a cabin, and ran a grist mill. Later, Clark got ill and had to have his right leg amputated. This was performed without today's modern drugs to kill the pain. Clark asked that two flute players and two drummers play outside for two hours during the operation.

Clark moved to Kentucky to live with his sister and her husband, where he later died. These words were spoken at his funeral:

"The mighty oak of the forest has fallen. . . . The father of the western country is no more."

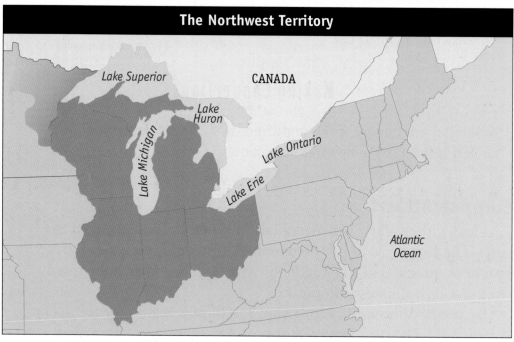

The Northwest Territory

What present-day states were once part of the Northwest Territory?

A territory is different than a state. People living in a territory cannot vote for all of their leaders. They cannot help make laws. They cannot vote for President of the United States. Only people in a state can do these things.

The Northwest Territory

Finally, after many years of war, the Americans won the war in the East. The United States of America was a new country. George Washington was the first president. The new nation extended all the way to the Mississippi River. However, the land west of the Appalachians was not yet divided into states. Remember that Virginia was governing the land of Illinois, but Virginia was finding it hard to govern a land so far away and so full of wilderness. Virginia leaders finally gave the Illinois region to the U.S. government.

The government made the large land region an official *territory.* They named it the Northwest Territory. It included the lands that would become the states of Ohio, Indiana, Illinois, Wisconsin, Michigan, and part of Minnesota.

The Northwest Ordinance

The U.S. government wrote a plan for the new land. The plan was called the Northwest Ordinance. An *ordinance* is a rule or law. The Northwest Ordinance set rules for the settlers in the Northwest Territory. The rules were supposed to get settlers to come and make the land their home. Here are some of the rules:

- Slavery would not be allowed.
- Education would be important.
- Settlers would have the freedom to follow any religion.
- Settlers who came to the territory would have the right to a trial by jury.

The Northwest Ordinance also set rough boundaries for how the territory might be broken up later into states. However, the Indians who had been on the lands first were not even considered. This mistake would lead to further unrest.

Illinois Becomes Part of the Indiana Territory

The Northwest Territory covered a large region of land. In fact, it was such a huge territory that it was hard to control. The people living there felt they didn't have enough protection from angry Indians. They felt like they had been forgotten by the government.

To solve this problem, Congress divided the Northwest Territory into smaller pieces. One of the smaller pieces was called the Indiana Territory. The new territory included the land that would later become Illinois.

What Do You Think**?**

After reading about the Northwest Ordinance, would you want to move to the Northwest Territory? List the pros and cons.

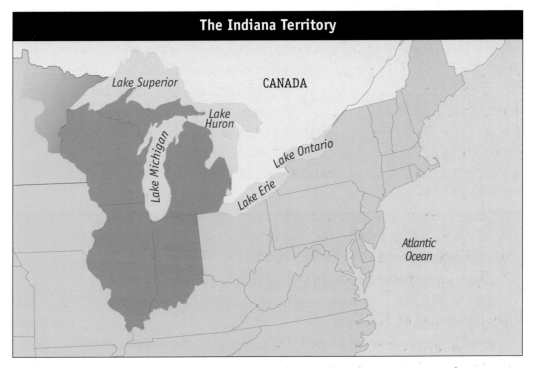

The Indiana Territory

Lake Superior

CANADA

Lake Huron

Lake Michigan

Lake Ontario

Lake Erie

Atlantic Ocean

Compare this map to the one on page 124. What present-day state was no longer part of the Northwest Territory?

The Illinois Territory

To the people living there, however, the Indiana Territory still seemed too big. The government leaders met in Vincennes. The settlers in Illinois complained that the government leaders were still too far away to really help them.

It took nine more years before Congress divided the Indiana Territory and made the Illinois Territory. Ninian Edwards was chosen to be the governor.

The Illinois Territory didn't look like Illinois does today. The northern border went all the way to Canada. It included land that would later become several states.

Ninian Edwards was the first governor of the new Illinois Territory.

Compare this map to the maps on pages 124 and 125 to see how the huge Northwest Territory got divided up into smaller regions. How was the size of the new Illinois Territory different from today's Illinois State? What was the capital city?

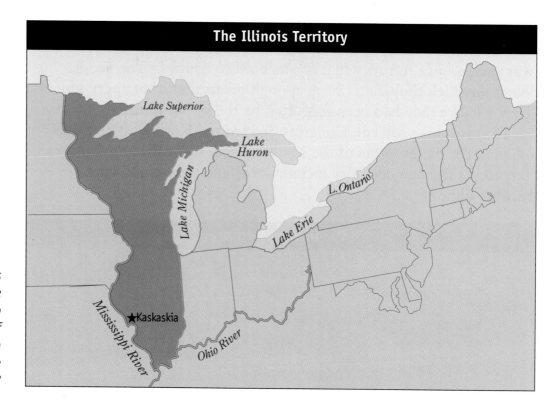

The Illinois Territory

Lake Superior
Lake Huron
Lake Michigan
L. Ontario
Lake Erie
Mississippi River
★Kaskaskia
Ohio River

② MEMORY MASTER

1. Why did Virginia give up the land of Illinois?
2. How did the U.S. government get settlers to move to the Northwest Territory?
3. What important issue was not covered in the Northwest Ordinance?
4. What is the main difference between a territory and a state?

Chapter 6 "Journey to Statehood"

Unrest in the Indian Territory

The land in the territory had been Indian land before the white Americans took over. The Indians, angry over their loss of hunting grounds, attacked American settlements. They stole horses, tore down fences, and destroyed crops. Sometimes they killed settlers.

Fort Dearborn

To protect the settlers living at the mouth of the Chicago River, the U.S. government sent soldiers to build a fort.

Fort Dearborn was made of sturdy logs placed upright in the ground. There were two log walls around the fort. If anyone attacked the fort, they would have to climb over the first wall before they could reach the second. The only holes in the walls were high above the ground. Soldiers inside the fort stood on walkways near the tops of the walls and aimed their rifles through the holes.

Inside the fort were houses for sleeping and storing supplies. There was a well for fresh water. A tunnel ran from the fort to the shore of Lake Michigan. If the people inside ever needed to escape, they could sneak through the tunnel to the edge of the lake. An American flag was raised above the fort.

PEOPLE TO KNOW

John Kinzie
Jean Baptiste Point du Sable

PLACES TO LOCATE

Chicago

WORDS TO UNDERSTAND

massacre

Fort Dearborn was built across the Chicago River from the old trading post and farm started many years before by du Sable. Would you feel safe in a fort like this?

Chicago Is Born

Du Sable's Trading Post

About four years before Fort Dearborn was built, Jean Baptiste du Sable, a black fur trader, had set up the first permanent settlement at the mouth of the Chicago River. Du Sable and his wife opened a trading post. They collected furs from Indians and other trappers and traded for metal goods, wool blankets, food, and other items. The family also farmed and sold vegetables to people who visited their trading post.

Du Sable built a large home. It had mirrors and pictures on the walls. These were rare in the wilderness. They built a stable and barn and raised cattle, hogs, and hens. Later, du Sable sold his trading post and his farm to settler John Kenzie and moved away.

Illinois PORTRAIT

Jean Baptiste Point du Sable
1745-1814

Jean du Sable was born in Haiti. His father was a French sea captain and his mother was an ex-slave. The du Sable family was Catholic. After going to school in France, du Sable worked on his father's ship. He also learned to be a carpenter. He later came to the Illinois region to trap furs.

Jean du Sable married a Potawatomi Indian woman and they had two children. During the American Revolution du Sable was captured by British soldiers. When he was set free, he moved to the north side of the Chicago River, opened a trading post, and ran a farm. In the du Sable home the first marriage in Chicago was performed, the first election was held, and the first court was held.

"Land of Stinky Onions"

A small community around the old trading post and Fort Dearborn grew to become the city of Chicago. What does the name "Chicago" mean? The answer is not clear. The name may have been the title for Indian chiefs. Indians also called the river and swampy region *Checagou.* Another form of the Indian words meant "the place of bad smells" because wild onions in the swamp sometimes smelled very bad!

Study this painting of Chicago in 1820 to learn how the land looked when only du Sable's old trading post (on the right) and the sturdy Fort Dearborn (on the left) stood at the place we now call the busy city of Chicago. See the winding river that Indians and early settlers used as a highway. Wouldn't these people be surprised to see today's Chicago, with its busy shipping ports and tall skyscrapers?

Some Indians joined with English soldiers to help them fight the Americans. The American farmer on the other side of the fence does not know he is about to be attacked.

The War of 1812

Long after the American Revolution had ended, the British still hoped to end America's dream of being independent. Another war between the United States and Great Britain began. It became known as the War of 1812. Indian groups who were angry with the American settlers helped the British fight the American settlers. One famous battle was fought at Fort Dearborn.

The Fort Dearborn Massacre

After British soldiers had captured a nearby fort, the community at Fort Dearborn knew it was not safe from attack. On a hot day in August, the soldiers at Fort Dearborn got orders to leave. They were told to take the settlers living nearby to Fort Wayne in Indiana. Friendly Indians warned them not to go. There were not enough soldiers to make the trip safely, they said. They would have to travel past hundreds of unfriendly Indians camped on the shore of the lake.

John Kinzie and other settlers agreed. The trip to Fort Wayne would be too dangerous. They had enough food and guns to stay in the fort for months. But the fort's commander felt he had to obey his orders. They would go to Indiana.

On August 15, 1812, the soldiers and settlers marched out of the fort. Fifes (flutes) and drums led the way. Before they had gone two miles, they were attacked. A bloody battle followed. The Indians killed or captured almost everyone. John Kinzie, his family, and a few other settlers escaped with the help of friendly Indians. The fort was burned the next day. The bloody battle has become known as the Fort Dearborn Massacre.

The war ended. The British could not win back the land they had once ruled. With the end of the fighting, American settlers began to come to Illinois again. Chicago grew.

A *massacre* is a horrible killing of a large number of people.

③ MEMORY MASTER

1. What do you think was the cause of the War of 1812?
2. Why did indians become allies with the Brittish?
3. Who is the founder of Chicago?

Ambush! Children followed their parents outside the safety of Fort Dearborn and hadn't gone far when they were attacked. The men fought back, but many died in the horrible massacre.

PEOPLE TO KNOW

Shadrach Bond
Daniel Pope Cook
Nathaniel Pope

PLACES TO LOCATE

Kaskaskia
Vandalia
Springfield

WORDS TO UNDERSTAND

Congress
delegate
reject

Congress is made of two groups of people—the House of Representatives and the Senate. Congress makes all the laws for our country in Washington, D.C.

Statehood

As the number of people in Illinois grew, so did their interest in becoming a state. Why did everyone want Illinois to become a state? What was wrong with being a territory?

Territories were allowed to send **delegates** to Congress in Washington, D.C. At this time, the delegate for the Illinois Territory was Nathaniel Pope. But there was a big problem. Nathaniel Pope could not vote in Congress. He did not have a say in the laws Congress made for his territory. That was because Illinois was not a state.

If Illinois became a state, its people would have a vote in Congress. A state would also attract more settlers. People wanted to settle in areas that were a part of the growing United States.

A New Boundary

The Illinois Territory was divided before Illinois became a state. The members of Congress wanted a state boundary 41 miles south of where it is today. Pope argued that this boundary line would not do, because Illinois needed the shoreline of Lake Michigan for trade with states in the East. Without the shoreline for docks and warehouses, Illinois could only trade by slower land routes.

Pope had another reason to worry about trade. If Illinois could not trade with eastern states, it would have to get most of its goods from southern states. The goods would enter Illinois by traveling up the Mississippi and Ohio Rivers. But something else might come along with the goods—slaves. Many white people in the southern states owned slaves. Pope did not want Illinois to become a state full of slave owners.

Pope's request for a new border was granted. Illinois gained the fourteen northern counties, including the rich Galena lead mining district and the port of Chicago on Lake Michigan.

What Do You Think?

Today, more than half of the people in Illinois live in the region that Pope won for the state with his brilliant efforts in Congress. How would Illinois be different without Chicago and its ports on Lake Michigan? Illinois would be a different state with a different history. Would your life be different?

Nathaniel Pope Asks for a Change

A territory had to have 60,000 people to become a state. In 1818, the Illinois Territory had less than 40,000 people. However, Nathaniel Pope and Daniel Pope Cook talked Congress into agreeing to let Illinois write a state constitution. If Congress approved the constitution, Illinois would become a state.

A Newspaper Pleas for Statehood

A young man named Daniel Pope Cook was Nathaniel Pope's nephew. He believed it was important for Illinois to become a state. He owned part of the territory's first newspaper, *The Illinois Herald*. He wrote articles in the paper that told people why Illinois should become a state. He pleaded with leaders in the Illinois Territory to work for statehood.

The Delegates Meet

In August, 33 delegates from around Illinois met in Kaskaskia. Their job was to write a constitution for the new state. The men had been elected by the people of Illinois. They were merchants, ministers, doctors, lawyers, sheriffs, and boatmen.

The constitution was short and simple, and the men approved most of it easily. But there was one matter the delegates argued and argued about, and that was slavery.

Nathaniel Pope worked to make Illinois a state.

The Question of Slavery

Slavery is one person owning another person. The owner makes the slave work long, hard hours without pay. When slaves were brought from Africa, they were treated horribly. They were made to live in shacks. They were not allowed to learn how to read or write. Often they were beaten and whipped if they upset their owner, or "master."

At the time, it was up to each state to decide if it would allow slavery. Most of the southern states allowed it. Many people in the South owned large plantations. They needed many workers to grow their huge crops of cotton, tobacco, rice, or sugar. They bought slaves to do this work.

In the North, there were many industries besides farming. There were farms, but they were smaller. In most cases, the families could do the work themselves or they hired men to help.

Many of the Illinois delegates wanted to allow slavery in the new state. They wanted slaves to work in the mines and fields. Others thought that slavery would take work away from poor white people. They also believed that it was wrong to buy and sell human beings as if they were property. They wanted Illinois to be a free state.

Finally, those who were against slavery won. Even the men who wanted slavery worried that Congress might *reject* their constitution if it allowed slavery.

A State at Last, 1818

When the new state constitution was finished, the people of Illinois waited for Congress to act. On December 3, 1818, Illinois entered the United States as the 21st state.

Choosing Leaders

Even before Illinois became a state, its people were allowed to elect government leaders. They elected Shadrach Bond as the first governor. They elected senators and representatives to the General Assembly. The General Assembly was like the U.S. Congress. It made laws for the state. The men met in Kaskaskia, the first state capital.

The General Assembly hired men to lay out a brand new town to be the new capital city. They called it Vandalia. After about two years a capitol building was built and the government leaders moved into their offices. Later, Springfield became the state capital.

An "overseer" on horseback kept the slaves working all day.

Making Connections

What do you think of when you hear the word "slavery"? What do you know about the history of slavery?

A new capitol building was built behind the old one in Springfield. This is the capitol building today.

This is the Old State Capitol in Springfield.

Springfield
1839

Vandalia
1820

Kaskaskia
1818

The capital was moved to Vandalia in 1820.
Vandalia was the capital until 1839, when it was moved to Springfield.

Kaskaskia was Illinois' first capital city. This was the first capitol building.

Shadrach Bond
1773–1832

The first governor of the new state of Illinois was Shadrach Bond. He had come to Illinois when he was 21 years old. He taught himself how to be a successful farmer. He was friendly and honest and became popular in Kaskaskia.

During the War of 1812, Bond was a captain in the army. Later, when Illinois became a territory, he was chosen to be the first delegate to Congress. Even later, when Illinois became a state, people voted for Bond to be the first governor. He was so popular that no one even ran against him. He worked to get better transportation for the state by building a canal, new roads, and bridges over rivers.

④ MEMORY MASTER

1. What did the delegates think about slavery?
2. What was the date Illinois became a state?
3. How many stars were on the flag of the United States when Illinois became a state?

PEOPLE TO KNOW

Chief Black Hawk
Andrew Jackson

PLACES TO LOCATE

Iowa
Wisconsin

WORDS TO UNDERSTAND

reservation
surrender
treaty
valid

Settlers Take Indian Lands

After Illinois became a state, more and more pioneers settled farther and farther north. The new settlers wanted land of their own. Most of them did not understand the lifestyle or the culture of the Native Americans living there. The Indians did not build fences to mark off their land, and they did not believe they could own any part of the earth. Instead, they felt their tribal lands were to share with everyone in the tribe.

The new settlers, however, felt they had a right to claim land just for themselves. They were moving onto the fertile lands where Sauk and Fox Indians lived. Soon there were problems.

The Government Responds

The U.S. government wanted settlers to come and live in the new states. Government leaders did not want settlers to worry about attacks from angry Indians, so they proposed *treaties,* or written agreements between the government and the Indians.

In exchange for money, food, and supplies, Indians agreed to leave their lands and move onto *reservations.* A reservation was a small area of land, usually just for one tribe. There the Indians could hunt, farm, and live in peace. Indians had to remain on the reservation if they wanted to be supported by the government.

Usually a U.S. agent was in charge of the reservation. The agent kept track of the tribe and reported to the U.S. government.

Indian Treaties

Sauk and Fox Indians made several treaties with the U.S. government. They traded their land, including Illinois, to the government in exchange for friendship and protection. They also received some money and other goods such as clothes, tools, blankets, and food. Indian families left all they knew and moved across the Mississippi River into Iowa.

Indian leaders felt they had no choice but to sign the treaties. Some tribes thought they were even tricked into signing.

As part of Andrew Jackson's Indian Removal Act, the Cherokee nation was forced to move to present-day Oklahoma. The Cherokee people called this journey the "Trail of Tears" because of the horrible hunger, disease, and death on the forced march. About 4,000 Cherokees died. The long march did not take place in Illinois.

Broken Treaties

Over the next few years, many of the treaties were broken. Often the Indians did not receive good food, clothing, or supplies. They were often paid late. Some of the reservation land was not good for farming. The people had to stay on the reservations, so they could not travel to hunt as they once had. They were given wheat, not the "mother corn" they had always eaten.

White teachers were brought in to teach the Indian children in schools. The teachers forced the children to speak English. The children had to wear clothes like the white people instead of the clothes they were used to.

The Indian ways began to be forgotten. Many tribal customs broke down. The people felt threatened as they saw more and more settlers moving west.

What Do You Think ?

How do you think the Indians felt as they moved from their homelands? Why do you think they chose to sign the treaties and move?

Indian Removal Act, 1830

President Andrew Jackson called for an Indian Removal Act that would mean the United States could move all Indians to lands farther west. President Jackson said:

This would open new farmland to whites while offering Indians a haven where they would be free to develop at their own pace. . . . Your white brothers will not trouble you, they will have no claims to the land, and you can live upon it, you and all your children, as long as the grass grows or the water runs, in peace and plenty.

The Black Hawk War

Black Hawk was an Indian leader who said the treaties were not *valid.* He claimed the Indians had been given alcohol to make them drunk so they would give up the land. He said they didn't understand that by signing the treaty they would be giving up their homeland. He said the settlers should be the ones to leave. He wanted to return to his homeland and the sacred burial ground of his people near the Mississippi and Rock Rivers.

For more than a year, tension grew. There were many battles between Indians and white settlers. Finally Black Hawk led his warriors and their families back onto the land in Illinois. U.S. soldiers followed Black Hawk throughout northern Illinois and into part of the land that is now Wisconsin.

Thousands of volunteer soldiers also set out after the Indians. After days of tracking, the soldiers found Black Hawk on the shore of the Mississippi River near the Bad Axe River. At the same time, a steamboat loaded with soldiers and cannons arrived. Black Hawk knew his people were trapped between the soldiers on land and the soldiers on the river. He waved a white flag of *surrender.* The soldiers on the boat fired anyway. Over and over, guns fired at the Indians. You can imagine the horrible sound of people screaming as they tried to get away. Indian men, women, and children died. Finally, the steamboat left.

Long before he became president of the United States, Abraham Lincoln served in the Black Hawk War. He later joked that he only fought mosquitoes.

What can you learn about the battle in this painting?

This painting shows Indian people fleeing after the terrible Battle of Bad Ax in Wisconsin, 1832. The battle ended the Black Hawk War.

The Indians who were still alive decided to try to cross the river the next day. They started building wooden rafts. Black Hawk and a small group decided to walk farther north to search for help from the Winnebago tribes.

Morning came. The Indians tried to cross the river, but enemy Indian tribes on the other side of the river attacked them. There was no hope left. Hundreds of Indians died in the battle or drowned trying to cross the river. Nearly the whole group was wiped out in just two days. Those who did not die were taken as prisoners.

Chief Black Hawk and others who had fled north finally surrendered. When the war was over, all Indian tribes were ordered out of Illinois. It was the last time large Indian groups lived in the state.

You have taken me prisoner with all my warriors. I fought hard. But your guns were well-aimed. The bullets flew like birds in the air, and whizzed by our ears like the wind through the trees in the winter. My warriors fell around me, it began to look dismal. I saw my evil day at hand.

The sun rose dim on us in the morning, and at night it sunk in a dark cloud, and looked like a ball of fire. That was the last sun that shone on Black Hawk. His heart is dead, and no longer beats quick in his bosom. He is now a prisoner to the white man; they will do with him as they wish. But he can stand torture, and is not afraid of death. He is no coward!

—Chief Black Hawk

What Do You Think ?

How can differing points of view cause conflict? Is there a way to know for sure who is right?

Black Hawk
1767–1838

Ma-ka-tai-me-she-kia-kiak (Black Sparrow Hawk) was born just north of Rock River. Like most boys of the Sauk tribe, he learned to hunt and fish. By age 15, Black Hawk had become a warrior. By age 45, he had earned the title of "war chief."

Believing that treaties removing his tribe to Iowa were not valid, Black Hawk re-crossed the Mississippi River with women, children, and about 300 warriors. He wanted to again live upon the ancient hunting grounds and reclaim the land for his Indian nation. He led an attack on the white settlers there. In response, the white militia attacked the Indians. Black Hawk was taken prisoner and exhibited in eastern cities before finally being returned to Iowa.

"... how different is our situation now, from what it was in those days! Then we were as happy as the buffalo on the plains, but now, we are as miserable as the hungry, howling wolf in the prairie!"

—Black Hawk

George Catlin, Artist

George Catlin was born in Pennsylvania and learned to read and write at home. Even in his early years, Indians had a strong influence on Catlin's life because they had once captured his mother.

Catlin was the first artist to travel to Indian lands and paint pictures of them. He wanted his Indian paintings to tell the story of the Indian people. He worried that their traditions and culture would be forgotten. After the Indians were taken captive by the government, Catlin painted this portrait of Black Hawk.

5 MEMORY MASTER

1. Why were there disagreements over who owned the land?
2. What did Black Hawk want his people to do?
3. What happened to Black Hawk and his people?

Chapter 6 Review

Activity

The State Seal

Once Illinois became a state, a state seal was approved. This picture shows the third design of the seal, created in 1868. Look closely at the details of the seal. It is similar to the seal of the United States of America. See if you can answer the following questions:

1. What does the bald eagle represent?
2. Why does the shield have 13 stars and 13 stripes?
3. What does the date 1818 remind us of?
4. Why is the grass under the eagle important?
5. What could the rising sun be a symbol of?
6. The eagle is holding a streamer with the state motto written on it. It says "State Sovereignty, National Union" What does that mean? Use a dictionary and talk about the word "sovereignty" with your teacher.

Activity

What's West?

A friend of yours is confused. He has heard that Illinois is in the Midwest. This chapter says Illinois was part of the Northwest Territory. When you look at a current map of the United States, Illinois doesn't seem to be out west at all! Can you explain how all of the descriptions could be correct?

Activity

The Power of Persuasion

Nathaniel Pope and Daniel Pope Cook talked Congress into letting Illinois become a state even though 20,000 fewer people lived there than were required for statehood. Write a persuasive speech the men might have given to convince Congress to overlook the rule. Remember that you will need facts to support your opinion.

Anchor It!

12,000 B.C.
First people in North America

1400s
Columbus discovers America.

1500s
America first appears on
the map.

1600s
Pilgrims arrive.

1700s
Declaration of Independence
George Washington

1800s
Abraham Lincoln
Pioneers go west.

1900s
Martin Luther King
Your parents were born.

2000s
A New Century
9/11 Terrorists attack the U.S.

A Changing Illinois

Timeline of Events

1811-1839
The National Road is built.

1820
Steamboats start bringing
settlers and goods into Illinois

1800   1810   1820   1830

1831
Cyrus McCormic
invents the reaper

142

Chapter 7

For years, travel to Illinois was very slow. A boy and girl might travel with their parents by wagon, then by boat on the river, then by wagon again. Then thousands of hard-working men made travel faster by digging canals so people could travel by boat. Steamships replaced the slower sailing ships and flatboats. Crews of workers from foreign countries came to clear trees and boulders and lay railroad tracks. It got easier and faster to get to Illinois.

Compare this drawing of early Chicago to the one on page 128 of the last chapter. What changes in transportation and settlement do you notice?

1838
The first train ride in Illinois takes place on the Northern Cross Railroad.

1846
Bishop Hill is settled. The Mormons leave Nauvoo.

1851-1856
The Illinois Central Railroad is built.

1840

1850

1860

1870

1837
John Deere invents the self-scouring plow.

1836-1848
The Illinois and Michigan Canal is built.

1865
The Amish settle in central Illinois.

PEOPLE TO KNOW

John Fitch
Robert Fulton

PLACES TO LOCATE

Ireland
Maryland
Indiana
Cairo
Decatur
East St. Louis
Galena
Jacksonville
Meredosia
Springfield
St. Louis
Quincy

WORDS TO UNDERSTAND

barge
canal
cargo
immigrant
steamboat

On the Move

As more and more settlers moved to Illinois, much of the prairie was being used as farmland. More people also started living nearer each other in towns and villages. They opened businesses to provide the many things people wanted.

The National Road

The U.S. government decided to build the first real road to connect the eastern part of the country with the new states on the western frontier. The new road went from Maryland all the way to the Mississippi River. It was called the National Road.

Building the road was not easy. Crews of men sweated all day, chopping down trees and digging paths through thick grass and over high ridges. It was hard work to cut through the mountain rocks in the East. The men built bridges over streams. In the heat of summer and the cold of winter, the men worked. They lived in nearby towns or in camps along the route.

All day long the National Road was used by people traveling on horseback, in wagons, and in high stagecoaches pulled by horses or mules.

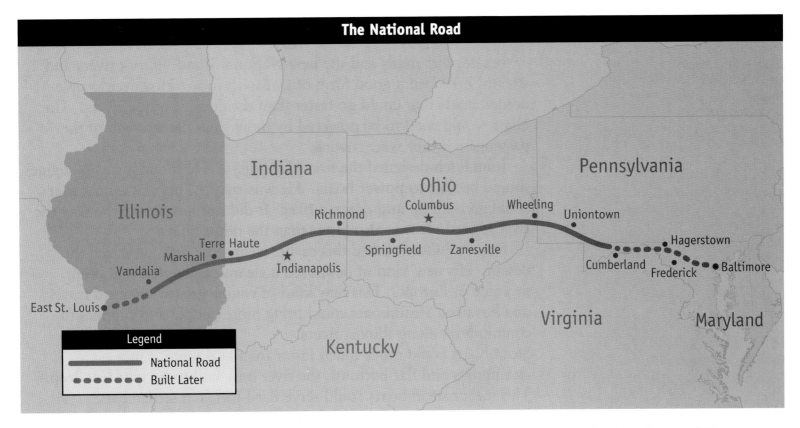

When the road finally opened, stagecoaches and wagons carried people and goods from town to town. Merchants used the road to sell goods in other places. Farmers drove herds of cattle, sheep, and pigs along the road to market. Letters and newspapers from towns in the East were sent to people in the West. Families who had moved far away from home were glad to read them. Before long, inns, trading posts, and new towns were built along the road.

In Illinois, the road first came through the town of Marshall and ended at Vandalia, which was once the state's capital city. Later, the state finished a road to East St. Louis. From there, people and goods traveled on the Mississippi River.

Towns Today

Today, towns along Highway 40 and Interstate I-70 are sitting where the National Road used to go. They include Marshall, Vandalia, Troy, St. Jacob, St. Elmo, Pocahontas, Mulberry Grove, Montrose, Livingston, Altamont, Casey, Collinsville, Greenville, and others.

The towns celebrated the road's 200th anniversary in 2006, which was 200 years after Congress approved a plan to start building it. There were parades, contests, and animal shows. If you live in one of these towns, pretend you see wagons, horses, and cows walking along the old road. Pretend you are a traveler on the National Road.

Steamboats Change Travel

Besides dirt roads and the new National Road, Illinois rivers and streams provided a good form of transportation. However, people needed boats that could go faster than the current of the rivers. The boats would need to be powered by more than the strength of the passengers if they were rowing.

John Fitch designed the first *steamboat.* He thought steam engines should be able to power boats. He was right. This was a boat that could go both up and down a river. It did not have to go the way the river flowed. It was also faster than the other boats.

Robert Fulton studied this earlier steamboat and improved the design. His new kind of boat used a steam engine that had been invented in Europe. This new kind of engine greatly changed travel and business. Steamboats could bring more people and supplies to communities along Illinois rivers.

Steamboats could move much faster than keelboats. Since steamboats had flat bottoms, the river only had to be four feet deep. This meant steamboats could serve hard-to-reach settlements. Their powerful engines helped them battle strong currents and carry heavy loads. Steamboats could even tow *barges.*

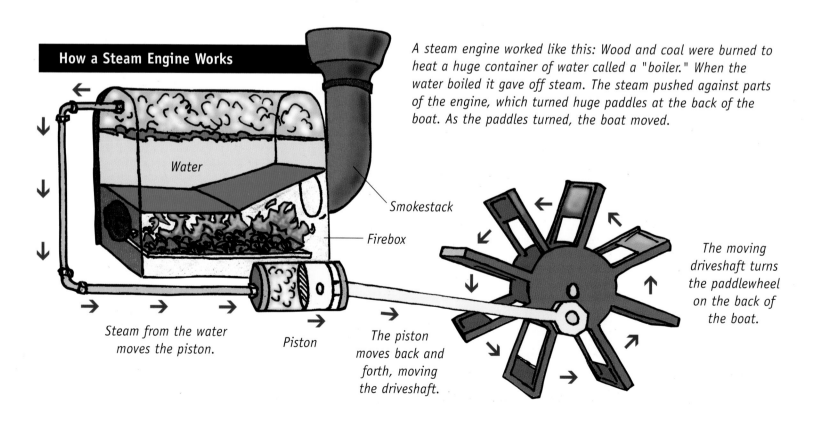

How a Steam Engine Works

Water

Steam from the water moves the piston.

Piston

The piston moves back and forth, moving the driveshaft.

Smokestack

Firebox

A steam engine worked like this: Wood and coal were burned to heat a huge container of water called a "boiler." When the water boiled it gave off steam. The steam pushed against parts of the engine, which turned huge paddles at the back of the boat. As the paddles turned, the boat moved.

The moving driveshaft turns the paddlewheel on the back of the boat.

Chapter 7 "A Changing Illinois"

Barges were long, flat boats that carried thousands of pounds of corn, other food, or manufactured goods along the rivers. The barges had no engines of their own and had to be pulled along the river.

Soon hundreds of steamboats were moving up and down the Mississippi River and along the Lake Michigan shore. The line of steamboats ran for more than a mile along the docks at Chicago, St. Louis, and Cairo.

Danger Ahead!

Of course, steamboat travel had its problems. Big rivers like the Ohio and Mississippi were often filled with floodwater. When floods came, logs, sandbars, and some islands were hidden under the water. Even the best riverboat pilots grounded their boats or sank them by running into hidden logs or sandbars. Sometimes the steam boilers exploded and fire swept through the boat, killing the passengers. Steamboat crews also faced the danger of pirates along lonely stretches of river.

Steamboats delivered the mail and brought supplies to river towns. Children pleaded with their parents to let them take a ride on a steamboat.

How many kinds of boats can you see in this drawing of the town of Cairo? What rivers flowed past Cairo?

147

Visiting A Steamboat

As a young man, the famous writer Mark Twain lived next to the mighty Mississippi River. He was a steamboat pilot. He called the river "a wonderful book" with stories and secrets to tell.

Making Connections

What kinds of boats have you ridden on? Paddle boats, motorboats, steamboats, or even a canoe? Were you going fast or slow? What powered the boats?

Suppose you could visit a steamboat in 1845. You stand at the edge of a pier, waiting for the boat to come into sight. You hear its deep whistle in the distance. Soon you see smoke over the trees. The smoke is coming from two smokestacks rising high above the boat. The smoke is thick and black. It's coming from coal and wood being burned as fuel. As the boat comes closer, you see that it carries many passengers. It also has a deck full of goods going to market. You hear someone playing the calliope (cah·lie·oh·pee). It is like an organ, but it is powered by steam. The song is lively and the passengers are enjoying the music.

As the boat gets closer, wooden ramps are swung out from the boat so people can easily walk onto the shore. You dash onto the boat. Strong crew members are wheeling crates from place to place. Passengers are picking up their belongings.

Climbing to the upper deck, you can't believe your eyes. The cabins are beautiful. Only the rich can afford to travel this way. Next to the cabins is the dining room. It has expensive wood on the walls and shiny brass railings.

The pilot blows the whistle once again. It's time for visitors to leave. From the dock, you watch the boat slip back onto the river. The calliope is playing again. Smoke billows from the stacks. You wonder, could there be a more wonderful job in the entire world than being a riverboat pilot?

In the South, bales of cotton were loaded onto steamboats and shipped to factories in Illinois.

The Illinois & Michigan Canal

With the use of steamboats, travel improved. But what if people wanted to travel between the Illinois River and Lake Michigan? They had to cross a narrow strip of land that made it almost impossible to ship goods or passengers quickly.

Plans were made to build a **canal** through the strip of land. A canal is a waterway made by people. The canal would connect Lake Michigan to the Illinois River. Then there would be an all-water route from Lake Michigan to the Gulf of Mexico and back again. The route would make traveling and shipping goods faster.

Building the Canal

Thousands of workers came to Illinois to build the canal. Many came from as far away as Ireland. They lived in camps they set up along the route. Workers earned about $1 per day. They worked 14 or 15 hours a day, six days a week.

Digging started in the town of Bridgeport, which is now part of Chicago. Digging a canal was really digging out a riverbed by hand. The men cleared the land of trees, rocks, and grass. They used picks and shovels to dig out the canal bed. They put the dirt into wooden carts and mules and horses carried it away. Finally, the canal bed was 60 feet wide and 6 feet deep in most places. After about 12 years, workers reached the Illinois River at La Salle-Peru. Water flowed into the canal. The hard job was done.

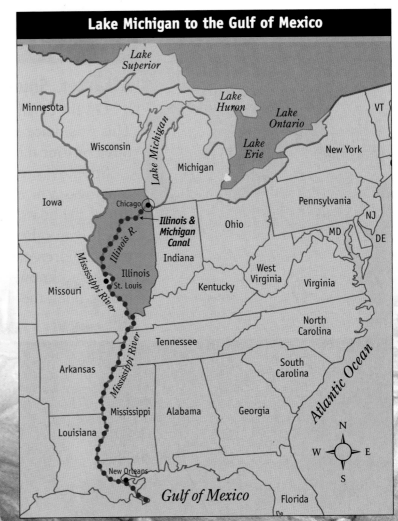

Lake Michigan to the Gulf of Mexico

Trace the route from the Gulf of Mexico along the Mississippi River to the Illinois River, then to Chicago and Lake Michigan. Can you see why the canal was important?

Canal boats were flatboats with a cabin for sleeping and a deck for storing goods and livestock. The boats had no engines, so towpaths were made along the canal. The boat was tied to a horse or mule that walked along the towpath and pulled the boat through the water.

A Faster, Smoother Trip

On the canal, passengers could zip along at almost six miles per hour. This was twice as fast as riding in a stagecoach that could only travel three or four miles per hour.

Speed was important to travelers, but so was comfort. The smooth canal was a nice change from rough roads. Travelers could sit on the top of the boats in good weather. They didn't have to sit inside a small coach with other passengers who smoked or snored loudly during the trip. Children on a canal boat had plenty of time to see the countryside and get to know the other people on the boat. They liked to watch the mules along the shore. They looked down at the water and tried to spot fish.

Canal Locks

When the land rose or fell, natural rivers had waterfalls or rapids. Canals had "locks" to raise or lower boats along their journey. Follow the diagram to see how a canal lock worked.

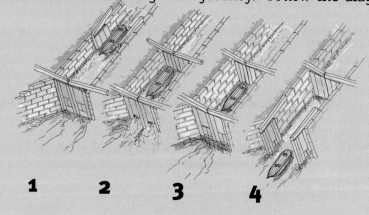

1 **2** **3** **4**

1. High water: a boat enters the lock.
2. The back gates close. Water is slowly let out of front gates.
3. The water level gets lower and lower.
4. The front gates open, and boat leaves the lock on a lower level.

Chapter 7 "A Changing Illinois"

Cargo on the Canal

Passengers were the main *cargo* on the Illinois & Michigan Canal when it first opened. Soon, however, passengers started riding on new railroads, and the canal was used mostly to haul wheat, corn, and beans from farms to Chicago, St. Louis, and New Orleans. Logs from Wisconsin were shipped to Chicago to be cut into boards. Then the boards were shipped to farms and towns in many states. Coal and other materials were put on boats headed for factories. Flour, wire, sand, and cement were picked up in towns along the canal and moved to other towns on canal boats.

The first year after the canal was built, Chicago became the nation's largest inland shipping port. Grain and coal from Illinois, sugar and coffee from New Orleans, and lumber from Wisconsin and Minnesota were shipped through the canal to Chicago.

The Railroad Boom

The people in Illinois wanted the state to spend money on canals and riverboats, but the governor thought the state should start laying track for railroads. He wanted to connect the state's major cities by rail. Plans were laid for new tracks that would be laid in the shape of a cross from one end of the state to the other.

One railroad would go from Galena in the north to Cairo in the south. This would be called the Illinois Central Railroad because it ran down the center of the state.

The Northern Cross Railroad would cross the state from Quincy to Jacksonville, then to Springfield and Decatur and finally all the way to Danville. This line was built first. Other lines were built later.

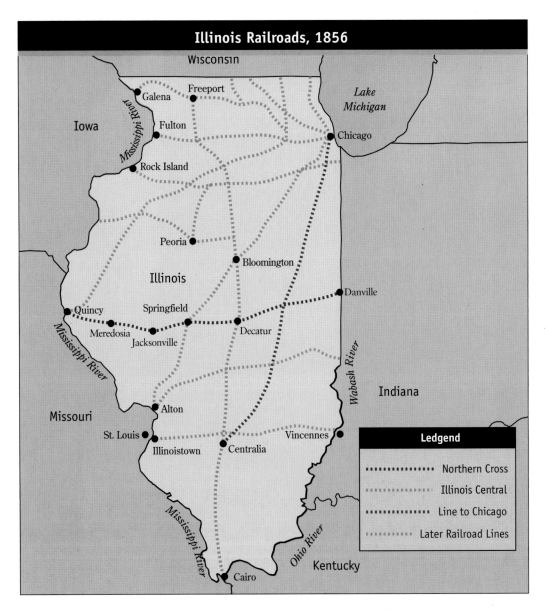

Illinois Railroads, 1856

Legend

.... Northern Cross
.... Illinois Central
.... Line to Chicago
.... Later Railroad Lines

Chapter 7 "A Changing Illinois"

The Northern Cross Railroad

On a crisp November day in 1838, a steam locomotive took a small group of people on the first train ride in Illinois history. It carried the group eight miles to the end of its track. Then it returned to Meredosia, on the bank of the Illinois River. The railroad's name was the Northern Cross.

The train was first built by the government. Years later, it was sold to the highest bidder. Track was built a little at a time, from city to city.

There were problems with the train's engines. They had been built in Pennsylvania, and it took months for parts to get to Illinois. For almost a year, train cars had to be pulled by oxen and horses.

Riding a train wasn't the smooth ride it is today. One author described a train ride on the Northern Cross like this:

> Along each wall of the coach ran a smooth stretch of bench like seat and a sudden lurch of the coach would often slide a sitter half the length of the coach and land him, or her, with a gruesome bump in the middle of the floor.

> When the train stopped at any "wooding" station, the whole train crew and some of the passengers joined in throwing the sawed wood into the great box of the tender. . . . Then the train could go on.

—George M. McConnel, Illinois Trails History

The seats in this train were different from the long bench seats of the Northern Cross. In this train, the seats faced each other. On long train rides, people cooked meals, slept in seats and bunks, and walked up and down inside the train cars. Men read newspapers and women knitted, read, and took care of children. A train car was almost like a tiny community.

The Illinois Central Railroad

A new railroad company needed help to build its railroad. The company asked the Illinois government for money. The state gave the company land on both sides of the route. The company could sell the land and use the money to pay to build the railroad.

Company officials went to cities in the eastern states and to Europe to find workers. They hung posters in railroad stations, hotels, and places where new immigrants might see them. The posters said the company would pay $1.25 a day in wages.

Workers saw the signs and came to Illinois to lay the tracks. About six years later, tracks connected Galena and Cairo. Another line went from Centralia to Chicago. The longest railroad in the world was ready for travel. The Illinois Central Railroad is still used today. Take a ride on the train!

It cost a lot of money to clear the land, lay tracks, and build stations for a railroad. To make money, the railroad advertised the sale of land on both sides of the tracks. What does this poster say to make people want to buy the land and move to Illinois?

Working on the Railroad

Thousands of workers helped build the great railroads. They came from Europe, Asia, and many parts of the United States. They worked all day in the burning heat of the summer and freezing cold of winter.

Building a railroad was hard work. Everything had to be done by hand. The work was dangerous, and many men got hurt. First, workers used picks, shovels, and plows to make a flat path. Next, workers laid the ties. Ties were heavy bars of wood. Across these, the men placed long iron rails. Finally, they pounded long, thick nails called "spikes" into the rails to hold them firmly on the ties.

An **immigrant** is a person who leaves his or her home and comes into a new place or a new country to live. Thousands of immigrants helped build our canals and railroads.

What Do You Think

How did work on the railroad compare to work on the canal?

1 MEMORY MASTER

1. Which two bodies of water did the Illinois and Michigan Canal connect?
2. How were canals and railroads important to the growth of Illinois cities?

John Deere
Cyrus McCormick

efficient
logo

This painting shows the public demonstration of the first reaper by Cyrus McCormick at Steele's Tavern, Virginia.

Inventions Make Farming Easier

When farmers first came to the Illinois prairie, they were not sure they had made the right choice. The soil was rich, but the grass was so thick it was hard to clear and plow the ground.

Cyrus McCormick's Reaper

Cyrus McCormick was from Virginia. His father had worked for many years to invent a machine that could cut the tall stalks of grain in the fields. At the time, farmers all used a tool called a "scythe" (SI·th) It was a long, curved blade attached to a handle. All the work had to be done by hand, swiping the scythe back and forth across the grass.

Cyrus learned from his father's mistakes, and after trying over and over to make it better, he made a large machine called a "reaper." It had long blades attached to wooden "arms" that went around and around as a horse pulled it through the fields. When he tested it, Cyrus could cut an acre of grain in an hour! A farmer using a scythe could only harvest half an acre in a whole day.

The reaper was a large machine pulled by a horse. The very noisy machine scared the horses, but it made farming much more *efficient.* Farmers could grow and harvest more crops with fewer workers. This lowered the costs of growing crops.

McCormick moved to Chicago. His reaper and the level Illinois prairie were made for each other. Instead of making the reapers by hand and selling them door-to-door like he had in Virginia, McCormick started a factory to make the reapers. He called it the McCormick Harvesting Company. Illinois farmers finally had a faster way to cut tall grasses and harvest their wheat and other grains.

What Do You Think ?

How could improved farming change the success of other businesses in the towns?

A Million-Dollar Idea

Cyrus McCormick had told his friends that his goal was to earn a million dollars. That was a lot of money when most workers earned only a nickel an hour. About 26 years later, McCormick had earned a million dollars! His reaper had also changed the way people farmed.

John Deere's Plow

Wooden plows could not cut through the thick roots of the tall grass. Iron plows were not much better. The rich prairie soil stuck to them like glue. Often a farmer had to stop plowing to scrape soil from the plow.

John Deere saw the farmers' problem. He wondered if he could make a plow that would clean itself. He made a curved steel blade from a broken saw. Farmers came to watch Deere try out his new self-scouring plow. It was a success! The soil slid right off the polished steel blade.

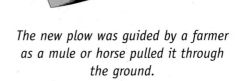

The new plow was guided by a farmer as a mule or horse pulled it through the ground.

Later, Deere opened a factory in Moline, and his business grew quickly. He advertised his invention all over the United States. Soon Deere's factory was making 10,000 plows per year.

With Deere's plow, Illinois farmers could plow large fields and plant more crops. With McCormick's reaper, they could harvest as much grain as they could plant. Wheat joined corn as a major crop.

John Deere
1804–1886

John Deere was born in Vermont. After completing his school education he worked as a blacksmith's apprentice. He then began his own career as a blacksmith. He was known for his high-quality work.

As pioneers began to move to the West, Deere decided to join them. He set out with a bundle of tools and a small amount of cash. After traveling many weeks by canal boat, lake boat, and stagecoach, he reached Grand Detour, Illinois.

John Deere worked there as a blacksmith and was busy shoeing horses and repairing plows and farmers' equipment. He learned of the trouble farmers were having with their plows. He invented a new self-scouring plow that was a great success.

Deere kept trying to make the plow even better. He even had the steel shipped from England. When one of Deere's partners said he was making too many changes in the design, Deere replied, "If we don't improve our product, someone else will."

Deere was one of the first men in the country to manufacture products and then advertise to sell them.

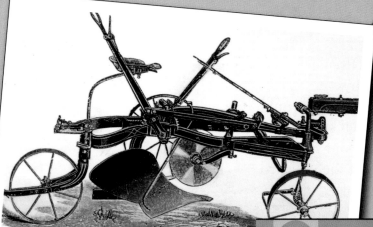

FIG. 3.—Deere's riding plow.

John Deere's riding plow was invented over 40 years after his first plow.

2 MEMORY MASTER

1. What was the main problem farmers were having on the prairie?
2. What personal traits made both McCormick and Deere successful?

Immigrants

In some European countries, disease had ruined crops and the people were starving. In other countries, wars had destroyed homes. There was no land and no freedom. Immigrants from these countries came to the United States to get jobs and a better life. They built roads, dug canals, and put down track for the railroads.

To get these workers, railroad companies posted signs in countries such as England, Ireland, and Sweden. They wanted immigrants to come and work for them. They advertised cheap land and lots of jobs. They told people the land would be more expensive in the future, so they should buy right away. They promised the soil would never wear out.

Immigrants already living in the United States also told people in Europe about this great place to live. They wrote letters to their *relatives* across the ocean. "Come to America," they said. "You can have a good life here if you are willing to work hard."

Thousands of people left their homes and families to start a new life in the United States. Steamboats, canal boats, and stagecoaches took people to towns throughout Illinois.

Immigrants from other countries and Americans from other states came for another reason. They had heard that Americans could belong to any church. This was not possible in many countries.

PEOPLE TO KNOW

Jakob Ammon
Erik Jansson
Joseph Smith

PLACES TO LOCATE

Sweden
Switzerland
Arthur
Arcola
Bishop Hill
Nauvoo

WORDS TO UNDERSTAND

descendents
relatives

The decks of ships were crowded with immigrants to the United States. They waved goodbye to family and friends on the shore, knowing they might never see them again.

Religious Settlements

The Mormons at Nauvoo

Members of The Church of Jesus Christ of Latter-day Saints, also called Mormons, wanted freedom of religion. The Mormons moved to Illinois after first being driven out of Ohio and Missouri. In the cold winter, thousands of Mormons escaped from angry mobs in Missouri and came to the town of Quincy, Illinois.

The people in Quincy were kind and gave the families shelter and food. Spring came, and the Mormons moved to a swampy place on the Mississippi River just north of Quincy. They drained the swampland beside the river, planted crops, and built a town they called Nauvoo.

Hundreds of Mormon families moved to Nauvoo from other states, Europe, and Canada. They built homes and farms, stores, a post office, a blacksmith shop, and other buildings. There were two docks where steamships could stop to get supplies and bring visitors. They even built a temple on the hill above the river. Their new city became the largest city in Illinois.

For a while, the Mormons lived in peace. But people in other towns did not understand the new religion, and many feared that the Mormons were getting too powerful. Joseph Smith was the leader of the church and also the mayor. He started a militia to protect Nauvoo in case of trouble. Volunteer soldiers in uniforms practiced marching up and down for all to see. This frightened people in other towns.

One night, some men printed a newspaper that the Mormons said was full of lies about them. When it came out in the morning, Mormon leaders held a meeting and agreed to destroy the printing press that night. This caused more trouble.

Joseph Smith was the Mormon leader in Nauvoo.

Within a month, Joseph Smith, his brother, and some other men were taken to a jail in nearby Carthage. Early the next evening, a mob of men, their faces painted black, broke into the jail. They shot and killed Joseph and his brother.

Again the Mormons were forced to leave their homes and farms. They could not find peace in Illinois. During the freezing cold of February, many packed up wagons and supplies. Wrapping their children in warm robes, they crossed the Mississippi River into Iowa and camped. The next summer, they traveled in wagons to a Utah desert no one wanted and built a new city. They called it Salt Lake City.

In February, the first Mormons to leave Nauvoo loaded their oxen and wagons on ferryboats. Later in the month the river froze solid and the people walked across it— oxen, wagons, and all. They left their new temple and homes behind to camp in the cold.

What Do You Think ?

Do people today accept and respect people of different religions?

The Bill of Rights

Part of the rules for our country is a document called the Bill of Rights. It lists freedoms that cannot be taken away from people in the United States. One of the freedoms is freedom of the press. Another is freedom of religion.

Bishop Hill

Bishop Hill was to be a perfect home for followers of Erik Jansson from Sweden. He did not agree with the state church of Sweden, but it was the only church allowed there at the time. Jansson was put in jail because of his beliefs. Religious books were burned by the government. After Jansson was released, the people decided they must leave Sweden. They had heard America was "the land of milk and honey." They had heard there was freedom of religion across the ocean.

Jansson led 300 followers to America. The journey was long and hard. After crossing the ocean and getting to Chicago, they still had to walk over 100 miles out into the rolling hills of the Illinois prairie.

The group started a village they called Bishop Hill. The first year they dug small homes called "dugouts" into the side of a hill. They made a front wall and a roof with logs. The weather was colder than usual. There was little food. Over 90 people died that first winter.

By summer, the families had started to build a church with apartments in it for some of the families. They planted crops to provide their own food. Over 1,000 more people came from Sweden, and they built homes, stores, a dairy, a bakery, and other buildings. The people made linen, furniture, brooms, and wagons to sell. They lived as a close community, enjoying the simple life for about 15 years. Then the land was divided up and many of the people moved away.

Some descendants of the first Swedish families still live at Bishop Hill. You can visit there and see what life was like for a child your age.

The Amish

About 20 years after the Swedes started Bishop Hill, Amish families began moving into central Illinois. The Amish are a religious group that was founded by a man named Jakob Ammon in Switzerland. They thought the church they belonged to was becoming too concerned with worldly things. They wanted to live a simple life. They formed a group and moved to Pennsylvania.

Over time, some Amish families moved west to Ohio and then to Illinois. They settled in Arthur and Arcola. They made their living by farming the rich land. They planted wheat, oats, clover, and corn.

As other towns started using new inventions such as electricity and automobiles, the Amish chose to keep their old way of life. They rode in horse-drawn buggies and used gas lamps instead of electricity. They grew their own food and made their own clothes. They wore the same kind of clothes as their grandparents had worn many years before.

There are still Amish communities in Illinois today. You can buy delicious food from their bakeries and furniture made by hand. You can drive behind a buggy and learn about Amish life that hasn't changed much over a hundred years.

③ MEMORY MASTER

1. What were two ways Europeans learned about jobs in Illinois?
2. How does the Constitution of our country protect religious freedom?

Lesson 2

Chapter 7 Review

— Activity —

Advertise Jobs in Illinois

Write an ad that might have been posted to convince men to work on the National Road. What will you pay them? Who do you represent? How do they get in touch with you?

Now pretend you have modern technology to advertise for the same job. Prepare a song or "jingle," design an ad on the computer, or think of a phone campaign.

— Activity —

Railroad Song

This is an American folksong sung by men working on the railroad. We don't know who first wrote the song. Irish immigrants may have sung it while working on the railroad. Dinah may refer to a woman OR a train engine. The horn means the call to lunch. Your teacher will know the tune, or listen to it online. Try singing the song as a round.

I've Been Working on the Railroad

I've been workin' on the railroad,
All the live long day.
I've been workin' on the railroad,
Just to pass the time away.
Don't you hear the whistle blowing?
Rise up so early in the morn.
Don't you hear the captain shouting,
"Dinah, blow your horn?"

Dinah, won't you blow,
Dinah, won't you blow,
Dinah, won't you blow your horn?
Dinah, won't you blow,
Dinah, won't you blow,
Dinah, won't you blow your horn?

Someone's in the kitchen with Dinah.
Someone's in the kitchen, I know.
Someone's in the kitchen with Dinah,
Strumming on the old banjo.

Fee, fie, fiddle-e-i-o,
Fee, fie, fiddle-e-i-o-o.
Fee, fie, fiddle-e-i-o,
Strumming on the old banjo.

Activity

Cause and Effect

With new roads and railroads crisscrossing Illinois, how was the landscape changed? Which natural resources were being affected? Discuss with your class the impact this had on the animal and plant life. Then write some cause and effect statements that show what you talked about.

Activity

Debate

Illinois leaders wanted to make travel around the state easier. They hired people to build roads and improve harbors and rivers. They started a canal and a railroad system. Illinois made big plans, but too many projects were started at one time. The state almost went broke. Imagine a debate taking place in the Illinois legislature.

Mr. Somerville thinks the best use of funds is to build a canal.

Mr. Swain thinks Illinois should help build the railroad.

Which do you think is the most important? Do some research and prepare to persuade the Illinois legislature to spend the money on one of the projects. Act out the debate with your class.

Activity

Persecution Newspaper Collage

Look through a newspaper and see if you can find articles or pictures of people being persecuted because of their religious beliefs. They might be people in other countries or people right in your city. Use these pictures to make a collage. Add words from the paper that tell how these people might be feeling. Underneath the collage write a statement to share how you feel about the situation.

12,000 B.C.
First people in North America

1400s
Columbus discovers America.

1500s
America first appears on the map.

1600s
Pilgrims arrive.

1700s
Declaration of Independence
George Washington

1800s
Abraham Lincoln
Pioneers go west.

1900s
Martin Luther King
Your parents were born.

2000s
A New Century
9/11 Terrorists attack the U.S.

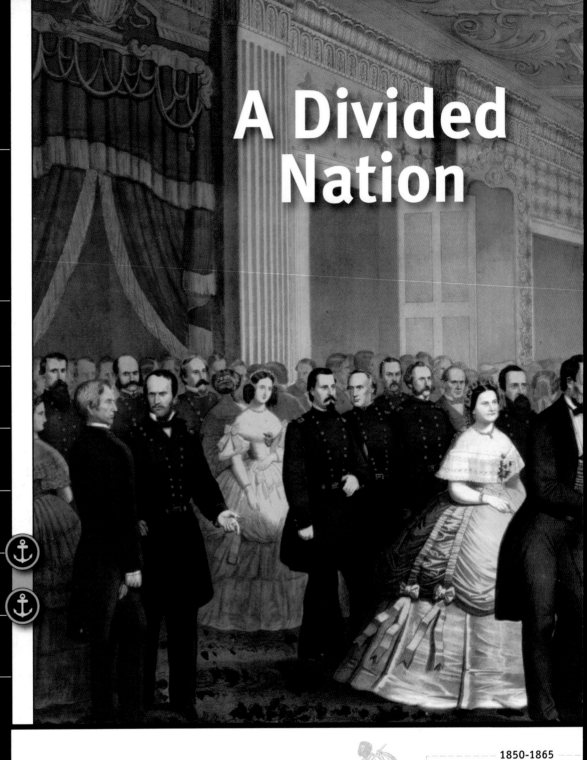

A Divided Nation

Timeline of Events

1840

1845

1850

1850-1865
Many slaves escape to freedom on the Underground Railroad.

1837
Elijah Lovejoy is killed for writing against slavery.

1850
The Fugitive Slave Act is passed.

There was a time when people in our country disagreed over important matters. They could not find a peaceful solution. Instead, the states in the southern part of the country left the United States and formed their own country. Abraham Lincoln had just been elected as president. He tried all he could think of to keep the country together. Despite his efforts, the country fought the horrible Civil War for five years.

In this picture, Abraham and Mary Lincoln greet war generals and others at a ball after Lincoln's second inauguration.

1858
Lincoln-Douglas Debates

1863 Lincoln issues the Emancipation Proclamation and later, the Gettysburg Address.
The Battle of Gettysburg is fought in Pennsylvania.

1860　　　　　　1865　　　　　　　　　1870　　　　　　1875

1861
Fort Sumter is attacked.

1861-1865
Lincoln is President of the United States; The Civil War

1865 Lincoln is shot and dies early the next morning.

167

A Nation Divided over Slavery

The United States had started calling itself the "Union," which meant a union of states joined together for a common purpose. Of course, the states were different in many ways. They were located in different parts of the country. Some states were along the coasts and had shipping ports. Some states had large cities, while others were farm regions with fewer people.

One issue divided the people of the country more than any other. Slavery was something everyone talked about. People had very strong feelings either for or against slavery.

The issues went deeper than whether or not slavery was wrong or right. It had to do with how people felt about each state having the right to decide about slavery. Slavery also affected how people in the state made money.

Americans who lived in the south part of the United States were called **Southerners.** Americans who lived in the north were called **Northerners.**

What Do You Think?

Remember when the new colonists did not want England to have power over them? They wanted their independence. Is this similar to the views of the people in the South?

State's Rights

Many people supported state's rights, which meant the right of the states to decide what was best for the people in the state. People in the South, for instance, thought the states should have more power than the national government in Washington, D.C. They did not want to be told what to do, especially when it involved the way they earned their money and the way they lived.

The Economy

Many people in the South said slavery was important to their economy, or the way they made money. Slavery was tied to the economy of the South in a big way. The people there were mainly farmers. The crops they grew, such as cotton, tobacco, rice, and sugar, needed many workers. Some had very large farms called *plantations.* The farmers said they could not run their plantations without the work of many slaves.

In the North, thousands of people in cities worked in factories. They also worked to build canals and railroads. People worked making barrels, wagons, and other goods for the factory, home, or farm. There were also many farms, but they were smaller than the large plantations. Families didn't need slaves to help them plant and harvest their crops.

As more territories were trying to become states, the question of slavery got more and more important to the country. Would the new states allow slavery? Southerners wanted all the new states to allow slavery. Northerners wanted the new states to be free from slavery.

Reading in Secret

Slaves were not allowed to learn to read and write. The masters were afraid that if their slaves could read and write, they could read maps and signs and try to escape. Still, many slaves learned to read in secret. Reading was a way of saying to the masters, "You can never own my mind."

There was plenty of work to be done outside the cabin. What do you think the man is doing?

African Americans in Illinois

The Illinois constitution said there could not be slaves in Illinois. However, this was thought to mean no new slaves. *Enslaved* men, women, and children still lived and worked in Illinois. Some whites started calling their slaves "servants," but they could not leave and did not get paid for their work.

Even though Illinois was a free state, free blacks were not welcome. They had a very hard time finding jobs or places to live. When they did find jobs, they were paid much less than white people. They had to go to court many times to prove that they were free. It was hard to prove they were free if a white man told the court he had found runaway slaves.

A few years after Illinois became a state, some people tried to change the state constitution and become a slave state. Almost half of the people of Illinois voted pro-slavery. It would be a long time until blacks were truly free in Illinois.

From Africa to America

Imagine you are taking a walk in Africa. Suddenly, strange men surround you. You find yourself trapped. You are put in chains and forced to leave your home, family, and everything that is familiar to you.

Africans did not become slaves because they wanted to. Men, women, and children were captured, taken from their homelands, and sold to slave traders. Slave traders chained the people together so they could hardly move. They crowded the frightened people into the bottom of wooden sailing ships. They gave them very little food. Many got sick and died on the long journey across the ocean.

When the ships landed, traders sold the slaves to the men who would pay the highest price. That kind of sale is called an **auction.** Parents and children could be sold to different owners called "masters." Masters took their slaves in a wagon to a plantation. They went from being free men and women to being someone's property.

Enslaved people had no rights. They worked without pay. They had to do whatever they were told to do. When children were born to slaves, the children also became slaves.

"My brothers and sisters were bid off first while my mother . . . held me by the hand. Then I was offered. My mother pushed through the crowd to the spot where [her master] was standing. She fell at his knees, begging him to buy her baby as well as herself."
— Josiah Henson, slave

Slaves were crowded onto a sailing ship. They were given very little to eat or drink. Many died on the voyage.

The Hard Life of a Slave

Slaves worked in many places in the country, but most lived on large cotton plantations in the South. From sunrise to sunset they worked, bent over in the fields, picking cotton. Picking cotton was backbreaking work. When it was time for lunch the workers could only rest for a short time. Lunch might be cold bacon and bread. Then it was time to pick more cotton.

One planter had 36 slaves picking cotton on his plantation. He wrote that a woman named Mary picked over 300 pounds in one day. A young boy named Adam picked 51 pounds. The best pickers could grasp the five white pieces of cotton from each plant with one hand, but they had to be careful. The open cotton ball (pod) was hard and prickly.

By late evening slaves could prepare their own suppers. They cooked meat over a fire and baked cornmeal to eat with it. Supper ended the hard day. As they went to sleep, they dreamed of Sunday, the one day a week they didn't have to work the fields. On Sundays they might go to church, work in their own gardens, or go hunting and fishing to get more food for their families. They also might walk many miles to visit part of their family who lived on another plantation.

We [lived] in log huts, and on the bare ground. In a single room we were huddled, like cattle, ten or a dozen persons, men, women, and children. . . Our beds were collections of old straw and old rags, thrown down in the corners and boxed in with boards; . . . The wind whistled and the rain and snow blew in through the cracks. . . the damp earth soaked in moisture till the floor was [muddy] as a pig sty.

—Josiah Henson

Look on the tags on your clothing. Is the shirt you're wearing made of cotton? Today, cotton is used more than any other fiber to make clothes. Today, all cotton is picked, cleaned, and made into fabric by machines.

While most enslaved men and women worked in the fields, others cooked and cleaned in the master's house and took care of the master's children. Some men worked as carpenters, blacksmiths or masons (bricklayers). Slaves drove mule teams that pulled wagons filled with cotton to warehouses. Workers cleaned the cotton, removed the seeds, spun it into cotton thread, and wove it into fabric.

What Do You Think ?

Our Declaration of Independence says, ". . . all men are created equal." But slaves were not thought to be equal to other people. Slaves were thought of as property, or something you own. What do you think it means to be equal?

African Traditions

In spite of the hard work and the terrible living conditions, slaves still tried to keep some of their African traditions. They sang songs in the field and at night. They told stories about their ancestors and their old country. They got married and had children. They tried to make something of their lives even though their freedom had been taken away. They could still make a choice about how they felt and what they thought about.

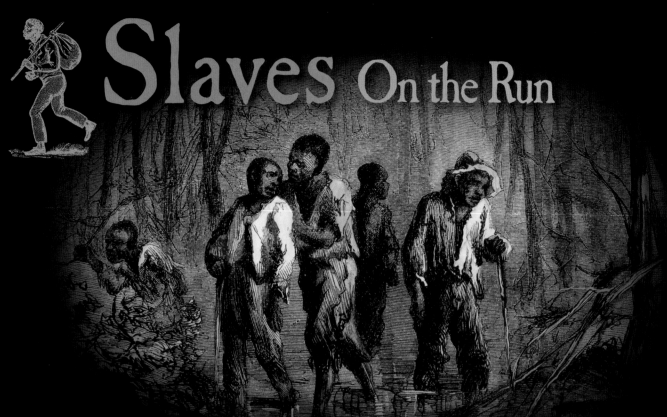

Slaves On the Run

Roads to Freedom

CANADA

Detroit
Buffalo
Boston
Chicago
New York
Wheeling
Cincinnati
Alexandria
Parkersburg
St. Louis

Memphis
Charleston

Atlantic
Ocean

Houston
New Orleans

Gulf of Mexico
THE
BAHAMAS

MEXICO

Legend

General routes of escape
Slave state—slavery permitted
Free state—slavery prohibited

CUBA

It is no surprise that people did not like living under such cruel conditions. Many slaves bravely tried to escape. Sadly, most escapes failed. If caught, runaways were beaten, jailed, or sold.

Still, many slaves tried to run away to the Northern states or Canada where they would be free. **_Abolitionists_** were people who wanted to end slavery. They wanted to make laws against slavery. They wanted masters to free their slaves. Many abolitionists helped slaves escape on the "Underground Railroad."

The Underground Railroad was not really a railroad. It was a system of secret routes that slaves in the South used to escape to the free states in the North. It wasn't really underground, either. "Underground" just means that the routes were kept secret from most people.

Runaway slaves were mostly men, but many women and children also ran away from masters and headed north into Canada, where they would be free. Illinois was on the route to freedom.

There were many paths through woods, over fields, and across rivers and swamps. Along these routes were "stations" such as farmhouses, barns, and churches where "conductors" hid runaways. Conductors were men and women who wanted to help the slaves escape.

Secret codes told the people when it was safe to move on. Women made quilts and hung them on their clotheslines. The patches on the quilts told the slaves which way to go. One quilt might mean it was safe to travel and another would tell runaways to stay hidden. Sometimes maps were sewn on a quilt as part of a design.

The Quakers were a religious group who thought slavery was wrong. Many Quakers helped slaves escape.

The Fugitive Slave Act

Slave owners were angry when people in the North helped slaves escape. They got Congress to pass the Fugitive Slave Act. The law punished anyone who tried to help a slave escape. The law said that even in free states, people had to return a slave to his or her master.

Harriet Tubman

Harriet Tubman never lived in Illinois, but she is known as one of the most **courageous** conductors of the Underground Railroad. She grew up as a slave. Then she escaped and later helped over 300 slaves to freedom. She was known as Moses, after Moses in the Bible. He led his people out of slavery in Egypt.

Slaves sang this song about Moses. The pharaoh was the leader of Egypt.

When Israel was in Egypt's land, let my people go.
Oppressed so hard they could not stand, let my people go.
Go down Moses, way down in Egypt's land,
Tell old pharaoh, let my people go.

Harriet Tubman had many ways of hiding runaway slaves. One time, she hid them under a load of fruits and vegetables in a wagon. Other times she dressed men up as women so they could hide from a master who was looking for them. Tubman taught the runaways to rub their bare feet or shoes with a red onion to keep the master's dogs from running after them.

About her own escape from slavery, Harriet said:

"I had reasoned this out in my mind; there was only two things I had a right to, liberty or death; if I could not have one, I would have the other, for no man should take me alive; I would fight for my liberty as long as my strength lasted..."

Owen Lovejoy and Safe Houses

Many stations on the Underground Railroad were right here in Illinois. One was in Princeton. It was the home of a preacher named Owen Lovejoy. He had a large house with many closets. In the days of the Underground Railroad, the closets hid many runaway slaves. When night came, the slaves hid under a pile of hay on a wagon. Then Lovejoy drove the wagon to the next station. A nearby river allowed slaves to escape by boat.

There were at least 38 known stations in Illinois. They were in Cairo, Quincy, Alton, Chester, Rockford, Chicago, and other towns. Today, people are working to have the sites preserved. They want to honor all the brave people who escaped and helped others escape.

The Old Slave House

On top of Hickory Hill in southern Illinois sits the Crenshaw house. John Hart Crenshaw owned the house. While people around Illinois were helping slaves escape, John was kidnapping free black people and selling them into slavery. It was like the Underground Railroad in reverse. The house has become known as the Old Slave House. Tourists visit to see the rooms where free blacks were hidden and sold.

Owen Lovejoy

● Princeton

What Do You Think?

Should we still keep places where sad things happened?

Elijah Lovejoy

Owen Lovejoy's brother, Elijah, was a newspaper editor. He believed strongly that slavery was wrong. He wrote against slavery in his paper. His views made some people angry—so angry that they became violent. Twice a mob attacked him for writing against slavery. They broke into his office and ruined his printing press.

Lovejoy moved from St. Louis, Missouri, to Alton, Illinois, to escape the mobs. But he was no safer in Illinois. Mobs destroyed another press. They told him there would be more violence if he kept attacking slavery in his newspaper.

Lovejoy was not willing to give up. He ordered yet another printing press. As soon as it arrived, the mob attacked again. Lovejoy was shot five times, and died a few days later on his 35th birthday. Angry men burned his warehouse and threw his new printing press into the Mississippi River.

1 MEMORY MASTER

1. What were the three main issues that divided the states?
2. Why were slaves important to the economy of the South?
3. Why was the slave escape route called the "Underground Railroad," and why was Illinois an important part of it?
4. Why did men want to destroy Lovejoy's printing press?

An All-Black Town

Brooklyn (also known as Lovejoy) is the oldest black town in the United States. It was named for Elijah P. Lovejoy. In 1829 a group of 11 families of runaway blacks fled slavery, crossed the Mississippi River, and started a small community. Five white abolitionists joined them. Even today, Brooklyn is an all-black town.

● Brooklyn
(St.Clair)

Making Connections

Who else have you read about who died defending something he or she thought was very important?

PEOPLE TO KNOW

Stephen A. Douglas
Abraham Lincoln
Mary Todd Lincoln

PLACES TO LOCATE

Indiana
Kentucky
Decatur
New Salem
Springfield
New Orleans, Louisiana
Washington, D.C.

WORDS TO UNDERSTAND

immoral

Young Abe Lincoln

Abraham Lincoln was born in a log cabin with a dirt floor on a small farm in Kentucky. He lived there until he was seven years old. Then the Lincolns moved to Indiana. They left Kentucky for two reasons. First, Abe's father, Thomas, lost his farm. The second reason was slavery. Kentucky was a slave state, and Thomas Lincoln believed it was wrong to own slaves.

The land the Lincolns settled on in Indiana was in the forest. Abraham had to work hard, helping his father clear the forest, build a new log cabin, and start a new farm. Abe's older sister, Sarah, helped with the housework and took care of the animals.

There was so much work to do that there was little time for school. Books and paper were hard to find. Even though he went to a few schools for short periods of time, Lincoln spent no more than one year in school in his entire life. Still, he learned to read, write, and work with numbers.

When Abe was only nine years old, his mother died, leaving Sarah and Abe alone with their father. It was a very sad time for everyone. The next year, however, Abe's father married again, and the new mother brought three more children to live in the cabin. "She proved to be a good and kind mother," Abe said of her. She helped Abe learn to read and write and took good care of him and his sister.

A Strong Worker

Lincoln grew to be a very tall young man and a good strong worker. This made him a favorite among other farm families. Whenever he could be spared from his father's farm, he worked for his neighbors.

At age 19, Abe was hired to help take a flatboat down the Mississippi River to New Orleans. For the first time, he saw how terrible slaves were treated. The people were being held in pens or locked in hot, crowded rooms, waiting for a buyer. Then they were taken away in chains. Abe's trip to New Orleans made him think even more about how wrong slavery was.

Lincoln was sometimes called "the rail splitter."

Lincoln Comes to Illinois

Abe's family settled on a farm near Decatur, Illinois. Abe helped his family get started on the new farm. A year later, the family moved again, but this time, Abe Lincoln did not move with them. He worked on another flatboat going to New Orleans. Then he moved alone to the small town of New Salem and got a job splitting logs to build fences. Someone gave him a job in a store and let him sleep in the back.

When he was not busy, Lincoln spent time reading and studying. He wanted to learn all he could about the law. He often walked to the county courthouse to watch the lawyers work.

Lincoln worked at several different jobs over the next few years. With a friend, he bought and ran his own store. They sold tea, coffee, sugar, salt, hats, shoes, and cloth to the people of New Salem. But in a few months the store failed. It took several years for Lincoln to pay off the debts from the store. He also worked as a surveyor. Lincoln worked as Postmaster (the person in charge of the post office) for New Salem.

At the urging of his friends, Lincoln first ran for public office when he was just 23 years old. He lost the election, but two years later, he tried again and won a seat in the Illinois General Assembly. Honest, brave, and friendly, Lincoln quickly made many friends.

Abe loved to read and learn. He borrowed books from anyone he could and read them by the fireplace at night. He even read while plowing.

"A friend is someone who finds me a new book to read."
—Abraham Lincoln

For a while, young Abe Lincoln worked on a flatboat on the Ohio River.

Lincoln Moves to Springfield

Lincoln moved to Springfield and worked as a lawyer. He opened a law office with another man. When people had problems, he helped defend them in court.

When he was about 30 years old, Abe Lincoln met Mary Todd at a dance. They made a strange-looking couple. She was just over 5 feet tall, and he was a tall, skinny man about 6 feet and 4 inches tall. A few years later, they married.

At the time, the Lincolns lived in a small room above a tavern. This was very hard for Mary, who was used to living in a fine house. Lincoln was working as a lawyer, but he did not want to bother people to collect the money they owed him. He didn't mind being poor—he was too interested in his work.

A Family of Boys

Finally, the Lincolns bought a home for the family that now included Robert, their first son. Then another son, Edward, was born. When he was four years old, Edward got very sick. The doctors could not help him, and he died. This was a tragic time for the family.

A third son, Willie, was born a short time later. Then another son came. He must have been a lively baby. He was called Tad because he wiggled like a tadpole.

Abraham and Mary Todd Lincoln

What Do You Think❓

Our state slogan is "Land of Lincoln." Do you think this is because he spent part of his life here, or because of the type of person Lincoln was? What do you think the slogan means?

This painting shows Abraham and Mary Lincoln with their sons, Robert and Tad. You can read a story about Tad on page 192.

Lincoln First Goes to Washington

Lincoln was elected to go to Washington, D.C., to work in Congress as a representative. He moved his young family to Washington. After his term in Washington was over, they returned to Springfield.

"If slavery is not wrong then nothing is wrong."
—Abraham Lincoln

A senator is a person elected to go to Washington, D.C. to help make the laws for our country. Both Douglas and Lincoln wanted to be senators, but Lincoln lost the election.

Lincoln-Douglas Debates

Back in Illinois, another man, Stephen A. Douglas, was a senator who wanted to win the election again. He was a short man whom people called the "Little Giant." People all over the country knew of him. Hoping to take Douglas's job as senator was Abraham Lincoln.

The debates were popular events. Brass bands played and cannons boomed. Thousands of people came from nearby towns and farms. The two men talked about the ideas of people all over Illinois and the country.

Lincoln believed that slavery was *immoral,* and that it should not be allowed to spread. "The real issue," he said, was the "struggle between right and wrong."

Douglas said that Lincoln was trying to start a war. "Let the people speak!" Douglas said. He believed the white people in each territory should decide if they wanted to own slaves.

The two great men debated the slavery question in cities across the state. In the end, Senator Douglas was re-elected. Lincoln had lost another election. Because of the debates, however, Lincoln had become known all over the country.

What Do You Think ?

What might be some of the reasons why Douglas defeated Lincoln in the election?

DU PAGE COUNTY CENTENNIAL
LINCOLN ★ DOUGLAS
DEBATE
AUGUST · 27TH
WEST CHICAGO

The President from Illinois

People liked Lincoln. They liked to hear him speak. Two years after the debate, Douglas and Lincoln met again. This time each wanted to be president of the United States. This time, Lincoln won. He became our 16th president.

Lincoln once again took his wife, Mary Todd Lincoln, and their sons to Washington, but this time they lived in the White House. The oldest son, Robert, often visited from college. The two younger boys, Willie and Tad, often interrupted important meetings. They ran through the halls and played out on the lawn. They also had pets in the famous house. The staff at the White House had never seen such wild boys! Then young Willie got a disease the doctors could not cure. After a few months of being very sick, Willie died in the White House. The president and his wife had now lost two of their sons.

Photography was a new invention at the time of Lincoln. Most of the pictures in this lesson were paintings and drawings done to illustrate Lincoln's life. However, this picture is a photograph. It was taken of the president and his son, Willie, in 1864.

2 MEMORY MASTER

1. List the types of jobs Lincoln had before becoming president. What do you think he learned from them?
2. How did Lincoln educate himself?
3. What made Lincoln popular to those he lived and worked with?

Chapter 8 "A Divided Nation"

The Civil War

People in the South did not like Lincoln's ideas. They did not want him to lead the country. When Lincoln was elected, seven Southern states *seceded,* or left, the Union.

People all over the country waited to see what President Lincoln would do. In his first speech he said he did not plan to change the South. He would not try to end slavery there. He also said that he did not plan to fight.

Soon after, confederate soldiers fired on Fort Sumter in South Carolina. While no one was killed, this was the starting of the Civil War. The new president faced the hard task of guiding a nation through its worst crisis.

PEOPLE TO KNOW

Mary Ann Bickerdyke
John Wilkes Booth
Jefferson Davis
Jennie Hodgers
Robert E. Lee

PLACES TO LOCATE

South Carolina
Cairo
Carbondale
Galesburg

WORDS TO UNDERSTAND

emancipation
rebellion
secede

One boy watching the fort wrote, "I had a splendid view. A perfect sheet of flame flashed out. There was a roar, a rumbling, and the war was on."

Union soldiers were inside Fort Sumter when they were surprised by loud blasts. The fighting did not last very long, and the soldiers left the fort, taking their flag with them.

A Nation Divided

After the battle, four more slave states in the South left the Union. The states formed what they hoped would be a new country. They called their country the Confederate States of America, or the Confederacy. Jefferson Davis was president of the Confederacy.

It was a very sad time in history. Each side formed an army to fight for their beliefs. Each side chose a general to lead their army. The Union fought to keep the country together. The Confederacy fought for the right to be a separate country.

War Songs

During the Civil War a Chicago man named George F. Root wrote war songs. Union soldiers sang his songs around campfires and on the battlefields. Songs such as "A Battle Cry of Freedom" helped keep their spirits up.

Battle Cry of Freedom

Yes we'll rally round the flag, boys, we'll rally once again,
Shouting the battle cry of freedom!
We will rally from the hillside, we'll rally from the plain,
Shouting the battle cry of freedom!

A Nation Divided— the Civil War

North

Name: Union
Nickname: Yankees
Color: Blue
Number of States: 23

South

Name: Confederacy
Nickname: Rebels
Color: Gray
Number of States: 11

President:
Abraham Lincoln

General:
Ulysses S. Grant

General:
Robert E. Lee

President:
Jefferson Davis

A Call for Soldiers

Lincoln asked for volunteers to defend the Union. The rush of young men from Illinois was greater than anyone had expected. Sometimes whole groups of teachers, firemen, or miners signed up.

At first, African Americans were not allowed in the army. But after two years they were allowed to join. About 1,800 from Illinois went to war.

Many young men joined the army thinking the war would be exciting and short. They dreamed of being brave heroes. But usually the war was not like that. Soldiers spent most days sitting in camp, waiting for a battle. When the battles came they were horrible. Men were shot and killed. Some lost an arm or leg.

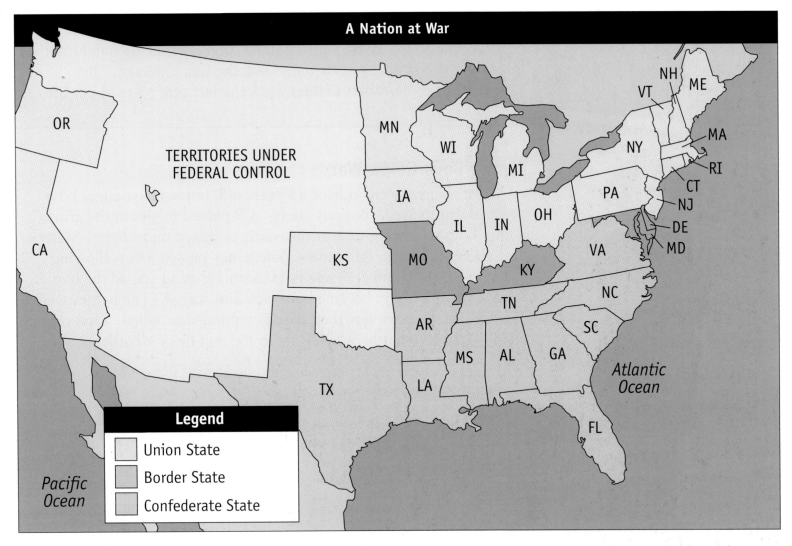

A Nation at War

TERRITORIES UNDER FEDERAL CONTROL

OR, CA, MN, WI, MI, NY, NH, VT, ME, MA, RI, CT, NJ, DE, MD, PA, OH, IN, IL, IA, KS, MO, KY, VA, NC, TN, AR, SC, MS, AL, GA, LA, TX, FL

Pacific Ocean

Atlantic Ocean

Legend
Union State
Border State
Confederate State

The border states were part of the Union, but people there still owned slaves. Can you find Illinois on the map? Was it a Union state or a Confederate state? What are the four border states?

Women in the War

Women volunteered to work without pay to help win the war. They set up hospitals. They made bandages and clothing for the soldiers. Many women ran family farms by themselves while their husbands and sons were at war. Others got factory jobs filling in for the men who were away. Some women served as spies. A few women even dressed up as men and joined the army.

Jennie Hodgers

Women were not allowed to be soldiers in the Civil War. But that didn't stop Jennie Hodgers. She joined the 95th Illinois Volunteers and fought for three years. How did she do it? She joined as a man called "Albert Cashier."

Jennie fought in many battles. After the war she was able to receive payment each month, but she worried that she might not get the money if the army found out she was a woman. She pretended to be Albert Cashier until the last few years of her life.

Young Boys Go to War

Most soldiers were at least 18 years old, but some younger boys went to war as well. Boys as young as 9 played bugles in the army. Other boys who went to visit their fathers stayed on to fight. Many lied about their age. Later, the Confederacy passed a law allowing boys under 18 to enlist. Some boys as young as 11 joined the battles.

Many of the boys became homesick and scared. The battles were terrible. Many boys saw their friends wounded or killed. One young man described what he was feeling in the middle of a battle:

I want to say, as we lay there and the shells were flying over us, my thoughts went back to my home, and I thought what a foolish boy I was to run away and get into such a mess as I was in.

—Elisha Stockwell

After the war, the government changed its rules. The Civil War was the last time large numbers of boys so young fought for our country.

Illinois PORTRAIT

"Mother" Bickerdyke
1817–1901

Mary Ann Ball Bickerdyke moved to Galesburg, Illinois, from Ohio. She touched so many lives she was called the "Mother" of the Union army.

Mrs. Bickerdyke was a nurse. While in church one Sunday, she heard about the awful conditions in army hospitals. One week later, she was on a train headed to Cairo. She had collected medical supplies from members of her church.

When Mrs. Bickerdyke arrived in Cairo, she went to the army hospital. What she saw made her angry. The hospital was just three tents. In each tent were ten men and a few cots. The other men had to sleep on straw on the ground. The straw had not been changed in weeks. The men were covered with dirt and flies. Their clothes had not been washed since they had arrived. The only supplies in the tents were buckets of water.

Mrs. Bickerdyke thought about what to do. She walked over to a group of healthy soldiers and asked them to follow her. They said they couldn't go unless they were given an order by one of their officers. But this wasn't going to stop her. She offered them a bribe: if they helped her clean up the hospital, she would cook them a chicken dinner.

The soldiers rounded up some barrels and sawed them in half. They scrubbed them with lye soap and then filled them with hot water. They brought the patients out from the tents and removed their tattered clothes. They washed the clothes. They also washed each patient and shaved his face and head. They cleaned the tents and moved the wounded soldiers back into a clean place in clean clothes.

Bickerdyke did the same thing at many hospitals in other places. Soon soldiers were all calling her "Mother."

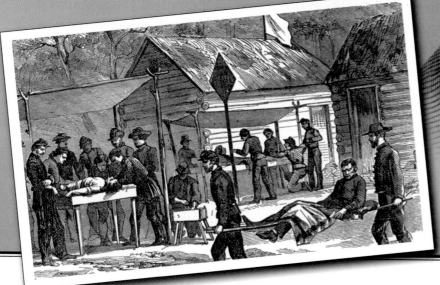

Wounded soldiers were brought from the battlefields to be cared for by nurses and doctors.

Lincoln tried to solve the slavery problem. He issued the Emancipation Proclamation that said: "All persons held as slaves within any state...in rebellion against the United States, shall be . . . forever free." In the North, people celebrated. In the South, slave owners paid little attention.

Battle at Gettysburg

War raged on. The South seemed to be winning. Confederate General Lee hoped to capture a major city, so he moved his army north.

Part of the Union army was in hot pursuit of the Confederate army. But neither commander knew exactly where the other army was. By complete accident, the two armies met at a little town in Pennsylvania called Gettysburg. This turned out to be one of the deadliest battles of the war. Even though the war lasted two more years, Lee and his army never recovered from their losses.

The Gettysburg Address

For months, the town of Gettysburg turned its churches and schools into hospitals. People worked to nurse and comfort the wounded. Dead soldiers were being buried all over town. A cemetery was made for the soldiers.

Workers moved thousands of graves to the new cemetery. Then they planned a ceremony. They invited President Lincoln to say a few words. He started his speech: *"Four score and seven years ago our fathers brought forth on this continent a new nation, conceived in liberty, and dedicated to the proposition that all men are created equal."*

After his short speech was over, it was very quiet. The president worried that it was not a good speech. But the opposite was true. The crowd thought it was a great speech! Newspapers printed it the next day.

Chapter 8 "A Divided Nation"

The speech helped people see the importance of liberty and equality. The war was finishing the work of the Declaration of Independence by making everyone free.

Illinois Supports the War

Much of the food needed for the war was grown in Illinois. The farm industry boomed. The great increase in farm products meant more jobs to sell and ship the goods. Chicago became a major center for shipping, storing, and selling corn and wheat.

Galena mined much of the iron need to make weapons used during the war. Men got jobs working in the mines. Towns grew up near the mines. This meant even more new businesses such as shops, stores, and offices were needed.

Cairo became the home of a huge Union military camp and supply depot. Soldiers and war materials were sent from Cairo down the river to support General Grant's troops. The growth spilled over into other nearby communities. The United States Navy built a new home for its Mississippi fleet of ships at Mound City. This gave many jobs to the men and women of Illinois.

Merchants brought grain, corn, lumber, and livestock into the state by train on a network of rails. In Chicago, workmen processed and packaged these materials and sent them on their way. With both the railways and waterways, Illinois became one of the busiest business centers in the United States.

The War Ends

After four long years and many battles, the Civil War finally ended. Some families celebrated as their husbands, fathers, and sons came home from war. In other families, tears were shed because loved ones had died and would never come home.

The war had shown everyone that Americans could not split their country in two. They had to stick together.

The Slaves Are Freed

After the war, slavery was ended by the Thirteenth Amendment to the U.S. Constitution. No longer could one person own another person. It was a time of great rejoicing among African Americans.

Illinois people supported the war in many ways. About 300,000 men and women from Illinois were soldiers or nurses. About 30,000 Illinois men lost their lives fighting to save the Union. Illinois towns grew because of the role they played during the Civil War.

What Do You Think?

Can you imagine what it would be like to be finally free after a lifetime of being a slave? What do you think the freed slaves looked forward to the most?

Memorial Day

The first Memorial Day was held a year after the Civil War ended, when the people of Carbondale gathered to honor those who had died in the Civil War. Memorial Day later became a national holiday to honor those who had died in all wars.

Activity

Our State Song and the Civil War

Two verses in our Illinois State Song remind us of the Civil War.

When you heard your country calling, Illinois, Illinois,
Where the shot and shell were falling, Illinois, Illinois,
When the Southern host withdrew,
Pitting Grey against the Blue,
There were none more brave than you, Illinois, Illinois,
There were none more brave than you, Illinois.

Not without thy wondrous story, Illinois, Illinois,
Can be writ the nation's glory, Illinois, Illinois,
On the record of thy years,
Abraham Lincoln's name appears,
Grant and Logan, and our tears, Illinois, Illinois,
Grant and Logan, and our tears, Illinois.

1. Which side in the war was the "Grey" and which side was the "Blue"?
2. In the second verse, who was Grant, and who was Logan? How can you find out?
3. What do the words "and our tears" mean?

Now it is your turn. Write a new verse to the song. What does it say about the Civil War or about Illinois?

Chapter 8 "A Divided Nation"

President Lincoln Is Assassinated

Just days after the war ended, a terrible thing happened in a theater in Washington, D.C. President Lincoln and his wife were watching a play when John Wilkes Booth, an actor, crept up to a special booth where the president was sitting. Booth shot Lincoln. Then he jumped down onto the stage, breaking his leg, and escaped out the back door. Booth was a Confederate and blamed Lincoln for the South losing the war. Lincoln was taken to a home across the street, where he died early the next morning.

A long funeral train took Lincoln back to Springfield to be buried. President Lincoln's funeral train was draped with black blankets and decorated with silver stars. It stopped in many towns along the route. People lined the streets for hours to say goodbye to the man who had led them through a terrible war and finally ended slavery forever.

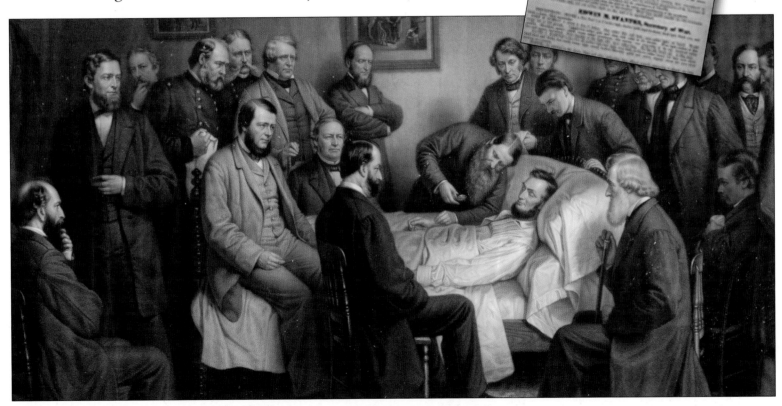

Abraham Lincoln was the first American president to be assassinated.

3 MEMORY MASTER

1. What did the people in the North call their country? What did the people in the South call their country?
2. How did Illinois men and women help during the war?

Chapter 8 Review

---- **Activity** ----

Freedom Isn't Free—Write an Essay

With your class, talk about the saying, "Freedom isn't free." What do you think it means?

Then pretend you are one of the following people and write an essay explaining the high cost of freedom and how you feel about your sacrifice.

- A Union soldier
- A Confederate soldier
- The child of a soldier who was killed
- A former slave
- A conductor on the Underground Railroad
- A soldier who lost his leg in battle
- A nurse in the war

---- **Activity** ----

Tad's Goat

At one time, Mary Lincoln and her sons left Washington for a while. While they were away, President Lincoln wrote his family a letter.

Read the letter. Tad was about your age at the time. What do you think Tad's reaction to the letter was? What do you think Tad might have written back to his father? What questions would he have had? What else might he have said to his father?

Hand write a return letter from Tad back to his father, President Lincoln.

Include not only questions, but also share information you think Tad would have wanted his father to know about what he had been doing with his family. Remember to think about the date, greeting, and how he would have signed the letter.

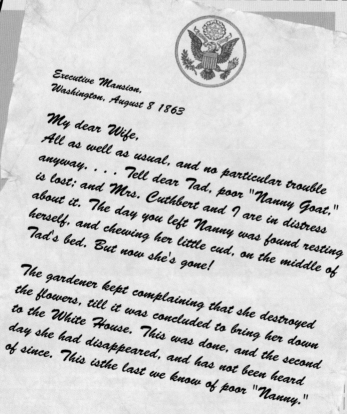

Executive Mansion,
Washington, August 8 1863

My dear Wife,
All as well as usual, and no particular trouble anyway. . . . Tell dear Tad, poor "Nanny Goat," is lost; and Mrs. Cuthbert and I are in distress about it. The day you left Nanny was found resting herself, and chewing her little cud, on the middle of Tad's bed. But now she's gone!

The gardener kept complaining that she destroyed the flowers, till it was concluded to bring her down to the White House. This was done, and the second day she had disappeared, and has not been heard of since. This isthe last we know of poor "Nanny."

Summarize the Civil War

On a piece of paper, draw a large web like this one. Now skim back through the chapter to review the important facts about the Civil War. Write down several bullet points (phrases) under each heading. Then use these details to write a summary paragraph about the Civil War.

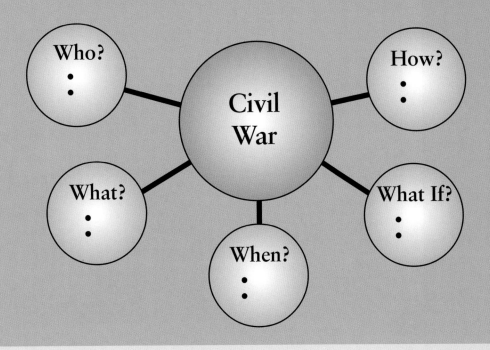

Finding Freedom Road

For this activity, work in groups of four.

1. Choose a place in your community that would make a good "safe house" for the Underground Railroad. Keep it a secret from the other groups.
2. Two students write a song that secretly tells how to get to the safe house. The other two students design a quilt with cut pieces of paper that secretly—without using words—shows directions.
3. Exchange songs and quilts with another group. See if each group can find the other group's safe house. (You will probably wish you had a conductor!)

12,000 B.C.
First people in North America

1400s
Columbus discovers America.

1500s
America first appears on
the map.

1600s
Pilgrims arrive.

1700s
Declaration of Independence
George Washington

1800s
Abraham Lincoln
Pioneers go west.

1900s
Martin Luther King
Your parents were born.

2000s
A New Century
9/11 Terrorists attack the U.S.

Times of Change

Timeline of Events

1860

1870

188

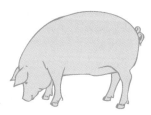

1865
Gurdon Hubbard starts a
meat packing business.
Union Stock Yard opens.
Marshall Field opens a
department store.

1871
Great
Chicago Fire

1872
Montgomery Ward
opens a mail order
business.

Chapter 9

Life changed in Illinois. Thousands of cattle were shipped to the Chicago stockyards on train cars. Marshall Field opened a large store that made shopping a lot more fun. People started using electricity for lights. They started driving cars. In 1893 Illinois held a wonderful World's Fair. It was called the Columbian Exhibition. This painting shows part of the Women's Building at the fair.

Notice the women's clothes and hair styles. How things have changed!

1886
Haymarket Square Riot

1894
Pullman Strike

1900
A new canal reverses the flow of the Chicago River.

1890

1900

1910

1889
Jane Addams opens Hull House.

1893
Chicago hosts the World Columbian Exposition.
Sears mail order business is started in Chicago.

PEOPLE TO KNOW

Marshall Field
Gurdon Hubbard
Alvah Roebuck
Richard Sears
Montgomery Ward

PLACES TO LOCATE

Minnesota

WORDS TO UNDERSTAND

mills
refrigerated
slaughter
stockyard

Early Industries

Farming had been the way most people in Illinois made their living. They plowed and planted, weeded, and picked the crops. Then they sold some of the grain or vegetables to make money. More and more, however, industry was catching up to farming. People worked in *mills* and factories, making things that were sold all over the country. One important thing that helped industry grow was the railroad.

What Do You Think ?

- How would you define industry?
- How does that relate to being industrious?

The lumber district of Chicago held stacks of wood for building.

This factory belonged to Friedrich Flersheim, who sold his farm and built this large factory to produce whisky. He made more than a thousand gallons a day.

Chapter 9 "Times of Change"

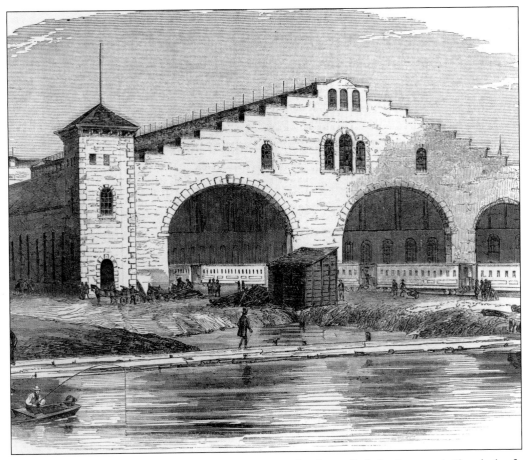

Illinois is called the crossroads of the nation. It is also called the transportation hub of the United States. This is the Great Central Railroad station in Chicago.

Railroad Expansion

In Illinois, railroads connected northern cities like Galena, Freeport, and Rock Island to southern cities like Alton, Centralia, and Cairo. The tracks passed through Quincy, Peoria, Springfield, and Bloomington. Chicago was usually their destination. From all directions, railroads and waterways led to Chicago.

Chicago became the world's largest railroad center. Over 100 trains entered or left the city every day. They brought wheat and corn to the flour mills and grain elevators of Chicago. Soon Chicago became the nation's most important grain market.

Trains also brought coal, clay, limestone, sand, gravel, and fluorite from Illinois towns. Trains carried logs from Wisconsin and Minnesota to mills in Chicago. Then the logs were cut into boards for building homes and furniture. The wood and the furniture was shipped out by train to cities in many places.

Trains also brought people to Chicago. Most of the newcomers were immigrants from Europe and other countries.

The Meat-Packing Industry

Farmers moved their live pigs and cattle by train to Chicago, where they were *slaughtered* (killed). The meat was cleaned, cut into pieces, and sold. The slaughtering took place mostly in the winter so the meat would stay cold.

Gurdon Hubbard got the idea to build a huge warehouse in Chicago to store the meat. He bought large ice blocks in other cities to keep the meat cool. His idea was a success. Packing and storing meat became big business. The meat was then shipped in new *refrigerated* railroad cars to other towns and cities. The train cars kept meat cool so it would not rot.

Barbed Wire

The barbed wire fence, improved by Joseph F. Glidden in DeKalb, was dotted with sharp pieces of wire that kept animals from rubbing against the fence and knocking it down. It was "horse high, hog tight, and bull strong," and it quickly replaced wooden fences in stockyards, farms, and ranches all over the country.

The Great Union Stock Yards in Chicago held thousands of cattle.

Chapter 9 "Times of Change"

Soon there were many *stockyards* around the city. A stockyard is a large fenced yard, usually with many smaller pens, in which cattle or pigs are kept until they are slaughtered or sold. The Union Stock Yard and Transit Company built hundreds of pens for animals. It also bought railroads and built meat packing plants.

Chicago's new stockyards brought business to the city. Chicago became the home of meat companies such as Swift, Armour, and Cudahy.

"In Chicago, meat packers use everything from the pig except the squeal." Every part of the animal was used. Leather goods, glue, soap, and medicines were some of the animal products besides meat that came as a result of the stockyards.

Making Connections

You may have heard the slogan, "Armour hot dogs . . . what kind of kids eat Armour hotdogs?" If you eat bacon in the morning, sliced lunchmeat on your sandwich, or hot dogs at a ball game, chances are some of it comes from companies that got their start in Illinois.

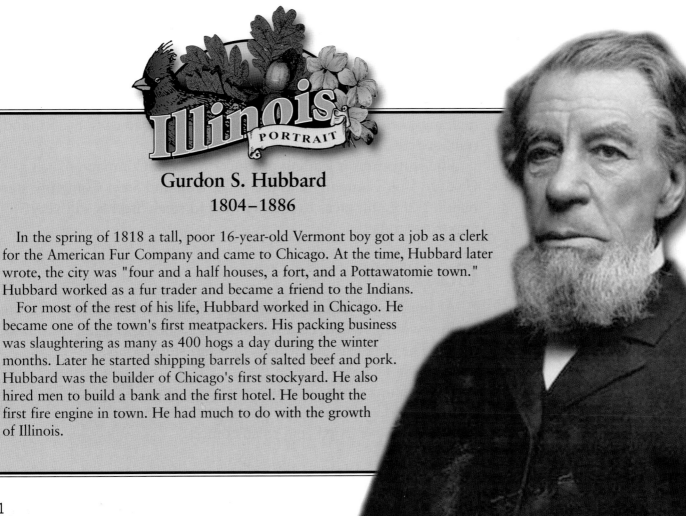

Illinois PORTRAIT

Gurdon S. Hubbard
1804–1886

In the spring of 1818 a tall, poor 16-year-old Vermont boy got a job as a clerk for the American Fur Company and came to Chicago. At the time, Hubbard later wrote, the city was "four and a half houses, a fort, and a Pottawatomie town." Hubbard worked as a fur trader and became a friend to the Indians.

For most of the rest of his life, Hubbard worked in Chicago. He became one of the town's first meatpackers. His packing business was slaughtering as many as 400 hogs a day during the winter months. Later he started shipping barrels of salted beef and pork. Hubbard was the builder of Chicago's first stockyard. He also hired men to build a bank and the first hotel. He bought the first fire engine in town. He had much to do with the growth of Illinois.

This large painting is called a mural. It covers part of a wall in the Lakeview Post Office. Study the painting to see how much of Illinois' history and industry you can see. Do you think the artist did a good job?

Iron, Steel, and Other Riches

Illinois wanted to keep industry growing. They needed iron and steel to do this. Iron ore had just been discovered in Minnesota mines. Once again, Chicago's location on Lake Michigan helped business. It was easy for ships from Minnesota to carry the iron ore through the Great Lakes to Chicago.

Iron was an important metal for making things that people used every day. Then people learned how to use iron to make steel. Steel was stronger than iron and it didn't rust easily. Steel was used to make tall buildings, bridges, farm machinery, tools, railroad cars, tracks, and train engines.

Illinois became a leading producer of steel. Companies such as the Chicago Iron Company and the Joliet Iron and Steel Company started building large furnaces to make iron and steel. Steel is still very important today.

What Do You Think?

Coal is a non-renewable natural resource. There will never be more coal underground than there is right now. What should companies do to make sure there will always be enough coal for our needs?

Coal

At first, coal was used mostly for heating and cooking. After steam engines were invented, coal was burned to boil the water that made steam. The steam turned wheels that ran steamboats, trains, and machines in factories.

Coal mining and railroads grew up together. The steam engines used tons of wood and coal to do their work. Those same engines pulled long trains that carried coal to customers.

Problems in the Coal Mines

Illinois coal mining was big business, but it was not without its troubles. Braidwood, one of the first coal towns, was filled with poor immigrants from all over the world. They did not speak English and had little education, but they worked hard for very little pay. Boys were put to work at the mines at an early age to help their fathers make a living. They spent so much time in the mines that they had no time for school or play.

Getting the coal from the ground was not easy. Underground work was dangerous, dirty, and often damp. Miners couldn't stand up straight. They picked and shoveled for 10 hours a day. Miners breathed dirty air and got sick with "black lung" disease. Gas explosions, cave-ins, and falling rocks hurt or killed miners.

Dark as a Dungeon

It's dark as a dungeon
and damp as the dew,
Where the danger is double
and pleasures are few,
Where the rain never falls
and the sun never shines,
It's dark as the dungeon
way down in the mine.

—Merle Travis

Young boys went to work in the coal mines. Mines were dangerous places. Sometimes they caved in or exploded. After a long day, the boys came home smeared with black dust and dirt. How old do you think these boys are?

One Boy's Story

This is the true story of Frank, a boy who had to quit school to work in a coal mine:

My childhood stopped when I was just 12 years old. I had always worked hard at school and helped with chores around home, but . . . after the sixth grade, I had to quit school and take a job in an underground coal mine. There were six children in my family and we needed the money I could earn.

Mining was very dangerous work. Walls caved in without warning. There were dangerous fumes inside the mines. But what I hated, most of all were the rats that lived inside the mine.

I made just over a dollar a day working in the mines. Sometimes the only daylight I saw was on Sunday, my one day off. It was not much of a life for a boy.

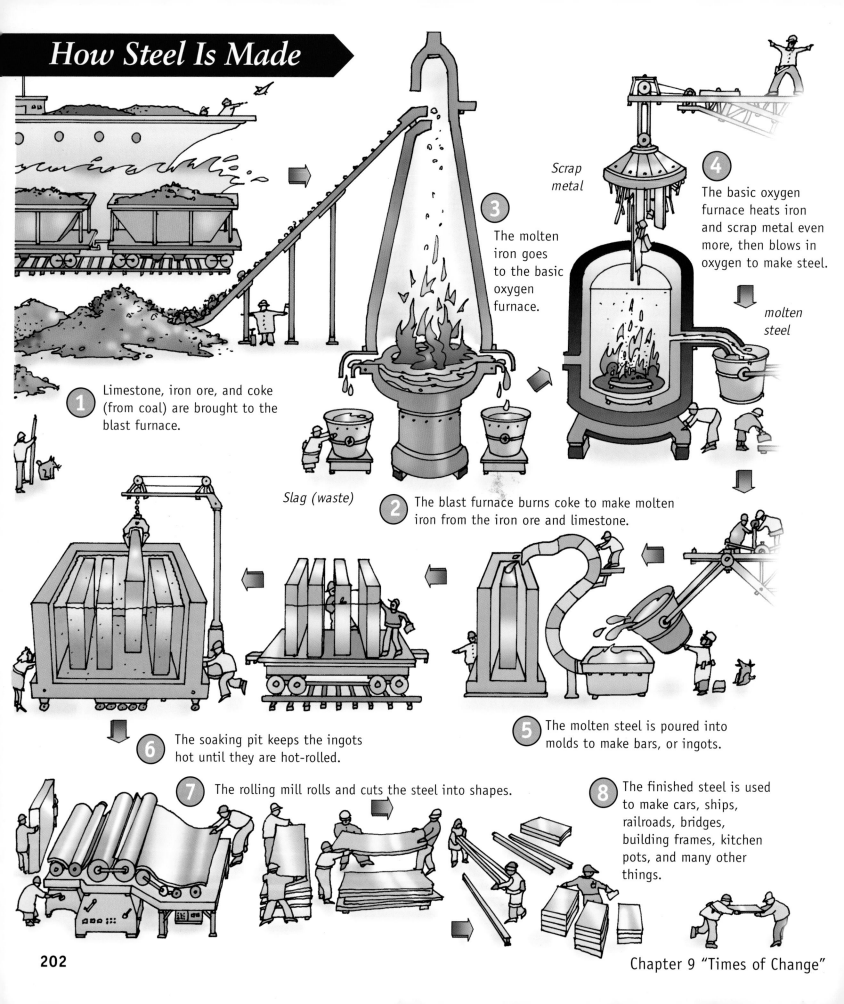

How Steel Is Made

1 Limestone, iron ore, and coke (from coal) are brought to the blast furnace.

2 The blast furnace burns coke to make molten iron from the iron ore and limestone.

Slag (waste)

3 The molten iron goes to the basic oxygen furnace.

Scrap metal

4 The basic oxygen furnace heats iron and scrap metal even more, then blows in oxygen to make steel.

molten steel

5 The molten steel is poured into molds to make bars, or ingots.

6 The soaking pit keeps the ingots hot until they are hot-rolled.

7 The rolling mill rolls and cuts the steel into shapes.

8 The finished steel is used to make cars, ships, railroads, bridges, building frames, kitchen pots, and many other things.

Department Stores Make Shopping Easier

Illinois is home to the modern department store. A department store sells many kinds of things. Before department stores, shoppers might go to a men's or women's clothes store, then a shoe store, then a furniture store, and then a bakery. A department store carried all of these things in one large building.

Marshall Field started one of the first department stores. He stocked his store with the best goods he could find. There were furs, carpets, and the latest fashions. He invited store owners in small towns to buy from the store. They could come to Chicago to look around and pick out items they wanted for their own stores.

The store was famous for service to its customers. Shoppers were greeted by a doorman. The clerks were trained to be friendly and helpful. Inside the store there was a library, a children's playroom, a restaurant, and a telegraph office. Goods that customers bought at the store could even be delivered to their homes.

Have you seen the clock outside the building? In 2006, the store's name was changed to Macy's.

The first Marshall Field Department Store was built in 1868. It burned to the ground in the Great Chicago Fire in 1871, but was built again, better than ever.

Shopping by Mail

Stores in cities were great for city people, but many families still lived out on farms. How could they shop? Shopping by mail from catalogs brought department store goods to villages and farms. The best at the mail-order business were Montgomery Ward and Richard Sears.

Ward arrived in Chicago at the age of 23. He worked for Marshall Field as a salesman, traveling to hundreds of small towns. Ward wondered why the same railroads taking him from place to place couldn't haul goods sold through a catalog. The idea stuck.

Ward opened a mail-order business. People could buy almost anything through the mail. Clothes, furs, eyeglasses, medicine, wigs, and even cars could be ordered. People who lived too far from a store were happy to be able to order what they wanted from the catalog. Soon Ward's catalog was the number-one supplier for farm families all over the country.

From a catalog, you could order a machine to wash your clothes.

Illinois PORTRAIT

Marshall Field
1834–1906

Marshall Field moved to Chicago when he was 21 years old and worked first as a stock boy, then as salesman, and then as a manager in a dry goods store. He saved half of his $400-a-year salary and sometime later, he and a business partner started Marshall Field & Company. His department store was a great success. The slogan for the store was: "Give the lady what she wants!"

As Field's business grew, so did his wealth. Near the end of his life he gave $1 million to start the Field Museum of Natural History in Chicago. He later gave $8 million to keep the museum running. Today it is one of the best natural history museums in the world.

Richard Sears Sells Watches by Mail

Richard Sears got started in business by paying for a box of pocket watches and selling them at a higher price than he paid for them. Then he bought more and sold them. At age 22, he started a watch-selling business in Minnesota. Then he moved to Chicago and joined with Alvah Roebuck, who made and repaired watches. The two young men started the Sears, Roebuck and Company mail-order business.

Sears wrote all the descriptions of goods and published a catalog to sell his watches and jewelry. Later he added shoes, women's clothes, wagons, buggies, bicycles, stoves, fishing rods, furniture, china, glassware, flutes and violins, saddles, guns, and baby carriages. Sears even sold over 100,000 kits to build homes. The first home kits cost only $400. People could get the wood already cut with directions on how to put the house together.

Sears offered lower prices than people paid in stores. The mail-order business was a huge success. Years later, Sears department stores opened in Chicago and other cities. Many are still in business today.

Making Connections

Does your family get catalogs in the mail? What do they sell? Maybe you also shop on-line. This is very similar to catalog shopping. What would you like to buy from a catalog?

① MEMORY MASTER

1 Why was industry becoming as popular as farming?
2. What new ways of shopping helped people get what they wanted?

PEOPLE TO KNOW

Alexander Graham Bell
Charles Duryea
Frank Duryea
Alva Fisher
Henry Ford
Ives McGaffey
Hieronymus Mueller

PLACES TO LOCATE

Canton
Peoria
Washburn

WORDS TO UNDERSTAND

commuter train
elevated
generator
self-propelled

A New Century

The 20th century began in 1900. A century is 100 years. People looked forward to the new century, but they had no idea how much the world around them would change.

Someone born in the early 1900s couldn't have imagined what life was going to be like. Maybe one of your great-great-grandmothers lived during that time. If so, she saw the world change before her very eyes.

What Do You Think ❓

What changes do you think will take place in your lifetime?

Electricity

Before the new century, if you wanted to cook food you had to use a stove that burned wood or coal. Today, you only have to turn a knob on a stove and electricity or gas creates heat that cooks your food.

To get light in the late 1800s, you filled a lamp with oil and burned the wick. It gave off a soft glow. Today, you just flip a switch, and a bright electric light comes on.

Electric *generators* were one of the most important new inventions in the early 1900s. Generators are machines that make electricity. Electricity is carried into homes through wire lines. The lines were strung across the tops of tall poles and from house to house. They made electric lights possible. Stoves, irons, and many other new inventions all used electricity.

Invention Timeline

1869 A vacuum cleaner is invented in Chicago.

1879 Phone service starts in Illinois. Electric lights are first used.

1860   1870   1880

1875 Telephones are first used in U.S.

In Chicago, Ives McGaffey invented a wood and canvas "sweeping machine" to clean rugs. The Whirlwind, as he called it, sucked dirt off the rugs. The machines were sold in the new department stores and in catalogs. Before the vacuums were invented, women swept rugs with a broom or got all the bigger boys in the house to help carry the heavy rugs outside, hang them on a line, and beat the dirt out of them with a "rug beater." Dirt flew everywhere! The new vacuum cleaner was a real help to the whole family.

One of the first electric washing machines was invented in Chicago by Alva J. Fisher. He called his machine the Mighty Thor. The machine was a large tub with a motor that swished the clothes back and forth. Someone still had to fill the tub with hot water and drain the soapy water out when the clothes were clean. Then clean rinse water had to be poured into the tub. The dripping wet clothes had to be wrung out and hung outside on lines to dry in the sun.

Telephones

"Hello! Hello! Can you hear me?" Alexander Graham Bell invented the telephone in the East, and within a few years people in Illinois could string phone lines from their house to the next one if they wanted to use the telephone. It was nice to call instead of walking across town to plan a picnic or invite friends over for dinner. Then telephone lines were strung from business to business and, finally, from town to town.

The Mighty Thor washed the clothes. Then a woman fed them between the rollers to squeeze out the water. Wet clothes were hung on lines to dry.

1892
The "EL" trains start running in Chicago.

1893 First Duryea car is made.

1905 Movies are first shown in theaters in U.S.

1920 Ford Model-T cars are popular.

1890 | **1900** | **1910** | **1920**

1887 Electric streetcars are first used in U.S.

1900 Automobiles are starting to be used.

1906 Radio stations begin broadcasting in U.S.

1908 An electric washing machine is invented in Chicago.

Radio and Moving Pictures

Two of the most exciting inventions were the radio and the movies. Everyone across the United States wanted a radio. At first there were not enough to go around. People visited friends who were lucky enough to own one. They gathered around to listen to their favorite programs. They were amazed. Imagine hearing voices and music that came from the air!

A well-known show in Illinois was "Uncle Bob." Children and their parents tuned in each night to hear him read bedtime stories and sing songs.

The first movies had no sound. If you were a child then, you might put on your best clothes and go with your parents to a theater in town. You would take your seat and wait for the movie to begin. At just the right time, you would see a piano player up on the stage place her fingers on the piano keys. When the movie started, she began to play along with the movie. She played happy music and sad music, fast music and slow music, and music to scare you!

After about 24 years sound was added to the movies. These newer movies were called "talkies."

Movies and radios brought our nation together. People everywhere saw the same movies and heard the same music. They hummed the songs as they worked. They heard the same news and talked about it at the dinner table. People in Illinois, California, and New York could all hear the crowd cheer as the famous baseball player Babe Ruth hit his home runs.

Making Connections

Wouldn't your great-great-grandmother be surprised by the many movies we see today? What movies have you seen this year?

The first radios were very large. A family gathered around the radio to hear music and action-packed stories.

Getting from Here to There

Streetcars Carry People Across Town

As cities grew, it was no longer easy to walk from one
end to the other. In a time when few people had cars and
there were no buses, a man in a city could hop on a
streetcar and ride to his office building across town. He
was grateful to have a ride and not have to walk or ride
in a carriage behind a clomping horse.

At first, horses or mules pulled the streetcars along tracks down
the middle of a street. Each streetcar carried many people. Then electric
streetcars got power from electric wires that ran above the tracks.
Horses and mules were no longer needed.

The "EL" Train System

Illinois had one of the first track systems in the country built partly
up off the ground. The "EL" was built with a series of *elevated*
tracks that connected Chicago to communities outside the city. Because
the tracks are up high, they cross over streets without having to stop at
corners. They only stop at stations to pick up riders. The trains were
not built to ship goods. Instead, they are *commuter trains* that carry
thousands of people to and from work each day.

*A train glides across an
elevated track above the
busy La Salle Street in
Chicago.*

*While it was first powered by steam, the "EL" is now run with electricity. It brings many
business people to the "Loop" in Chicago.*

Stuck again! What might the men be thinking about the horse and the car? Which one would be easier to get out of the mud?

Automobiles Are a Hit!

Automobiles would change the way of life for people everywhere. At first, only wealthy people could afford one. They drove their shiny black cars mostly for fun. Henry Ford opened a factory that made Ford Model T cars in Michigan. He joked that people could have any color car they wanted, as long as it was black. The cars became less expensive, and soon more and more people drove cars. People started seeing both cars and horses "parked" in front of hotels and stores downtown.

Driving in those days was not easy, however. Cars often broke down. There were few gas stations or repair shops. Roads were a real problem for cars. Most roads outside of the larger cities were still dirt roads. If it rained, the roads turned to mud and the cars got stuck. When the weather was dry, people choked on the dust. Then Illinois started to build new and better roads. They raised the money for the new roads by putting a small tax on gasoline.

A hundred car companies went into business at different places in Illinois. None of them lasted very long. Hieronymus Mueller, living in Decatur, was one of the first, but his effort ended in disaster. He died from an explosion while building his car. Dr. James Selkirk, of Aurora, built only one car!

The First Gasoline-Powered Cars

Charles Duryea was born in Canton, Illinois, and his brother, Frank, was born in Washburn. When Charles grew up he went into the bicycle business in Peoria. He left his brother in Massachusetts to start building a car they had designed.

One cool night in September, 1893, after many hours of hard work, the brothers pulled the "car" out of the shed for the first test run. It was no more than a simple wagon with a motor, but it reached a speed of 5 miles per hour. The first time it went 25 feet. After some adjustments, it went over 200 feet!"

Frank built a second car and drove it to win a race put on by the *Chicago Times-Herald* on Thanksgiving Day. Here is a narrative of Charles Duryea as if it was spoken by the inventor himself:

In the newspaper I saw an entry for the first **self-propelled** vehicle race. We had to transport our car all the way to Chicago. Only six cars were going to race. Frank was chosen to drive the car from Chicago to Evanston and back through the snow. It took over 10 hours at a speed of about 7.3 miles per hour, but we won!

The brothers used some of their $2,000 cash prize to open the first company in the United States to make gasoline automobiles. Later, they moved their company to Peoria. However, there were problems, and the company closed after making only 13 cars.

2 MEMORY MASTER

1. How many years are in a century? When you see a certain year, how do you figure out which century it is in?
2. What were some of the inventions that changed the way of life for people in Illinois? How do you benefit from those same inventions today?
3. How could listening to the radio or watching a movie compare to the stories told by a pioneer father to his family?

What Do You Think

- Cars have made travel much easier. What ways have cars changed people's daily lives?
- Cars have also caused problems. What are they? How can we solve them?

PEOPLE TO KNOW

Jane Adams
Dwight L. Moody

WORDS TO UNDERSTAND

ethnic
slums
tenement

Making Connections

How do you think children felt about leaving their things behind? What would you pick?

More Immigrants Come to Illinois

Papa said that it was no longer safe for a Jewish family in Russia, so we are going to America. . . . Papa and mama are busy selling most of our belongings. Mama told me and my little sister, Anna, to each pick one book and one toy to bring with us. Anna cried. She's only four. But I'm ten and must be brave and reasonable, Mama says.

—Alvin Sandrovitch

Like Anna and Alvin, millions of immigrants came to our country. People throughout Europe had heard stories about America. They called it the "land of opportunity." Why would so many people leave their homes and families and risk a dangerous trip across the ocean?

The people who came here were looking for a better life. Some who came were looking for a place where they could be free to follow their own religious beliefs. Others left their homelands because of war. Some came because in America there was land and the promise of jobs. Some immigrants had to leave their countries simply to survive. In Ireland there was a famine. People were starving.

At first, most immigrants came from England, Ireland, Germany, and Sweden. Soon new groups joined them. Poles, Austrians, Russians, Italians, Greeks, and Romanians came. For the most part they settled in Chicago, Rockford, Aurora, Joliet, and Elgin. In these cities the

Thousands of immigrants crossed the ocean on ships that took them to Ellis Island in the New York Harbor. After a few days they were taken by boat into the city. From there they took trains or other boats to get to new homes in America.

newcomers could find work in factories. Chinese and Japanese people came from Asia. Mexicans also came hoping to find work.

A large group of men and women living in the countries of Russia, Poland, and Germany were Jews. It was very important to them to live their Jewish religion and keep their traditions. However, they were often driven out of their homes because of their religion. Many came to the United States for safety.

By Foot, by Boat, by Train They Came

No matter what country they came from, the people had a long journey ahead of them. Just to leave their homelands they had to walk great distances or take trains to get to the nearest port. Then they often had to wait days or weeks for the next ship. Many people were seasick. The ships moved slowly, taking several months to reach America.

When the ships reached America, many immigrants still had to travel to places like Illinois. They rode trains or on boats up rivers. Sometimes they were out of money and walked to the next town.

Making Connections

Today, you can visit many different cultures by visiting ethnic neighborhoods. What is your neighborhood like?

The Top Reasons People Came to America

1. To escape poverty and find jobs
2. To enjoy freedom of religion
3. To escape war and bad governments
4. To join other family members

Immigrants like these came as laborers to work on the railroads and in mines and factories.

Ethnic Neighborhoods

Can you imagine how hard and frightening it would be to start living in a place where you didn't speak the language, didn't know how to get around the city, and didn't know anyone? Those things were hard for the new immigrants too. That is why the immigrants often settled in cities and neighborhoods that were already filled with people from their homeland. Sometimes they moved in with relatives until they could find another place to live.

Ethnic groups are people sharing a common race, language, culture, or religion. Ethnic neighborhoods grew up where groups of immigrants settled. There they could speak their own language and keep their traditions. They felt more at home. It was easier to find a job or go to school.

Struggling in a New Land

Immigrants helped build the railroads and canals. They started farms, stores, and businesses. They worked in steel mills, factories, and meatpacking plants.

The people worked long, hard hours. For all their work they were paid very low wages. The wages were so low that often the women and children in a family had to go to work so there would be enough money for food and rent. People who did not speak English had to take the lowest-paying jobs.

Tenements

In the cities, some ethnic neighborhoods became **slums.** Children had to play in the streets or alleys. There was more dirt than grass. There were few trees or flowers. The slums had many crowded **tenements.** Tenements were large apartment buildings for poor people.

The owners of tenements didn't keep them safe or clean. They didn't repair walls or broken stairs. The families usually had a stove to give heat in the winter, but the rooms were very hot in the summer. The children and their parents climbed up to the roof at night and slept outside in the cooler night air.

Tenements were good for children in one way, though. There were always other children to play with. There was always something exciting going on.

Helping Chicago's Poor

Some people tried to clean up the slums and make life better for the poor people of Illinois. Dwight L. Moody spent much of his life bringing religion to poor people. He especially liked to help children, teenagers, and adults who had nowhere to live or play. Moody helped build the first YMCA in the country. It was a place open to anyone who needed help or a free place to sleep at night.

Another such person was Jane Addams. She started the first "settlement house" in Chicago. A settlement house was a clean, safe, place where the poor could come to get help.

Illinois PORTRAIT

Jane Addams
1860–1935

Jane Addams was born into a wealthy family, but from a very young age she was concerned about poor people. On a trip to England, Jane saw something called a settlement house. When she got home, she made a plan. She would move to Chicago and start a settlement house there. The settlement house would offer all kinds of help to people in need.

Jane and her friend, Ellen Gates Starr, found an old mansion in a poor area of Chicago. The mansion had once been the home of a wealthy man named Charles Hull. Jane bought the mansion, fixed it up, and moved in. She named it Hull House.

Hull House started a kindergarten and clubs for children. It was a place for people of all ages to meet and talk with neighbors. They could also take classes and learn to speak English, cook American dishes, and sew. Hull House helped new immigrants learn to live in their new country and take better care of their families. It helped them make friends and feel better about themselves.

Jane Addams worked very hard all over the world to help people and support peace. She also worked to get women the right to vote. She became the first woman to win the Nobel Peace Prize for helping spread peace in the world.

3 MEMORY MASTER

1. Why did immigrants want to live in America?
2. What is an ethnic neighborhood? How did they help new immigrants?
3. Describe some of the problems the immigrants faced in their new country.

Working in Factories

Immigrants often found work in factories in the cities. Illinois factories made all kinds of products. They worked sewing clothing, rolling cigars, or making glass bottles or other products to sell. People also worked in offices and sold things in department stores, drug stores, and grocery stores.

However, the growth of cities and industries led to new problems. People saw many things that needed to be changed. *Poverty*, child labor, long working hours, dangerous workplaces, dirty streets, unsafe water and food, no garbage collection, and no street cleaning were growing problems. People began to think about what to do to solve them.

Children at Work

There were laws against hiring children under the age of 15, but many bosses never asked young people their ages. Children as young as 9 years old worked in sweatshops. Sweatshops were factories or smaller businesses where working conditions were terrible. The hours were long. The lighting was dim. There was not enough fresh air. It got

These boys are taking a noon-hour break from work at the Illinois Glass Company in Alton, 1910. The boys on the front row are Frank, Joe, Henry, Frank, Emil, William, and Fred.

In this sweatshop on Maxwell Street in Chicago, women and men made clothes. They cut out the cloth from patterns and then sewed by hand and with sewing machines.

very hot in the summer and people used to sweat all day long. Parents wanted their children to go to school, but they needed the 10 cents a day the children made at work. Sometimes children went to school part of the day and worked the rest of the day. Sunday was the only day off.

Danger at Work

Many factory owners did not care much about the workers. Owners did not try to give workers a nice place to work. They pushed them to make more and more and to work faster and faster.

The people worked 12 to 14 hours a day in factories that were often unsafe and unhealthy. Machines were noisy and dangerous. Workers often got hurt. If anyone complained, he or she was fired. There were so many other people looking for jobs that the owners could easily find someone else.

Unions Help Workers

Workers began to come together and fight for change. Coal miners, railroad workers, iron makers, and other workers formed labor **unions.** A union is a group of people who join together to get better working conditions and higher pay. Unions tried to get the government to make laws about how long the workday could be. As a result, Illinois was the first state to make a law that said people only had to work eight hours a day.

One way workers tried to change poor working conditions was to go on **strike.** A strike is when all the workers stop working until they get at least some of what they want. Often the strikes led to violence.

Making Connections

How long is your day in school? How long are your parents at work? How long should a regular workday be?

What Do You Think?

- Talk to an adult you know about some of the problems at work places today. How can we make work places better?
- Do you think having a strike is a helpful way to improve working conditions?

Riot at Haymarket Square

A *riot* is when a large number of people create a wild or dangerous disturbance. One riot began in Chicago when workers at McCormick's reaper factory went on strike. They were striking for an eight-hour day.

Fighting broke out, and the police shot several men. The leaders called for a meeting at Haymarket Square so workers and owners could solve their problems. When the police tried to break up the large crowd, someone threw a bomb that killed seven policemen and hurt many others. Other men in the crowd were also killed.

The Pullman Strike

George Pullman invented the railroad sleeping car. His sleeping cars were made in his Chicago factory. Pullman thought of a way to avoid strikes and unhappy workers. He would build a town for his workers where they could live a safe and comfortable life. He built apartments, stores, parks, churches, and factories in his town. He named it Pullman, after himself.

But the workers were not happy. Pullman owned everything in the town. He controlled the prices. He made the rent higher than it was in Chicago. When business slowed down, he cut the workers' wages, but he would not lower their rent. The workers felt it was unfair. Their union went on strike and fighting broke out. Pullman's dream town turned into a nightmare.

The poster shows men sitting in the dining car of a Pullman train.

The Haymarket Riot started when a bomb exploded among the policemen.

Laws Made Things Better

Here are some things that people did to solve the problems at home and at work. They passed laws so that:

- Children under the age of 14 could not work in mines.

- Workers could not be fired for joining a labor union.

- Bosses had to pay their workers no less than a certain amount of money.

- Mines had to have rules for safety.

- Workers hurt on the job could still get paid.

- Milk sold in stores would have to be clean and fresh.

- Companies could not pollute the air and water.

- Cities would collect garbage regularly.

- Cities would put in the sewer systems needed for indoor bathrooms. At that time most people still had outhouses.

Coal Strikes

Trouble in the coal industry lasted for some time. One of the biggest coal wars took place at the Leiter mine near Zeigler. Joe Leiter had bought a coal mine and also built a town for his workers. His mine became the largest in Illinois.

The miners wanted the company to recognize their union. They wanted to be paid the same as miners working nearby. They wanted only members of their union to work in the Leiter mine. The company said no, so the workers went on strike.

Without workers, Leiter could not mine coal. He hired black miners from the South to come to Illinois. He also hired immigrants from Europe. As the new workers arrived, angry men met them. The strikers yelled and even shot at the new workers. Many of them fled in fear for their lives, but some stayed and worked.

Zeigler

The River that Flows Backwards

One problem in Chicago had an amazing solution. In the 1880s and 1890s many Chicago children became ill. Some of them died. The trouble was the city's drinking water. Chicago got its drinking water from Lake Michigan. After heavy rains, city waste from the stockyards and other industries ran into the Chicago River. Then the river carried it into the lake. As the city grew, it became very hard to keep the lake water near Chicago clean enough to drink. Something had to be done.

"What if the flow of the Chicago River could be reversed?" some people asked. Then the polluted water would flow away from Lake Michigan.

A canal called the Chicago Sanitary and Ship Canal had to be built to make this happen. Locks at each end controlled the flow of the water. For ten years Chicagoans worked to dig the canal. Thousands of immigrants helped.

The canal helped the pollution problem. It also connected the Chicago River to the Des Plaines River and then to the Illinois River and the Mississippi River all the way to the Gulf of Mexico.

Most canals were dug only 6 or 8 feet deep, but the new canal was dug 25 feet deep! Why? Shallow water usually flows into deeper water. The water of Lake Michigan would flow into the Sanitary and Ship Canal only if the canal was very deep.

The Idle Tile Factory in Ottawa could ship their product by boat much easier than on the roads.

Chapter 9 "Times of Change"

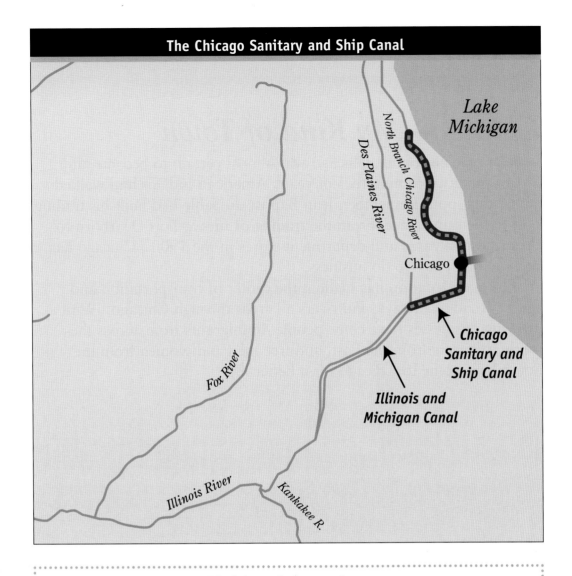

The Chicago Sanitary and Ship Canal

Lake Michigan

North Branch Chicago River

Des Plaines River

Chicago

Chicago Sanitary and Ship Canal

Illinois and Michigan Canal

Fox River

Illinois River

Kankakee R.

Sanitary Canal

The word "sanitary" means clean and free from disease. Why would the canal have that word in its name?

Making Connections

Where else did we read about canals and locks? If you have taken a boat ride on the Chicago River, you have seen how the locks work.

④ MEMORY MASTER

1. What problems in cities needed to be solved?
2. What were some of the hardships factory workers faced on the job?
3. What does it mean to go on strike?
4. Why were people unhappy about living in Pullman's town?

PEOPLE TO KNOW

William Jenney
Frank Lloyd Wright

WORDS TO UNDERSTAND

architect
exhibit
midway
skyscraper

Chicago—My Kind of Town

From the beginning, Chicago was almost certain to become an important city. For hundreds of years, American Indians had walked across this spot. Remember, Jean Baptist du Sable had built his trading post in the same place. From the trading of furs at Fort Dearborn to the busy stockyards and department stores in the 1900s, Chicago has been a good place to do business.

Chicago's location has made it the center of transportation and trade. Roads, railways, and rivers all cross through Chicago. With growing businesses have come people. Immigrants from across the world, pioneers from the East, and free men and women from the South have come to Chicago for a better life.

Today, Chicago is the third most-populated city in the United States.

Chicago's Flag

If you visit Chicago and look up at a flag pole, you will see another red, white, and blue flag flying under the American flag. This is the flag of the city of Chicago. The flag helps us remember the important events in Chicago history.

The three white sections stand for the north, west, and south sides of the city. Each side has its unique culture, business, and people. The top blue stripe represents Lake Michigan and the North Branch of the Chicago River. The bottom blue stripe represents the South Branch of the Chicago River and the Great Canal.

The four red stars stand for four major events in the history of Chicago. It is easy to remember these events because they all start with the same letter. Think of:

- fort (Fort Dearborn)
- fire (Great Chicago Fire)
- fairs (two world fairs: the Columbian Exposition and the Century of Progress)

In an earlier chapter of this book you read about Fort Dearborn and the settling of Chicago. Now, let's look at the other main events.

The Great Chicago Fire

It seemed as if nothing could stop Chicago, but in 1871 it was almost destroyed. It had been a very hot and dry summer with little rain. All summer the fire department kept busy putting out fires. The combination of scorching temperatures, no rain, and a "city of wood" added up to disaster.

The city had wooden houses and wooden barns with wooden roofs. Downtown buildings up to six stories tall were built of wood. Sidewalks were made of wood. Even the streets were paved with wooden blocks. It was a disaster ready to happen.

O'Leary's Cow

Tragedy began in a barn behind Catherine and Patrick O'Leary's cottage, just south of downtown. It was just after 9:00 p.m. Local legend says that a cow kicked over a lantern and started the barn on fire.

Very soon the fire was out of control. Fanned by a strong wind, it spread quickly toward downtown. When the fire alarm sounded, Chicago's firemen were already weary from fighting fires the night before. Some of the equipment didn't work. As the fire spread, the engine house at the waterworks burned, stopping the water supply to the firemen.

The firemen worked hard, but nothing helped—not even the Chicago River. During the night, the wind carried sparks and pieces of burning wood across the river. Even the buildings across the river were beginning to scorch in the heat.

A City in Flames

The flames brought down grand hotels, the Tribune Building, the Federal Building, the Courthouse, department stores, homes, and everything in its way.

All night and all of the next day, the fire burned. Great clouds of dark smoke filled the air. The heat was intense. People fled the city with carriages, horses, and wagons. Those who stayed ran to the lake and stood in water up to their necks, hoping it would keep them safe from the fire.

One woman wrote this story about how she rode away from the fire in a carriage behind a fast-moving horse:

Everybody was out of their houses, . . . and the sidewalks were covered with furniture and bundles of every description. The middle of the street was a jam of carts, carriages, . . . and every sort of vehicle. Many horses were being led along, all excited and prancing, some running away. I scarcely dared look right or left, as I kept my seat by holding tightly to the trunk. I had to use all my powers to keep on. I was glad to go fast, for the fire behind us raged, and the whole earth, or all we saw of it, was a yellowish red.

—Mary L. Fales

Finally, around midnight, a soft rain began. By the next day the fire was over, but Chicago was in ruins.

Up from the Ashes

Downtown Chicago and most of the north side of the city was in ashes, but all was not lost. Businesses on the south and west sides of the city were still working. Trains could still come into Chicago.

The city's faith in itself was shown by *The Chicago Tribune*. The newspaper's office had been destroyed, but from a rented space, the newspaper came out within two days. It carried a story that gave everyone hope. The message was clear:

"CHEER UP! . . . CHICAGO SHALL RISE AGAIN!"

Right away the people set to work rebuilding. This time they used brick and stone. There was work for everyone. Homes, apartment buildings, schools, churches, stores, factories, train stations, and bridges had to be built. Streets had to be paved. All of the jobs brought thousands of new workers to Chicago.

The O' Leary house on DeKoven Street did not burn down. Today, the Chicago Fire Academy stands on the same spot. Men and women there learn how to fight fires.

The first building built after the fire was this real estate office on Washington Street.

CHEER UP.

In the midst of a calamity without parallel in the world's history, looking upon the ashes of thirty years' accumulations, the people of this once beautiful city have resolved that CHICAGO SHALL RISE AGAIN

Building to the Sky

The fire gave business owners a chance to make a great name for their city. The city also began to push upward. William Jenney was a young *architect*. He designed a method to make buildings extra tall—so tall that they were called *skyscrapers*. For the first time, Mr. Jenney used a steel skeleton, or frame, to hold up a building. The walls hung on the frame like curtains. They could be thinner and the windows could be bigger to let more light inside.

Louis Sullivan also designed skyscrapers. He created a new American architecture style. He designed many of the new buildings for the world's fair to be held in Chicago.

Frank Lloyd Wright was one of Sullivan's students. His buildings blended with their natural surroundings. Open rooms flowed from one space to another. He is famous for his "Prairie Style" buildings and is still thought to be one of the greatest American architects. He designed over 100 buildings for Chicago alone, and hundreds of others.

One Congress Center was one of the first skyscrapers designed by William Jenney.
(Right) The Moore-Dugal home was designed by Frank Lloyd Wright.

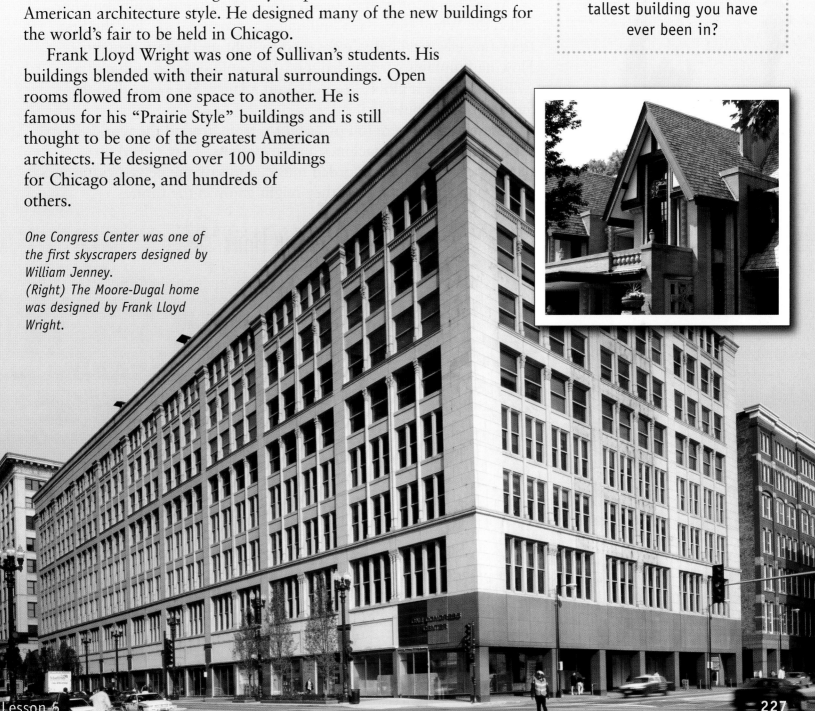

Making Connections

You have probably seen a skyscraper and maybe even ridden up the elevator to look out over the city. How many stories tall is the tallest building you have ever been in?

The Columbian Exposition, 1893

One red star on the Chicago flag stands for a world's fair held in Chicago. The World Columbian Exposition on the shores of Lake Michigan welcomed visitors from around the world. The giant world's fair was supposed to open on the 400th anniversary of the explorations by Columbus in 1492, but it was a year late. The fair showed the world that Chicago had risen from the ashes of the great Chicago Fire just 20 years earlier.

At the center of the fair was a group of glistening white buildings called the White City. Each building was like a palace. For the first time, tiny electrical lights were used to light up the fair at night. Flowing fountains surrounded a 65-foot gold-covered statue of a woman holding a globe, an eagle, and a lance. She was called the Statue of the Republic.

The buildings were full of *exhibits* from around the world. People could see many new machines and inventions. They talked on telephones, listened to recorded music, and saw the newest fire trucks. They got a glimpse of what they might enjoy in the future.

What Do You Think ?

What do you think the globe, eagle, and lance on the statue symbolized?

Opening day of the fair was a crowded event.

Next to the exhibits was the *midway* with music, lights, rides, and good food. The world's first Ferris Wheel had 36 cars, each of which could seat 60 people! One of the cars carried a band that played whenever the wheel was in motion.

Nearby, Buffalo Bill's Wild West Show performed. There were all types of performers from around the world. For the first time, people ate Cracker Jacks (small boxes of popcorn with peanuts), and chewed Juicy Fruit gum.

Another World's Fair

In 1933, Chicago hosted another world's fair. One of the stars on the Chicago flag stands for this later fair. You will read about it in the next chapter.

⑤ MEMORY MASTER

1. The four red stars on the Chicago city flag represent what historical events?
2. What caused the Great Chicago Fire to spread so quickly and create such damage?
3. Why was the Columbian Exposition important?

Top: The Grand Court at night glittered with electric lights.

Activity

Graphs Tell an Interesting Story

Use the graphs to answer the questions.

1. Did the number of people living on farms go up or down from 1910 to 1970?
2. Were more people living on farms in 1870 or one hundred years later?
3. How much money did farm goods bring in 1890?
4. How much money did farm goods bring in 1930?
5. Did the money made from other goods rise or fall from 1890 to 1930?

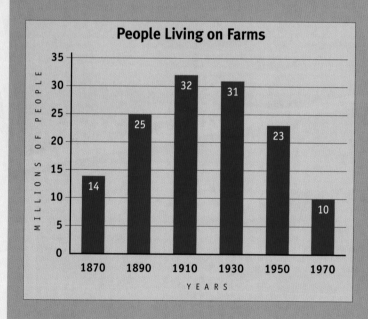

People Living on Farms

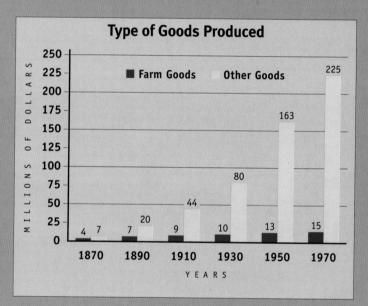

Type of Goods Produced

Activity

Lemons to Lemonade

There is a saying that says "When life hands you a lemon, make lemonade." This chapter shows many examples of taking an event that was really "sour" and turning it into something "sweet." Talk about this idea with your class. Make a list of the examples from the text and then write several examples from your own life.

Invention Riddle Poster

1. Make a list of the new inventions discussed in this chapter.
2. Go online to learn more about some of these inventions, or choose others to learn about. Choose several inventions to include in a riddle poster.
3. On scratch paper, write a simple riddle to give clues about each invention. Check over your work and make any corrections you think are needed.
4. Write the clues for each invention on the front of a large index card or small piece of paper.
5. Attach the card or small piece of paper to a larger sheet of construction paper by taping only across the top. The hints can be read, and the card can be lifted up to see what is behind it.
6. Under the card or small piece of paper, draw and color a picture of the invention. Label the drawing with the name of the invention, and the date it was invented.
7. After you have several flaps on your paper, write a title for your project.

Here is one example of clues for one card:

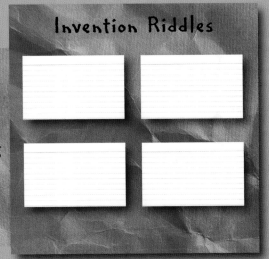

invented in Chicago

called the Mighty Thor

had to be filled with hot water

Answer under the flap: ← electric washing machine, 1908

Invention Riddles

Collect Data and Make a Graph

As a class, take a simple survey:

1. How many students were born in the United States, and how many were born in other countries?
2. What countries did parents, grandparents, or other ancestors come from?
3. List the countries and group them by continents.
4. Show your findings in a simple graph. You could make a bar graph or a pie graph.
5. Would you have similar results if you surveyed a different class or a different grade? What if you surveyed a different school in a different part of town?

12,000 B.C.
First people in North America

1400s
Columbus discovers America.

1500s
America first appears on
the map.

1600s
Pilgrims arrive.

1700s
Declaration of Independence
George Washington

1800s
Abraham Lincoln
Pioneers go west.

1900s
Martin Luther King
Your parents were born.

2000s
A New Century
9/11 Terrorists attack the U.S.

Timeline of Events

Modern Times

1909
The NAACP is
founded in New
York.

1917
U.S. enters the war.
East St. Louis
Race Riots

1920s
Roaring
Twenties

1930s
Great Depression

1939-
1945
World
War I

1900   **1920**   **1930**   **1940**

1913
Illinois
women win
the right to
vote.

1914-1918
World War I

1920 All women in the
U.S. win the right to vote.

1914 The Great Migration brings
blacks from the South. Blues and
Jazz come to Chicago.

1933
Chicago hosts
the Century of
Progress
Exposition.

1941
Japanese
bomb
Hawaii.
U.S. enters
the war.

Chapter 10

The 1900s, like all other times in history, brought both good times and bad times. New inventions such as light bulbs, telephones, record players, and automobiles became popular. Immigrants still moved to Illinois from many different countries.

Sadly, the people of the world did not always treat each other well. There were wars and riots. Then new laws were passed to help people of all races enjoy American freedoms and opportunities. More and more, people thought it was important to get along and respect each other.

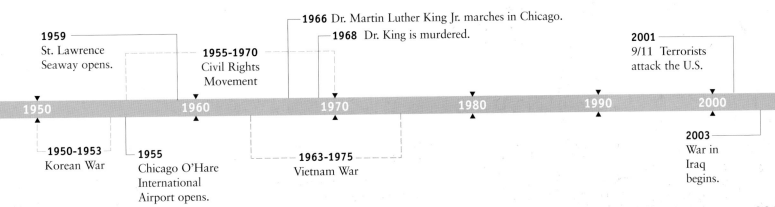

1959
St. Lawrence Seaway opens.

1955-1970
Civil Rights Movement

1966 Dr. Martin Luther King Jr. marches in Chicago.

1968 Dr. King is murdered.

2001
9/11 Terrorists attack the U.S.

1950   1960   1970   1980   1990   2000

1950-1953
Korean War

1955
Chicago O'Hare International Airport opens.

1963-1975
Vietnam War

2003
War in Iraq begins.

PEOPLE TO KNOW

Al Capone
Franklin D. Roosevelt
Eugene Williams
Woodrow Wilson

PLACES TO LOCATE

Chicago
East St. Louis
New Orleans

WORDS TO UNDERSTAND

alcohol
civilian
depression
gangster
military
submarine

World War I

Soon after the new century began, a war started in Europe. The fighting soon involved so many countries that it was called a "world war." It was also called the "Great War." Later, people called it World War I. It lasted about four years. Before it was over, World War I had claimed the lives of 10 million people.

At first, President Woodrow Wilson tried to keep Americans out of the war, but when German *submarines* attacked our ships, Americans got angry. The president and Congress decided we should join the war. Soldiers from Illinois were soon fighting in Europe.

New weapons made war deadlier than ever. Such weapons included machine guns, tanks, airplanes, submarines, and poisonous gas.

The government printed posters to get Americans to plant gardens and grow their own food. Why do you think this was important?

Will you have a part in Victory?

WRITE TO THE NATIONAL WAR GARDEN COMMISSION — WASHINGTON, D.C. for free books on gardening, canning & drying.

"Every Garden a Munition Plant"

Families wave goodbye to soldiers who are leaving Chicago to go to war.

Doing Their Part

Civilians are people, just like you, who do not work in the *military.* The military relates to war. It includes soldiers and their leaders and places that train them for war.

During the war, civilians helped support our soldiers in many ways. Women's clubs made bandages at Red Cross centers. They knitted socks and made clothing. They planted "victory" gardens and bottled fruits and vegetables to save for winter.

In Europe, many farms were destroyed during the fighting. People there needed food, and Illinois farmers helped. Boys from the cities went out to the farms and helped harvest the crops. They sent some of the crops overseas to feed the hungry boys and girls in war-torn towns. Families had meals without meat and wheat so they could send more food overseas to feed the soldiers.

Many tanks and weapons were made in Illinois factories. In fact, one in every three items made in our state went toward winning the war.

Making Connections

Do you eat meat and wheat? What would you have to cut out from the meals you are used to eating if you suddenly didn't have them?

What Do You Think ?

- Is a member of your family in the military?
- What sacrifices are some children making today in times of war?

Illinois Does Its Part

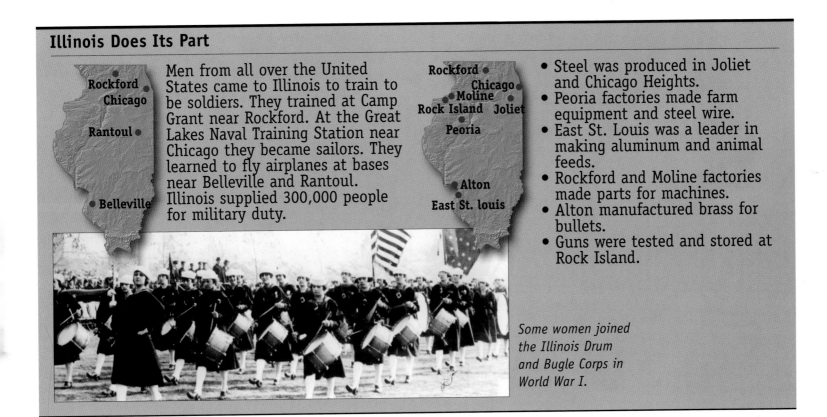

Men from all over the United States came to Illinois to train to be soldiers. They trained at Camp Grant near Rockford. At the Great Lakes Naval Training Station near Chicago they became sailors. They learned to fly airplanes at bases near Belleville and Rantoul. Illinois supplied 300,000 people for military duty.

- Steel was produced in Joliet and Chicago Heights.
- Peoria factories made farm equipment and steel wire.
- East St. Louis was a leader in making aluminum and animal feeds.
- Rockford and Moline factories made parts for machines.
- Alton manufactured brass for bullets.
- Guns were tested and stored at Rock Island.

Some women joined the Illinois Drum and Bugle Corps in World War I.

The Roaring Twenties

Finally, the war ended. Factories switched from making war materials to making things people wanted at home. People wanted to forget about the war and just have fun. In the cities, there were goldfish-swallowing contests and all-night dances. Couples danced a new dance called the Charleston. For the first time in America, women cut their hair in a short bob and wore shorter dresses. The 1920s became known as "the Roaring Twenties."

Women Win the Right to Vote

After many years of hard work, women earned the right to vote. For the first time, millions of women were allowed to vote for the president and other leaders. Most women celebrated. Their long, hard fight to get to vote was over. Other women thought men should control the government and women should stay at home and take care of the house and their children.

A lady wears a sash and carries a sign that says, "Help us win the vote." What do the words on this ballot box say?

These young women show their desire for fun by dancing the Charleston on a rooftop ledge at Chicago's Sherman Hotel.

Gangsters and Bootleg Gin

There was a lot of music and dancing after the war, but violence often made the headlines during the 1920s. One reason was *alcohol.* Since alcoholic drinks were outlawed in the United States, those who still wanted to drink went to "wet clubs" where they could drink. *Gangsters,* such as Johnny Torrio, Al Capone (Scarface) and "Babyface" Nelson supplied the alcohol.

"Bootlegging" (secretly buying and selling alcohol) became big business. Soon Capone was considered the boss of this kind of organized crime. His gang was known all over Chicago.

Al Capone was the boss of crime in Chicago.

Johnny Torrio

Several kegs of beer are being dumped into Lake Michigan. Some men jumped into the water to drink it!

The Great Depression

The good times of the Roaring Twenties ended when a depression began. A *depression* is a time when many people can't make enough money to take care of their families. They want to work, but they can't find jobs. The depression of the 1930s was the worst depression the United States had ever known.

People without jobs stopped buying things such as radios, cars, and washing machines. That left stores with goods they couldn't sell. Factories did not need to produce as much, so they sent more workers home. Without paychecks, workers couldn't spend as much as they had before. More businesses slowed down. People who could not pay their rent had to move, but unless they had a relative who would take them in, they had no place to go.

People stood in long lines to get free soup and bread. They grew gardens in their backyards. They saved everything they could. They mended old clothes again and again. When children wore holes in the bottoms of their shoes, they put cardboard inside.

The New Deal

President Franklin D. Roosevelt (often called FDR) wanted people to start working again. He had a plan called the New Deal. The government loaned farmers money so they could stay in business. Young people were trained for jobs. Children got free school lunches.

The government put men to work fixing roads, bridges, and campgrounds in state parks across America. One of these was Starved Rock State Park in Illinois.

Artists were hired to paint murals on walls of post office buildings and other places. Historians were hired to write the histories of towns. They talked to people to learn what their lives were like. They talked to people who had been slaves and wrote down their stories. Finally, the depression ended. Times got better for most people.

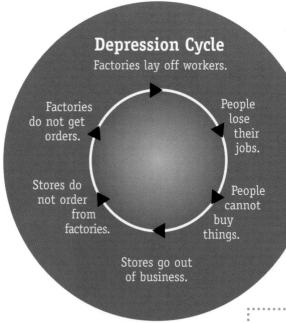

Out of a job, men sold apples to earn money.

Depression Cycle

Factories lay off workers.

People lose their jobs.

People cannot buy things.

Stores go out of business.

Stores do not order from factories.

Factories do not get orders.

Making Connections

Roosevelt thought he could improve things even though times where hard. Can you think of a time when you tried to improve your life even when it was hard?

The Century of Progress Exhibition

During the years of the Great Depression, Chicago people created a world event that helped people have good times again. The city hosted a second world's fair to mark the city's 100th birthday.

Bright colors were used to create a "Rainbow City" on the shore of Lake Michigan. The fair showed new scientific discoveries and how much industry had changed. Car makers showed off their dream cars. General Motors had a working model of an assembly line. Henry Ford showed off his work in the Ford Building.

The midway had a Sky Ride that took visitors from one end of the fair to another, high above the crowds. The exposition boasted an Enchanted Isle with a "Magic Mountain" that children could climb.

The first Major League All-Star Baseball Game was held at Comiskey Park as part of the fair. The American League beat the National League 4-2. Even though it was intended to be a one-time-only event, the All-Star game is still played today.

The fair was such a success it ran for a second year. The building that held the Museum of Science and Industry is still used today.

Remember the fourth red star on the Chicago flag? It stands for this world fair.

The Ford exhibit at the fair brought in thousands of visitors.

1 MEMORY MASTER

1. How did people in Illinois help during World War I?
2. What is meant by the term "Roaring Twenties"?
3. What was the Great Depression?

PEOPLE TO KNOW

Franklin D. Roosevelt
Adolph Hitler

PLACES TO LOCATE

Germany
Japan
Hawaii
Cicero
Des Plaines
Kankakee
Oak Brook
Seneca

WORDS TO UNDERSTAND

Holocaust
interstate
ration

A Second World War

President Roosevelt's New Deal was helping to end the Great Depression. Then something happened that changed the depression cycle.

In 1939, another world war began in Europe. It is called World War II. The United States did not get involved for the first two years. Then the Japanese bombed our navy base in Pearl Harbor, Hawaii. After that, the United States joined the war. Our soldiers fought in Europe and Asia.

Like thousands of 18-year-old guys, I reported for basic training in the U.S. Army. . . . I was shipped overseas, . . . along with 18,000 other soldiers. We sailed in 1944, taking a zigzag course to avoid German submarines and planes in the North Atlantic Ocean.

—Robert Kennedy, from the Illinois WWII Memorial

Illinois Helps in the Cause

Illinois was a leader in the war effort. Soldiers and pilots were trained at bases such as Great Lakes Naval Air Base and Camp Grant. Women served as nurses, drivers, office workers, photographers, and pilots.

Illinois factories and farms went into high gear. The largest factory in the world was built in Chicago to make airplane engines. Illinois even made boats for the navy. The Western Electric Company in Cicero made radar equipment. A plant near Kankakee made over one billion pounds of explosives. The Pullman Company made tanks and airplane parts.

Workers in the town of Seneca made huge ships for planes to land on. Seneca became known as the "Prairie shipyard." The huge ships were floated down the Illinois and Mississippi Rivers to the ocean for use in the war.

Farms led the nation in soybeans. Farmers also raised large amounts of cheese, hogs, and corn for Americans at home and soldiers at war.

Help from Home

People who stayed at home did their part. It was hard to get such things as coffee, nylon stockings, and alarm clocks. The materials that went into making those items were being used to make bullets, parachutes, and other war goods.

With so many men off fighting in the war, more women went to work at jobs that had only been done by men. Women trained to be mechanics, welders, truck drivers, and carpenters. For many women, it was their first paying job.

Children also did their part. They collected pots, pans, and tin cans that could be turned into metal for making ships and airplanes.

The War Ends

Countries on both sides of the war tried to build a super bomb. Scientists in the United States, including those working secretly at the University of Chicago, finally figured out how to make a bomb. It was more powerful than any other bomb in history.

To end the war with Japan, the United States dropped the world's first atomic bomb on a city in Japan. Still, Japan did not surrender. When a second bomb was dropped on another city, Japan surrendered. It was a horrible time of death and suffering for the people of Japan.

Many workers were needed during the war. Some teenagers were allowed to quit school and work in factories.

What does this poster want the people to save? Why?

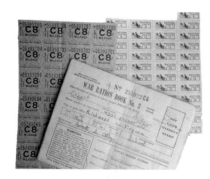

Ration coupons had to be used to buy certain food at the store.

*Food got scarce because so much was needed to send overseas to feed soldiers. The government started to **ration** many items. This meant people could buy only so much sugar, meat, butter, or coffee. Each family was given ration stamps every month.*

The Holocaust

A young Jewish girl wrote:

"Next year would have been my last year at school, but I won't be able to graduate . . . the schools have closed. The Nazis have forced more than 5,000 Jews to live in one small area of the town."

One terrible time during World War II was the *Holocaust.* It happened across the Atlantic Ocean in Europe. In Germany, Adolph Hitler believed that Germans were better than other kinds of people. He thought the world would be better without all different kinds of people. He especially hated Jewish people.

Hitler's troops rounded up all the Jewish people they could find. They sent them to horrible places called concentration camps. At the camps, there was hardly anything to eat. People slept on wooden platforms stacked up three layers high. It got very cold in the winters and very hot in the summers. The people were forced to do hard labor. People who were too old, too young, or too weak to work were killed. About 6 million Jews died in the camps. So did 6 million other people.

When the war ended, American soldiers freed the people in the camps who were still alive. The soldiers were horrified when they saw the people looking like walking skeletons. The men and women who were still alive started searching for family members. Many came to live with relatives in the United States, and some came to live in Illinois towns.

Prisoners at concentration camps were given so little food that thousands starved to death. This photograph shows the prisoners being rescued after the war ended.

Chapter 10 "Modern Times"

A Booming State and Nation

People had little to spend their money on during the war. Factories were busy making goods to help win the war. That changed when the war ended. Factories started making refrigerators, stoves, washing machines, furniture, televisions, radios, lawn mowers, and cars.

Fast food restaurant chains also started at this time. The first McDonald's Restaurant opened in Des Plaines. Before long, McDonald's could be found from coast to coast. Today, their national headquarters and training center are in Oak Brook.

On the ground, people needed better roads. A new type of highway called the *interstate* was made all over the country. These roads connected one state to another. Most of the interstates had few stop lights so people could travel farther and faster than before. Large trucks used the new roads to ship goods in and out of Illinois. Today, we call these roads freeways.

At the same time, the people wanted a better way to ship goods by water. The U.S. and Canadian governments got together and built the St. Lawrence Seaway. It has locks, canals, and channels connecting the Great Lakes and the Atlantic Ocean. After it was finished, the largest ships could sail from Chicago all the way to the Atlantic Ocean and then to Europe or Asia. Some say if there was a fifth star on the Chicago flag, it would stand for the St. Lawrence Seaway.

Better Transportation

During World War II, the country needed a place to build aircraft that was far away from the coasts of the Atlantic and Pacific Oceans. People worried that the enemy might try to bomb places close to the coasts. Chicago, far inland, seemed like a good choice. A site where O'Hare International Airport now stands was chosen. For many years airplanes were manufactured there. Later, the airport was built. O'Hare is now one of the busiest airports in the world.

After the war, Illinois factories began to build television sets. At first, only a few families had a TV set, and they showed programs only in black and white. A lucky child who had one invited friends over after to school to watch Lassie, Annie Oakley, Zorro, Howdy Doody, and Roy Rogers. By 1960 almost every home in Illinois had a TV.

② MEMORY MASTER

1. How did people in Illinois help win the war?
2. What was the Holocaust? Where did it happen?
3. Why were the new forms of transportation so important?

PEOPLE TO KNOW

Robert Abbott
Louis Armstrong
Martin Luther King Jr.
Eugene Williams

PLACES TO LOCATE

Afghanistan
Iraq
Korea
Persian Gulf
Springfield
New York City
Washington, D.C.

WORDS TO UNDERSTAND

character
civil rights
discrimination
prejudice
protest
refugee
segregation
terrorist

Separation of people by race is called *segregation.* Do you see any segregation today?

The Great Migration

While the nation fought for the freedom of others across the seas, there were still many problems among the people in our own country. Part of the problems had to do with prejudice between blacks and whites.

The problems had started many years earlier. At the beginning of the 1900s, most African Americans lived in the South. They worked as farmers and other jobs that slaves had done in earlier years. They barely made enough to buy food and shelter for their families. Then they heard about all of the jobs in factories and mines in the North. Families packed up and moved to start a new life. This movement to the North is known as "the Great Migration."

Blacks in the South hoped to find jobs, better housing, and more fair treatment in the North. Instead, most found discrimination.

Soon thousands of black people were moving north to Chicago and other cities. Even in the North, however, they found life very hard. They were treated unfairly. They were not allowed in movie theaters or clubs. They could not sit and eat with everybody else in restaurants. Public places had separate bathrooms and drinking fountains for blacks and whites. At work, black men got paid a lot less than most white men. Women got paid even less.

Signs like these were painted in many places. They kept blacks separate from whites. In movie theaters, blacks had to go upstairs and sit in the balcony. In restaurants, blacks could not eat in the same room as whites. Blacks had to use separate restrooms.

The NAACP

In the summer of 1908, the country was shocked by the account of the race riots at Springfield, Illinois. Here, in the home of Abraham Lincoln, a mob containing many of the town's "best citizens" raged for two days, killed and wounded . . . Negroes, and drove thousands from the city.

—Mary White Ovington, 1914

What did these words mean? What was happening in Springfield? If you were a black child living in Springfield then, you might have to move to a new home in another town. Some white people of Springfield did not want any blacks living there. This meant your father and mother would have to find new jobs. You would hear people fighting in the streets. Your mother would tell you not to be afraid, but you were anyway.

The fighting finally stopped, but the problems did not go away. The next year, a group of both black people and white people met in New York City to try to stop the unfair treatment. They started a group called the National Association for the Advancement of Colored People, or the NAACP. The group made plans to travel around the country and teach people to respect the rights of black people. They also planned to get Congress to make new laws to end *discrimination.*

Six blocks of Walnut Street were reduced to rubble from fires started during race riots in East St. Louis in July, 1917.

Chicago Blues and Jazz

The Blues

When black people moved north as part of the great migration, they brought a new kind of music. It first came from old slave songs. Usually the songs were about sadness, lost love, or other hardships. Most of the time a man or woman sang to the music of a guitar.

Jazz

Many jazz players moved north. There were better jobs in northern cities such as Chicago and New York City. Chicago became famous for its jazz. Like the blues, jazz music began in the South, in New Orleans. Blues songs and African American folk music developed into a new art form. It had a new kind of rhythm, and some of the notes were played off beat. Musicians made up melodies as they went along.

The Original Creole Orchestra arrived in Chicago in 1914. They started the South Side of Chicago swinging with the sounds of jazz. Soon other bands were formed, and jazz clubs opened around the city.

Blues Today

Today, Chicago is the blues capital of the world. Famous musicians come to perform. Each year Chicago has free blues festivals. Harmonicas wail and guitars strum while drums and basses keep the beat. They make life seem a little easier.

Have you ever "sung the blues"? We use the phrase "singin' the blues" to mean feeling sad.

Illinois PORTRAIT

Louis Armstrong
1900–1971

Louis Armstrong was born in New Orleans, where jazz music was born. His family was very poor. His father left the family when Louis was very young. His mother, Mary Ann, worked as a maid and left the children to be raised by Louis's grandmother. How did Louis get into music?

Louis and his sister often wandered the town, looking for adventure and getting into trouble. At age 12 Louis was taken by the police to the Colored Waifs Home. The home had a band, and Louis learned to play a bugle. Later, he earned money by singing on the street. He played on trains, joined a riverboat band, and got jobs playing in clubs. Since he never had any private lessons, he learned all he could from older players.

Finally, Louis and his wife and young son came to Chicago and played the trumpet in King Oliver's Creole Jazz Band. The group played almost every night and made records that were sold all over the world. Over the years, Louis, who by now was called by his nickname "Satchmo" played in 30 films, wrote his autobiography, and composed songs. He started his career as a trumpet player but ended mainly as a singer. Audiences loved Satchmo. He finally left Chicago to live in New York City.

247

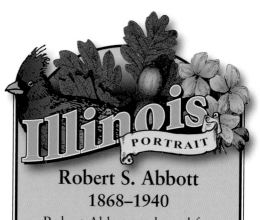

Illinois PORTRAIT

Robert S. Abbott
1868–1940

Robert Abbot graduated from law school, but was not allowed to practice law because he was black. He decided to use his skills in another way. He started publishing the *Chicago Defender*, a weekly newspaper, with only $25. He sold advertising and subscriptions by walking around the city and knocking on doors.

After a while, over 100,000 people were buying the newspapers each week. The papers were passed from person to person and were read aloud in churches and other places where people talked about the problems of discrimination. The papers were even read by blacks in the South. Stories in the paper attacked racial prejudice everywhere. They urged blacks to move north for a better life.

Because of the paper, over a million blacks left the South and moved north. Robert Abbott's paper was so successful he became one of the first African American millionaires.

Prejudice Explodes

Prejudice against blacks and other groups went on all through World War I, the Roaring Twenties, and the Great Depression. During the depression, problems had been even worse for blacks than for everyone else. If a company had to fire an employee because there wasn't enough business, a black man was almost always the first to be fired. Still, African Americans, like the rest of the people, managed somehow.

Eventually, racial prejudice exploded into violence. A riot broke out in East St. Louis. For hours angry white mobs threw bricks, shot guns, and beat people. They burned homes and destroyed businesses. African Americans were killed. About 6,000 were driven from their homes.

Eugene Williams Drowns in Lake Michigan

Over the next few years, riots took place in other cities and towns in the United States. One of the worst started when Eugene Williams was swimming in Lake Michigan. White swimmers did not like where he was swimming. They said he was in water that was just for whites. Arguments broke out and people began throwing stones at each another. Williams could not come out of the water without getting hurt, so he hung onto a piece of wood as long as he could. Finally, he could not hang on any longer, and he drowned.

Rumors spread that Williams had been stoned to death. Five days of rioting between blacks and whites followed. Men on both sides were killed and many were hurt. Soldiers had to be called in to stop the fighting.

The crowd leaves the beach after the drowning of Eugene Williams.

The Civil Rights Movement

In the South, white people made laws that black people had to follow. The laws were called "Jim Crow" laws. Jim Crow laws were used to keep white people separate from black people. Black students had to attend schools just for blacks. They had to sit in the back of buses. Even cemeteries were *segregated*. If a black person broke the laws, he or she had to pay a fine or go to jail. White people who let African Americans brake the laws were also fined.

Segregation took place all over the country. Real estate agents would not even show blacks certain houses in "white" neighborhoods. If black families did move into a home, garbage might be dumped on their lawns. People might break their windows.

Civil rights are the rights that should naturally belong to all civilians, or all citizens of a place, no matter what race they are or where they or their family moved from.

What Do You Think ❓

Why do you think people had such strong feelings against people they didn't even really know? Does this still happen today?

Police oversee a man leaving the South Side of Chicago after the riots of 1919.

Dr. Martin Luther King Jr.

Young black leaders worked hard to end segregation. One leader was Dr. Martin Luther King Jr., a minister from Georgia. He led peaceful marches and *protests.* He reminded everyone that our nation was founded on the belief that "all men are created equal." Both white people and black people joined his marches.

Dr. King often came to Chicago. He came to join in the fight against segregated schools. He also joined with community leaders to promote fair housing and put a stop to the horrible, rundown slums where many blacks lived. To see what life was like for blacks in Chicago, Dr. King came to the city and rented an apartment for his family in the West Side ghetto. He led two protest parades into all-white neighborhoods to promote fair housing.

Sadly, Dr. King was murdered a few years later as he stood out on his hotel room balcony in Memphis, Tennessee. Thousands of people were so upset after the murder that they burned buildings and smashed windows in cities. There were riots in Chicago and other Illinois towns. This would have made Dr. King very sad. He always spoke for peaceful change.

In Illinois and other states, the third Monday in January is Martin Luther King Jr. Day. The holiday helps us remember what he did for all Americans.

Civil Rights Laws

The struggle for civil rights grew stronger and stronger. Finally, the courts made it clear that all people should be treated equally. Congress passed laws to make sure all people could vote and all people could live

Black children marched to end segregation in schools.

In Washington, D.C., Dr. King gave his famous "I Have a Dream" speech.

or work wherever they chose. There could no longer be segregated schools, theaters, or neighborhoods. As Martin Luther King had said, only a person's *character,* not his or her color, should count.

More Wars Overseas

Our country has fought in other wars after World War II. Our soldiers fought a long war in Vietnam. Not everyone agreed about fighting these wars. Many used their right to protest. Others were grateful that the United States was working for freedom around the world.

At the end of the war in Vietnam, many refugees came to the United States for safety. The story of a boy who escaped from his home country might sound like this:

I am 10 years old. My brother and I escaped from Vietnam. Ten of our family started, but only four of us made it. I was very frightened, but we had to run and hide in the jungle until we got to the ocean. We had little food and no belongings. When we got to the water, we had to pay hundreds of dollars to get on a small boat. We did not have enough money for all of us, so some had to stay behind. We hope we will see them soon. It has been hard getting used to our new life here, but I am learning English and going to school. My life is better now.

What Do You Think

Do you think all people are treated equally now? What would Martin Luther King think?

A *refugee* is a person who flees for refuge, or safety, in time of war.

Some Americans saw the Vietnam War as a fight for freedom. Other Americans believed we had no business fighting in Vietnam.

September 11, 2001: Terrorists Attack the United States

The people of Illinois welcomed a new century on January 1, 2000. What people were not looking for was an event on September 11, 2001. Early in the morning, two airplanes crashed into the World Trade Center in New York City. Then a third airplane crashed into the Pentagon in Washington, D.C. Another plane crashed onto the ground in Pennsylvania.

Foreign **terrorists** had taken over the planes to hurt Americans. In Springfield, Illinois, thousands of workers were sent home from different state buildings. Power plants, airports, and public buildings increased security. In Chicago, everyone left the Sears Tower and other tall buildings. They thought the buildings might be attacked just like the tall towers of the buildings in New York. At airports, passengers were searched carefully. Bags were X-rayed for signs of weapons.

A month after the attacks, military forces from countries around the world entered Afghanistan looking for terrorists. In 2003 the United States sent soldiers into Iraq. For the second time in this new century, Americans fought terrorism. Soldiers from Illinois fought in the war.

In cities across the state, people held memorial services after the attack on September 11. This boy's father died in the attack. Other boys lost fathers and brothers who died overseas during war.

Men and women from Illinois and all the other states fought in Iraq. Why do you think this soldier has a dog?

How do we all benefit by going to school with people from other cultures?

Recent Immigrants

Thousands of people have come from other places to live in Illinois. They have come from other states. They have also come from other countries, such as Mexico, India, China, Japan, and Vietnam. They have come from the Pacific Islands, the Middle East, and many other places.

Hispanic/Latino

The new century brought even more Hispanic people to Illinois. Most came to find better jobs than they could find in their homelands of Mexico and other countries. The Mexican community is the largest ethnic group in the Chicago region.

You can take part in the culture of two Mexican American communities in the Chicago area. You can gaze at the rich colors of murals on the walls of buildings in Little Village and Pilsen. Visit the nation's largest Latino museum, the Mexican Fine Arts Center Museum. Workers at the museum sponsor events and exhibits that promote Latino culture.

Hispanic children are the second-largest ethnic group in Illinois. Their parents are working to provide a good life for their children.

You Can Be Part of a Safe World

How can you help Illinois be a great place to live? You can be aware of prejudice and treat others with respect. You can be kind and helpful. You can help children from other countries learn English. You can invite them to play. You can study hard in school. You can be part of a safe world.

Toward the Next Century

What will Illinois be like in the next century? What new inventions and discoveries might come in your lifetime? What challenges do people face if they are to have a better future?

Here are some things the people of Illinois are working on today:

- Cleaning up the environment so people can enjoy clean air and water.
- Protecting agricultural land so we can continue to raise crops.
- Providing better public housing.
- Taking care of children by improving schools and day care centers.
- Making sure they are people of good *character*.

What do you think should be added to this list?

Everyone deserves a good home, good food, and a good education. We all want a beautiful, clean environment. Are you a good friend? Do you help your family? Are you doing your part to make Illinois a better place?

③ MEMORY MASTER

1. Explain why civil rights are important to everyone.
2. Why is Martin Luther King Day a holiday?
3. When did terrorists attack the United States? What happened?

Chapter 10 Review

---- **Activity** ----

Famous or Infamous?

What is the difference between being "famous" and being "infamous"? Look up the two words in a dictionary. Can you find a synonym for each? Now find one person from the chapter that fits each definition. Tell why you chose each person.

---- **Activity** ----

Listen to Blues and Jazz

Go to the library or the Internet to find jazz or blues music, and listen to it in class or at home. Look for the names of the performers in this chapter. Talk about what the music reminds you of. Does everyone feel the same way about it? Now share your favorite type of music. Are there ways your music is similar to jazz or blues?

---- **Activity** ----

The Census: It Counts!

Census forms ask people what race they are. Look at the graph to see what the census said about Illinois for the year 2000. Then answer the questions:

1. Where did your ancestors come from?
2. What group do you think you are in?
3. If your ancestors lived here before Columbus came, what group would you belong to?
4. If you or your ancestors moved here from China, Japan, or Vietnam, what group would you belong to?
5. If you moved here from Mexico, what group would you belong to?
6. If your ancestors came from a country in Africa, what group would you belong to?
7. What does "mixed race" mean?

Illinois Census, 2000	
White (Non-Hispanic)	67.8%
Black	15.1%
Hispanic	12.3%
Asian	3.4%
American Indian	0.2%
Mixed Race	1.9%

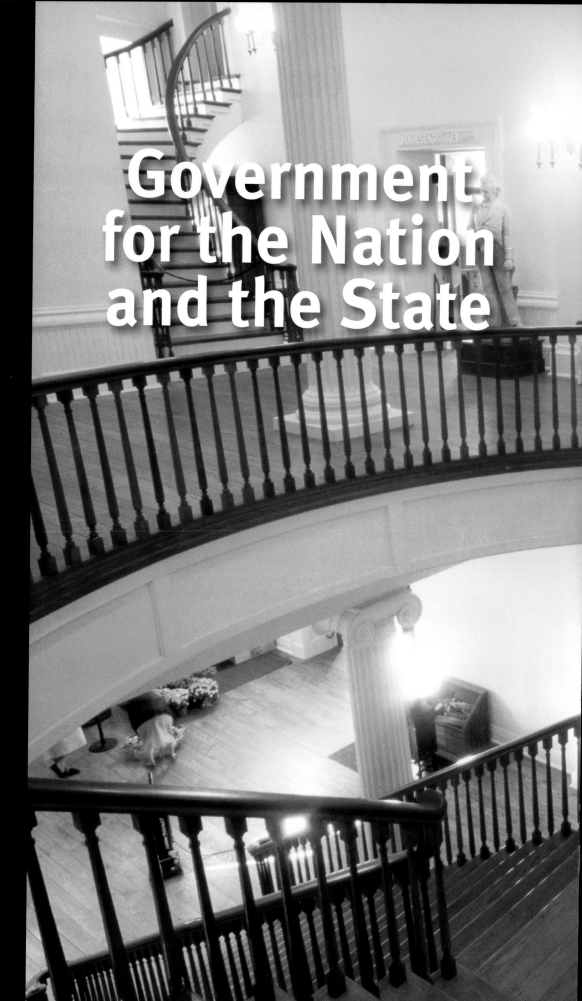

"Don't interfere with anything in the Constitution. That must be maintained, for it is the only safeguard of our liberties."

— President Abraham Lincoln

"Government of the people, by the people, and for the people, shall not perish from the Earth."

— from the Gettysburg Address, President Abraham Lincoln

Government for the Nation and the State

Chapter 11

When you walk down the stairs in the Old State House in Springfield, you are walking back in time. You are walking where Abraham Lincoln walked. Lincoln argued many cases before the Illinois Supreme Court in a room of the old state capitol. After he died, thousands of people viewed his body there before he was buried.

During the 1960s the Old State House was taken down and then rebuilt to look just as it did when Abraham Lincoln lived in the town. Today, our state government offices are in our newer State Capitol Building in Springfield. Have you visited the building there? What did you see?

WORDS TO UNDERSTAND

federal
intersection
national
public school
service
tax

Our Government

Government. That is a big word mostly used by adults. Does government have anything to do with kids? Well, if you are sitting in *public school* right now, the government probably paid for your school buildings, your desk, your books, and the paper you write on. The government even pays your teacher and your principal!

The government provides other *services*, too. Calling 911 in an emergency or having your trash collected are also part of government. The truth is, government affects all of us, no matter how young or old we are.

There are many different levels, or kinds, of governments. There is a *federal* or *national* government for our whole nation, state government for Illinois, and local government for the city you live in. Your school may even have a student government that decides certain things.

Governments help in many ways. They make laws and rules, provide protection, and offer many services.

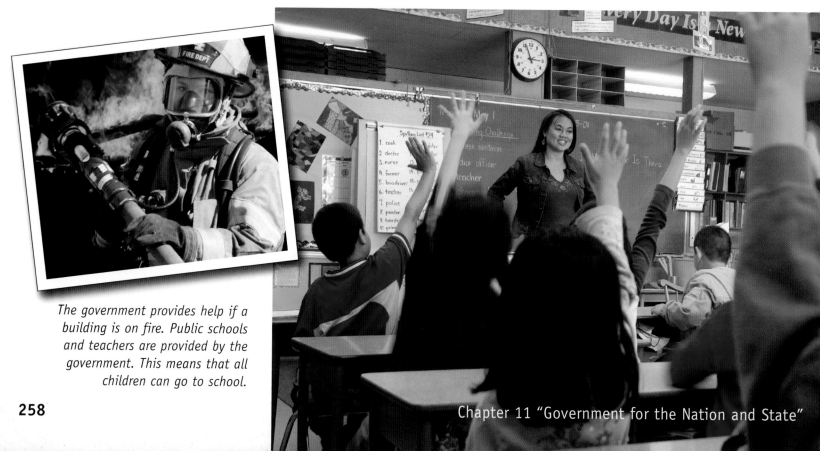

The government provides help if a building is on fire. Public schools and teachers are provided by the government. This means that all children can go to school.

Here are some of the most important things governments do:

Making Rules and Laws

What if there were no traffic lights or stop signs, and three cars came to an *intersection* at the same time? If none of the cars stopped, there would be an accident. How do we know whose turn it is to go through the intersection? We know because we have rules. Rules tell us who should go and who should stop. Rules make things run smoothly. They make things safer.

People in a community and in our nation agree to follow certain rules or laws. If someone breaks the law, he or she might have to pay a fine, provide community service, or go to jail.

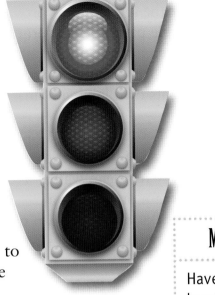

Making Connections

Have you seen someone break a rule or law? What happened?

Protect Rights

One of the most important things our government does is protect our rights. Let's say you park your new bike outside. While you are inside playing, someone steals your bike. You are angry because you know that is not fair. That bike was your property. What can you do?

You can go to the police. They will try to find your bike and the person who stole it. We have laws against stealing. These laws protect your property rights.

You also have personal rights. These are things like your right to state your opinion without being arrested and your right to belong to the religion of your choice. Our laws protect these important rights.

Provide Services

The government pays workers who build and staff our public schools, police and fire departments, and public libraries. They build and maintain public parks and swimming pools, roads and sidewalks. They take care of snow plowing streets and collect the garbage every week.

Taxes Pay for Services

How do governments pay for the services they provide? They get money from *taxes.* A tax is money people pay to the government. Tax money helps pay for services the people can use. Taxes come in many forms. People and businesses pay taxes on the money they make. When you buy clothes or games, you pay a sales tax. If your parents own land, a home, or a building, they pay property tax.

What is tax money used for? Taxes pay for making and fixing local streets. They pay for plowing snow. Taxes pay for libraries where you can check out books. Cities use tax money to pay for clean water. They have garbage picked up. If you play soccer on a city team or swim in a city pool, you are using a city service. Cities also pay for parks where you can play ball and have picnics. Taxes help people on welfare. They pay for places where people go to find jobs.

Taxes pay for public education. If you go to a public school, your building, the materials, and your teachers' salaries are paid for with tax money. However, parents who send their children to a private school must pay for these things.

The Common Good

Government leaders have to make choices about how to use tax money. They think of what would be best for most of the people. Services that keep our towns safe, protect our natural resources, or educate the children are for the common good of the people. "Common good" means it helps most of the people.

School

POLICE

HEALTH CARE

LIBRARY

WATER

1 MEMORY MASTER

1. What are the three levels of government?
2. How does the government help children and adults?
3. In this picture, which services are paid for with tax money?

PEOPLE TO KNOW

Thomas Jefferson
James Madison
George Washington

PLACES TO LOCATE

Philadelphia

WORDS TO UNDERSTAND

executive
judicial
jury
justice
legislators
republic
responsibility
volunteer

Thomas Jefferson wrote these words in the Declaration of Independence: "We hold these truths to be self-evident, that all men are created equal, that they are endowed by their Creator with certain inalienable rights. Among these are life, liberty, and the pursuit of happiness."

The History of Our Government

In past chapters you read about the beginnings of our national government. The people who fought to free our country from England wanted the United States to be a *republic.* This meant there would be no kings or queens, princes or princesses. Instead, the people would elect their leaders.

George Washington, James Madison, and other leaders met in Philadelphia to put into writing how our country could be run. They thought a lot about how to make the best government. They wanted it based on liberty and justice.

The Declaration of Independence, 1776

On July 4, 1776, men from the 13 colonies approved a document called the Declaration of Independence. It was a letter to the king of England explaining why the colonists wanted to form a new and independent country. The Declaration listed all the unfair things the king had done to the colonists. The first battles of the American Revolution had already begun. After a long war, we became a separate country. We became the United States of America.

The Declaration of Independence was first announced to the people in Philadelphia, far away from Illinois. What can you learn about the people of Philadelphia from this painting?

The Constitution, 1787

About four years after the war ended, our nation organized a new, stronger government. George Washington, James Madison, and other leaders gathered to write a new Constitution. Our national government is based on our Constitution. The Constitution is one of the most important documents in the United States.

The Constitution says the power to rule the nation comes from the people, not from a king or queen. The people can vote for their leaders. The Constitution also splits the government into three branches. The three branches divide the power. This is a very important part of our government.

The Bill of Rights, 1791

The first leaders of our country did another important thing. Several years after the Constitution became the law of the land, the leaders added a Bill of Rights. It lists rights the government cannot take away from people.

One of these rights is the freedom to belong to any religion. People can speak freely. They can write and print what they think is important. These are rights people in some other countries do not have.

James Madison studied governments from other places in the world. He chose what he thought would be the best government for the new United States of America. Because he wrote so much of it, he is often called the "Father of the Constitution."

What Do You Think ?

Does freedom of speech mean you can write graffiti on public property? Can you tell lies that harm others? How can we use our freedoms so they don't hurt anyone else?

"We the People" are the opening words of the Constitution of the United States of America. Why do you think these words were chosen?

With Rights Come Responsibilities

Having rights means we also have *responsibilities.* They are jobs we are in charge of doing. Adults have a responsibility to take part in government. This is what "government by the people" means. Voting is one way adults take part in government. Here are some other examples:

Vote.

Run for office.

Right	Responsibility
You can vote when you are 18 years old.	You should learn about the candidates and issues.
You have the right to go to any church you want or meet with any group as long as you don't hurt others.	You should respect those same rights in other people.
You get to help make the laws.	You must obey the laws.

Be a Resposible Citizen

One of your responsibilities is to be a good citizen. There are lots of things people can do to be good citizens. One of the first steps is to learn how government works. You are doing that right now!

Here are some other things you can do:

- Settle conflicts peacefully. Listen to the other person's point of view.
- Obey all of your family and school rules.
- Tell the truth.
- Be polite and helpful.
- Help keep your own home and yard clean.
- Never litter or ruin someone else's property.
- Ask adults in your family to vote. Talk with them about what is going on in your town, state, and country.
- Write a letter to the editor of your town's newspaper.
- Volunteer to help in your community.

Go to town meetings.

Red Cross volunteers get ready to send supplies to the survivors of Hurricane Katrina in 2005.

Volunteers

Volunteers often work for the community without getting paid. They do things that help others. Some adults work at voting booths, others pick up litter along the streets. Older students volunteer to help younger children with their homework after school.

Some groups, such as the Red Cross, volunteer when there has been a bad storm or flood. They help families find a safe place to stay. They give them food and water. They help people who are injured.

Making Connections

Boy Scouts and Girl Scouts provide service to their community. They clean up parks, plant flowers, make birdhouses, make visits to the elderly, and collect food for the poor. What ways have you volunteered in your school or community?

Lesson 2

Branches of Government

The Constitution gives power to three branches of government. Each branch has the power to do only certain things, so that no single branch can become too powerful. No one branch can make laws. Each branch checks the others and balances the power.

Look at this giant government tree to see all the important things that go on in each branch.

Executive Branch

The *executive* branch carries out the laws. The president is the head of the executive branch. Find the reporters asking questions. Find the people who are talking with the president.

Judicial Branch

The courts make up the *judicial* branch. Courts decide what the laws mean. They must make sure laws do not go against the Constitution and its Bill of Rights. They try to settle problems in a peaceful way.

A judge listens to cases and rules in a court. A *jury* is a group of people who also listen to cases and decide if a person is innocent or guilty. If a person is found guilty, a judge decides what the punishment will be.

Find the judge, jury, and court reporter. The court reporter writes down everything that is said in court.

▲ Drawing by Jon Burton

266

Legislative Branch

The men and women who make our laws are our representatives. They are also called *legislators.* On the legislative branch, find the people who are giving speeches about the laws they want passed.

Voting

It is important to remember that the people choose their leaders. Most people who are citizens of the United States, are at least 18 years old, and are registered can vote for the leaders they want.

If representatives don't make laws the people want, the people might vote for someone else in the next election. Find the people voting. Then find the leaders climbing up the tree to serve in one of the branches of government.

What Do You Think?

Do you think 18-year-olds are responsible enough to vote for government leaders? Why or why not?

Levels of Government

In the United States, we not only have three branches of government, we have levels of government:

- **Local governments** make decisions for people in towns, cities, or counties.
- **State governments** make decisions for people in each state.
- **The national government** makes decisions for everyone in the country.

Each level of government has different jobs. Look at the chart to see what some of them are.

Every country has laws. Our Founding Fathers wanted laws to protect our rights and freedom. In our country, no one—not even the president—is more powerful than the law. This is called the **rule of law**.

Level	Place	Examples of Power
National	United States	• National defense • Printing money • Relations with other countries
State	Illinois	• State lands and resources • State roads • Driver's licenses
Local	Cities and counties	• City police and firefighters • County roads and bridges • Water and sewer

Representatives of the People

Does your school have a student council? Each class elects a student council member. Members from all of the classes vote for changes in the whole school. They are representatives.

Just like a student council, representatives from Illinois and all of the 50 states go to Washington, D.C., to make laws for the whole country. They serve in Congress. Congress is made up of two parts— the Senate and the House of Representatives.

The U.S. Senate

Like all the states, Illinois sends two people to serve in the U.S. Senate. This means there are a total of 100 senators in the United States.

The U.S. House of Representatives

Illinois also sends representatives to the U.S. House of Representatives. The number of people sent to the House of Representatives is based on each state's population (the number of people who live in the state). This means states with more people send more representatives. States with fewer people send a smaller number of representatives.

Illinois sends 20 people to the U.S. House of Representatives. They serve for two years unless we elect them more than once. If our population grows larger, someday we might send more people to represent us.

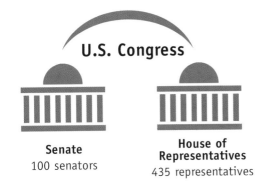

U.S. Congress

Senate
100 senators

House of Representatives
435 representatives

To pass a law, the Senate and the House of Representatives must each vote. This is the U.S. Senate in Washington, D.C.

② MEMORY MASTER

1. Name the important document that is the basis for our national government.
2. How can you help your community?
3. Why do we have three branches of government?
4. What do the men and women in the legislative branch do?
5. What are the three levels of government?

PEOPLE TO KNOW

Rod Blagojevich
Richard J. Daley
Harold Washington

PLACES TO LOCATE

Arizona
California
Illinois
Louisiana
Utah
West Virginia
Wisconsin

WORDS TO UNDERSTAND

agency
governor

State Government for Illinois

The 50 states of our country are not all alike. They have different geography, people, and industries. Each state has different problems. Each state has its own state government to solve these problems.

In the West, Arizona and Utah make laws about how water can be used. Water is very important there because they are desert states. In California, government workers inspect crops. They don't want insects to get into the fruit and vegetable plants. Wisconsin makes laws about fishing in its many lakes and rivers and logging in its forests. Louisiana has laws about its docks, where ships load and unload their cargoes. West Virginia makes laws about safety in its coal mines.

Illinois makes laws about transportation. It is important that the many people who use the trains, roads, rivers, and airports are safe.

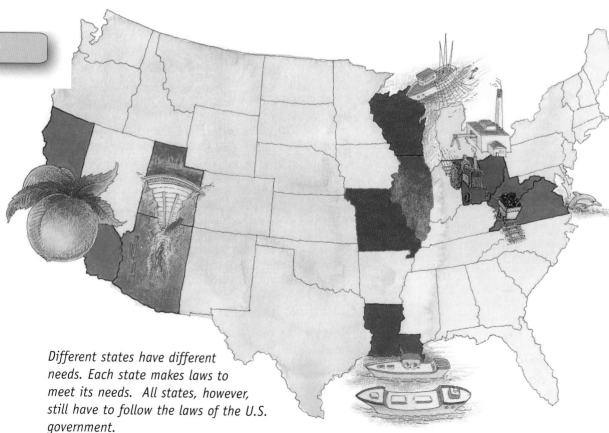

Different states have different needs. Each state makes laws to meet its needs. All states, however, still have to follow the laws of the U.S. government.

Shadrach Bond, our state's first governor, raised his right hand and vowed to lead the new state with honor.

Our State Constitution

Illinois has a constitution that tells how our state government works. Our first constitution was written in 1818, when Illinois became a state.

As Illinois grew and changed, new constitutions were written. Over the years, there have been four different constitutions for our state. The last one was written and voted on by the people of Illinois in 1970.

Our state constitution contains a Preamble (introduction), a Bill of Rights, and then gives the rules for how our state government must be organized for the common good of the people.

Here is the Preamble to the Illinois constitution. Talk with your class about what the words mean. Why are they important?

PREAMBLE:
We, the People of the State of Illinois—grateful to Almighty God for the civil, political and religious liberty which He has permitted us to enjoy and seeking His blessing upon our endeavors—in order to provide for the health, safety and welfare of the people; maintain a representative and orderly government; eliminate poverty and inequality; assure legal, social and economic justice; provide opportunity for the fullest development of the individual; insure domestic tranquility; provide for the common defense; and secure the blessings of freedom and liberty to ourselves and our posterity—do ordain and establish this Constitution for the State of Illinois.

Branches of State Government

The national Constitution gave each branch important powers. In this way, no branch can become a bully and take all the power. Like the national government, our state government is also divided into three branches. Each branch has certain duties. This way the power is spread out. How does this work?

Legislative Branch

The legislative branch makes the laws. In Illinois, our General Assembly is the legislative branch. It is a group of people who are elected by the people of the state to make the laws.

The General Assembly is divided into two groups called the Senate and the House of Representatives. Both groups meet each year to decide which bills become new laws.

Executive Branch

The executive branch carries out the laws. The *governor* is the head of the executive branch and is elected by the people of Illinois. Here is a list of some jobs the governor does. Which do you think are most important?

- Sees that state laws are carried out
- Signs bills into law or vetoes (rejects) them
- Commands state military forces
- Makes a budget of how state money will be spent

Many people help the governor by working in state *agencies.* Some agencies help farmers sell their crops or inspect farm animals. Other agencies run state parks, work on state roads and highways, collect taxes, and help run the state's schools and colleges.

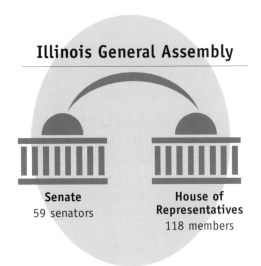

Illinois General Assembly

Senate
59 senators

House of Representatives
118 members

Governor Rod Blagojevich, 2007

Making Connections

Who is the current governor of Illinois? Do you know the names of any of our senators or representatives? Maybe you have seen them on TV or riding in a parade. You can read about them in the newspaper.

Chapter 11 "Government for the Nation and State"

Judicial Branch

The courts are another branch of our state government. Judges and juries are part of the courts. They make up the judicial branch of our state government. The judicial branch interprets the laws, which means they decide exactly what the laws mean.

Courts decide if a person is guilty of a crime. The jury must decide if the person on trial is guilty or not. If the person is found guilty of the crime, the judge decides how the person should be punished.

In another kind of case, a person might feel that he or she has not been treated fairly. A person might ask the courts to decide who was to blame for an accident. The court will listen to both sides and then decide on a way to settle the argument.

Our State Capitol Building

Springfield is our state's capital city. The Senate and the House of Representatives have their meetings at the Illinois State Capitol Building there.

The current building replaced the older, smaller building in 1888. The new building took 20 years to build. You can go online to see the inside of the capitol at: Ilstatehouse.com

Local Government

Since different places have different needs, local governments are very important. In some places in Illinois there are factories. In other places, there are farms. In large towns, you can see many buildings. City roads and sidewalks are crowded with cars and people. Other places are quieter, with very few people.

Local government is government close to home. County and city governments are two examples of local governments. You may not ever think about it, but these levels of government help take care of your needs.

Harold Washington

1922–1987

Raised in Chicago by his father, Washington was smart, witty, and friendly. He attended DuSable High School. Then he was the only black student in his class at Northwestern University Law School.

Washington was elected as an Illinois representative and then a senator. He ran for mayor of Chicago, but lost that election. Several years later he ran again, and this time, he won. He was Chicago's first black mayor. He worked to reduce crime, help public education, and develop better neighborhoods. After winning the same office again, Washington died suddenly of a heart attack.

County Government

Illinois is divided into 102 counties. Each county has a town that is the county seat. There is usually a courthouse there, where court is held. The courthouse is also a place where birth, death, and marriage certificates are recorded. If your family owns property, a map of your property is recorded in your county courthouse.

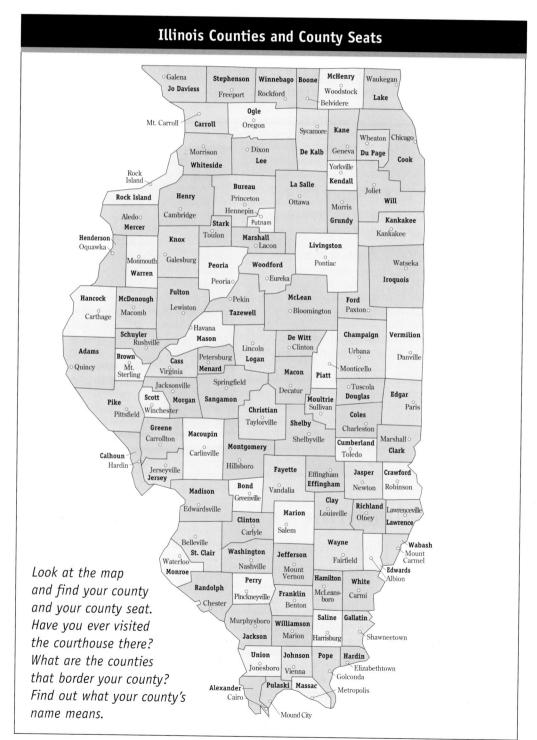

Illinois Counties and County Seats

Look at the map and find your county and your county seat. Have you ever visited the courthouse there? What are the counties that border your county? Find out what your county's name means.

Chapter 11 "Government for the Nation and State"

City Government

Government even closer to home is city government. A mayor or a city manager is in charge of departments that provide services for the town. Some of the services are clean water, garbage removal, sewage systems, health care, and fire and police workers.

Cities and towns make rules about what kinds of buildings can be built in different parts of town. They often keep houses separate from businesses. They make sure schools are in safe places. They make laws about speed limits on the roads. Cities also have city courts.

Making Connections

Does your city or town have a mayor? Who is he or she? What are the jobs of your mayor?

Illinois PORTRAIT

Richard Joseph Daley
1902–1976

Born on Chicago's South Side near the stockyards, Richard Daley was an only child of immigrant parents. He attended Catholic elementary and high schools, then took night classes to earn a law degree. Daley became the longest-serving mayor of Chicago. He was elected six times and served for 21 years as the "boss" of Chicago.

While Daley was mayor, Chicago became known as "The City that Works." The O'Hare Airport, the Sears Tower, and many new skyscrapers and highways were built during his terms. Daley was known for his strong leadership skills and his ability to make things happen. During the Civil Rights Era, however, many people thought he didn't do enough to solve the issues of segregation and make life better for blacks. Daley was mayor when Dr. Martin Luther King Jr. was murdered and urged the police to take strong action against those who rioted in Chicago after the murder.

Daley and his wife, Eleanor, had three daughters and four sons. Three of his sons have served in government positions, including mayor.

③ MEMORY MASTER

1. What do the people elected to the General Assembly do?
2. If someone has broken a law, which branch of government decides what his or her punishment will be?
3. The governor is head of which branch of state government?
4. Who is the head of city government?

Chapter 11 Review

Activity

Volunteer in Your Community

Community leaders have the job of solving problems in their cities, but each citizen can help solve local problems. Some things leaders might be working on are:

- helping poor people
- protecting the environment
- making sure people have jobs
- teaching kids and adults to read and write
- improving and building roads
- helping their community grow

1. What are some problems in your community?
2. As a class, choose one problem and think about how you might help solve it. List your ideas on the chalkboard. How do you propose to solve the problem?
3. Volunteers are people who give their time to help others. Can you volunteer to help?

Activity

The Pledge of Allegiance

I pledge allegiance to the Flag
of the United States of America,
and to the Republic for which it stands:
one Nation under God, indivisible,
With Liberty and Justice for all.

School children all across the country say this pledge every morning. They have been doing this since 1892! The words have been changed several times. They may change again. Even so, the words show our respect for our country and our flag.

When you say the Pledge of Allegiance you must stop, stand, face the flag, and put your right hand over your heart. If you are a scout or soldier in uniform, you must salute the flag instead.

Do you know what these words in the pledge mean?

I Pledge Allegiance to the flag	I promise my loyalty to the flag of the United States of America.
And to the Republic for which it stands	I pledge my loyalty to our government, where the people elect their own leaders to make laws.
Indivisible	The country cannot be divided up. All states join together in unity.
with Liberty	The people of this nation have freedoms guaranteed in the Bill of Rights.
and Justice for all.	Everyone is entitled by law to be treated justly and fairly.

Rules, Rules!

Whatever we do, wherever we go, we have to follow rules. If you get a new game for your birthday, you and your friends read the rules before you play.

Your family has rules, such as "You can't say up late on a school night." We learn many rules when we are young. We hardly even think about them as we grow up. Brainstorm with your friends and write down all the rules you can think of for each category.

Did you each think of different rules? Do you all think these rules are fair?

1. Home Rules	2. Classroom Rules
3. Rules of Your Favorite Game	4. Town Rules

Branches of Government Flip Book

A four-page flip book can be made by using two pieces of unlined paper. Layer them one on top of the other, leaving a half-inch space at the bottom of the bottom page. Holding the two pieces together, fold the top edges of the papers down at the same time, again leaving a half-inch space between each sheet. Now you have a flip book with a cover and three pages.

Write a title and your name on the cover, and draw an illustration.

On the bottom of each of the other pages, write the name of a branch of government. Then write a brief summary of the job of that branch and who governs it. Draw a symbol to remind you of that branch of government.

You could make another book about the three levels of government.

Griffin Hale's Flip Book

Legislative Branch

Executive Branch

Judicial Branch

"*All money means to me is a pride in accomplishment.*"
—*Ray Kroc, founder of McDonalds*

Economics for Illinois

Chapter 12

Our economy is important. It affects how adults earn a living so they can buy what they need. It affects the goods they produce and the goods they buy. People in Illinois work at many kinds of jobs to earn money. They build homes and apartments and produce food, clothes, games, sports equipment, books, and electronics. They provide medical care and radio and television programs. People fix your car when it breaks down and fix your teeth if you have a cavity. Other people ship goods in and out of Illinois every day.

Fast food restaurants are in every small town and large city. They produce food and sell food. The first McDonald's restaurant in the world began in Des Plaines, Illinois. Many years later, McDonald's had a day to remember the first McDonald's. People lined up to buy hamburgers for 15¢ and fries for 10¢.

279

Does a doctor provide a service or goods when she examines a child who has a sore throat?

Goods and Services

All people have needs. They need food, clothing, and shelter. They also have wants. They want things like cars, books, and bicycles. They want different kinds of foods. These things they want and need are called *products* or *goods.* The people who make them are called "producers."

People also need care from doctors. They need education from teachers. They want people to fix their car or mow their lawn. These are called *services.* Bankers, teachers, and firefighters provide services.

Who buys all the goods and services other people produce? Both adults and children are *consumers.* When you drink milk, wear shoes, or get a present for your birthday, you are a consumer. You are part of the economy.

When we are children, adults usually make sure our needs are met. When we grow up, we must earn a living to meet our needs. Most adults work at jobs to earn money for their families. At work, they provide goods and services for other people. In this chapter, we will see how people in our state earn money to meet their needs and wants.

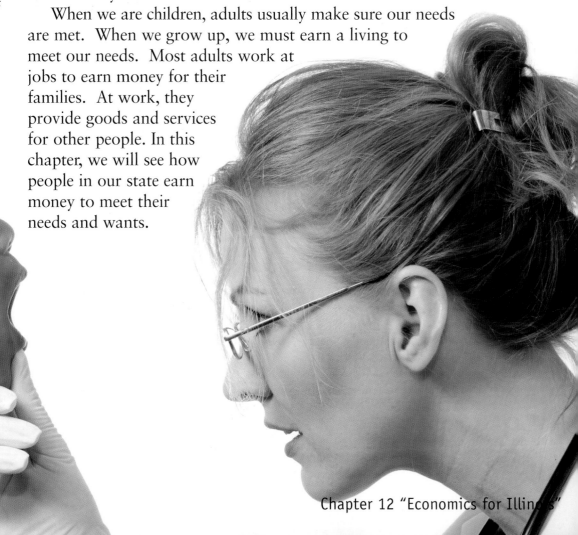

How Are Goods Produced?

To make goods or products, workers must use many kinds of resources. Look at all the products in your classroom. Which resources do you think were used to make all the products?

Natural Resources

Soil, sand, gravel, stone, water, trees, minerals (metals), and even sunshine are natural resources. They are used to produce many kinds of goods. Some of these natural resources help grow food and make food products. Others are used for building homes and offices, for making cement and paint, and for making furniture, clothes, and even cardboard boxes.

Supplies to make goods are often kept in a warehouse before they are shipped to factories or construction sites.

Capital Resources

Capital resources are goods or supplies that are used to make a new product. The tools used to make bicycles are capital resources. The money to rent a building, pay workers, buy tools and supplies, and run a business is also called "capital."

Economics is the study of how people make money and spend it. It is also the study of how people produce, buy, and sell the goods and services they need and want.

Human Resources

Business owners usually hire other people, called "employees," to work for them. The owner pays the employees. In economics, we call workers "human resources." Without workers, there would be no goods or services.

The owner of a business often holds planning meetings with employees. Are your parents employees of a business?

Working in a Bicycle Factory

People earn a living by providing goods and services. A farmer knows how to plant wheat and just the right time to harvest the crop. An electrician, however, knows how to get electricity into a house so the freezer will keep the chocolate ice cream from melting. Both workers have

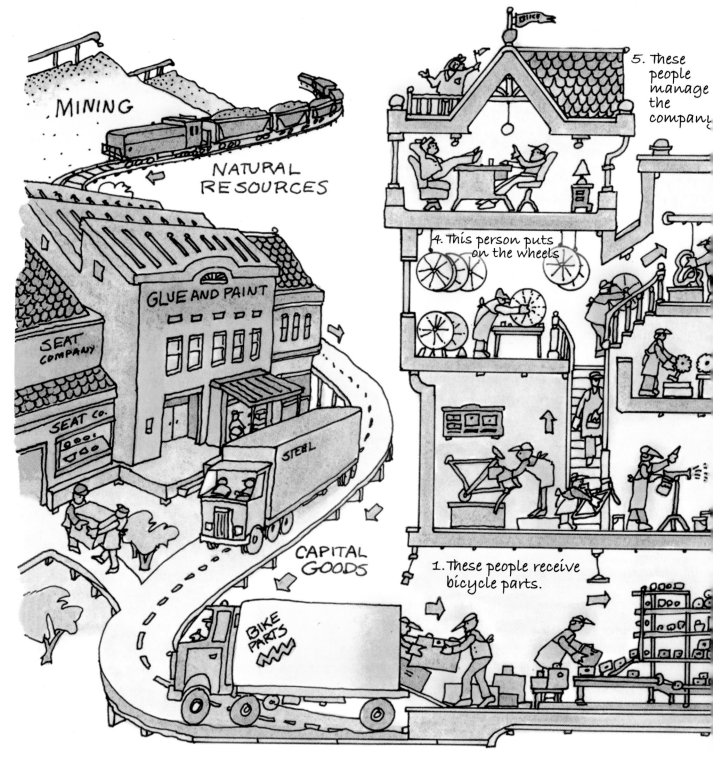

MINING

NATURAL RESOURCES

GLUE AND PAINT

SEAT COMPANY

SEAT CO.

STEEL

CAPITAL GOODS

BIKE PARTS

5. These people manage the company

4. This person puts on the wheels

1. These people receive bicycle parts.

Chapter 12 "Economics for Illinois"

special skills. *Specialization* is when people produce only one kind of product or are skilled at one job. They usually have to have special training and practice to get really good at what they do. Look at this picture of the different jobs in a bicycle factory. Start at number 1 in the lower left corner. Then find number two, and so on. Can you see why it would be hard for one worker to make a bicycle alone?

What Do You Think ❓

Which of these workers would you like to be? What skills do you think you would need to do your job? What type of education and experience would you need?

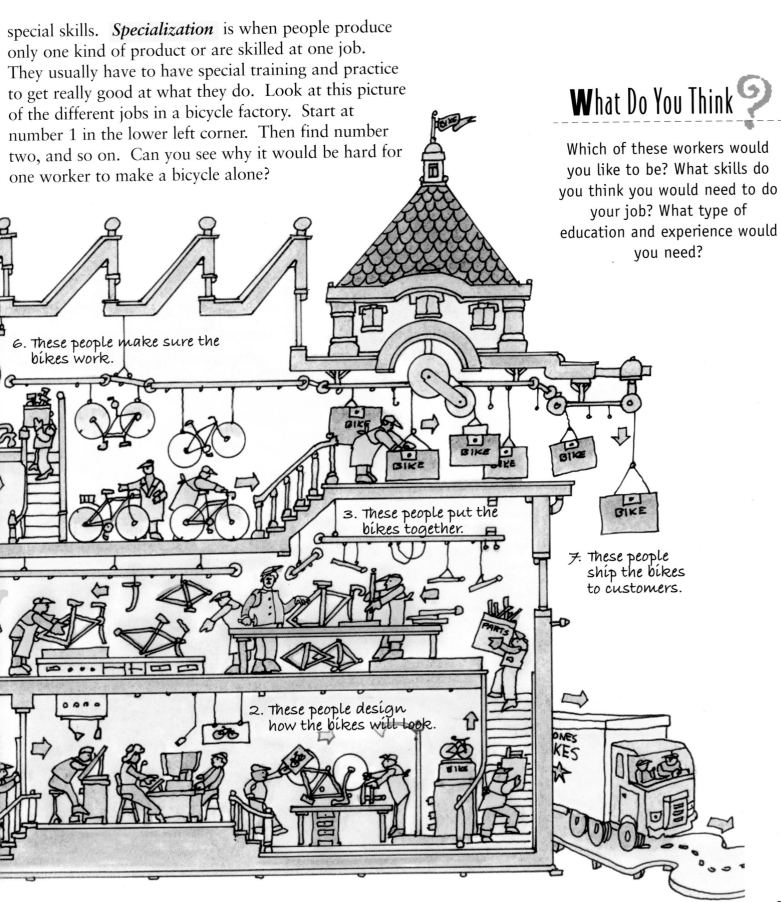

6. These people make sure the bikes work.

3. These people put the bikes together.

7. These people ship the bikes to customers.

2. These people design how the bikes will look.

Lesson 1

283

Oscar Mayer
1859–1955

At the age of 14, Oscar F. Mayer arrived in the United States from Germany with the dream of owning his own meat market. He worked as a butcher's boy in Detroit and then as a worker in Chicago's stockyards.

Then he and his brother took over a meat market and made it a success. They sold sausages, hams, bacon, and wieners.

Oscar used his friendly personality and sales ability to grow a family business. The men were known for their quality work, and soon business grew.

The company was one of the first to spend money to advertise their products. Little Oscar and his Wienermobile—a small chef in a hot dog-shaped vehicle—drove up to outdoor events and rode in parades. The company hired someone to write jingles for TV advertising too. Have you heard these jingles?

"Oh, I wish I were an Oscar Mayer wiener; that is what I'd truly like to be,"

"My bologna has a first name, it's O-s-c-a-r. My bologna has a second name, it's M-a-y-e-r."

In many school lunch boxes today, the sandwiches will be made with Oscar Mayer meat.

Immigrants Start Businesses

When immigrants came to this country, most of them got jobs working for other people at very low wages. The workers wanted better jobs. They needed more money to pay for the things their families needed. Many immigrants became *entrepreneurs*. An entrepreneur is someone who has an idea and takes a risk to start a business. They must ask themselves many questions. What products or services will they provide? How will they do it? Where will they get enough money to start the business? What if no one buys their products? Will the business make enough money?

When immigrants started a business, the whole family often helped. Sometimes even the children sewed, hammered, chopped, ran errands, or whatever needed to be done. When the business grew, the family hired other employees.

Some entrepreneurs sold goods. Maybe they made hats, rugs, or wagons. Maybe they farmed and sold extra corn or hogs.

Some entrepreneurs sold services. They may have delivered groceries, painted homes, or taught classes. They may have opened their own barbershops and cut hair.

What Do You Think?

Does it take courage to open a new business? What risks are involved?

Producing Goods for Sale

Supply and Demand

How do business owners decide how much to charge for their products? The selling price depends on a lot of things. For coats, it might depend on how much the cloth and zipper cost.

The price may also depend on how many coats are for sale. If a coat becomes popular, the company might not be able to make enough for all the people who want one. If people want a coat, they may be willing to pay more.

Sometimes a store has too many coats. If people don't want to buy the coats, the store may need to lower the price so more people will buy them. This is all part of *supply and demand*.

Competition

A company may want to lower its prices so it can sell more products. What if two or more companies make the same thing? What happens if one of them charges less for its products? More people would probably buy the products that cost less.

Price is one way companies compete, but there are many other ways. Companies may choose to make new products. They may work to make better ones. They may offer better services. That is *competition*.

ZOOM

What Do You Think ?

How does competition help consumers?

Hoop Magic has more basketballs than consumers are willing to buy. A sale lowers the price of basketballs. At the lower price, the demand by consumers might increase.

What Is Scarcity?

Scarcity is part of supply and demand. Scarcity is when there is not enough of something that people want.

Think of the gasoline in your family car. Gasoline is made from oil. A lot of the oil we use in the United States comes from other countries. Sometimes there are problems with buying oil from these countries. There might also be problems in our own country in shipping the oil to a place called a refinery. A refinery makes oil into gasoline. What if the refinery is hit by a terrible storm and has to shut down? There would be a scarcity of gasoline.

Scarcity can also be caused by lack of natural resources. If we use up our nonrenewable resources, companies will not be able to produce what we want to buy. For example, people are concerned we will not have enough energy to heat our homes or run cars and buses if we run out of oil or gasoline.

When products are scarce, the price goes way up. Talk with your class about products that are scarce in your town.

Making Connections

What does gas cost per gallon where you live? What decisions in your family are made based on the price of gasoline?

Over 20 cars lined up to buy gas when there was a scarcity of gasoline. Do you think the price of gas was high or low?

Choices and Trade-Offs

Most people want to spend their money wisely. They compare different products to find the best deal. They try to get the most for their money. They sometimes compare prices at different stores.

Whenever you buy something, you are making a choice. Sometimes you have to make a trade-off. A *trade-off* is choosing not to buy one thing so you will have enough money to buy something else.

Pretend you have $20 to spend. You want to buy a book and a video game, but you don't have enough money for both. Which would you choose to buy? What trade-off would you make?

Adults often have to think about trade-offs when they decide how to spend their money. Should they buy a house or rent an apartment? Should they buy a newer car or keep the one they have so they can pay for all the sports the children want to play? Should they take the family on vacation or stay home and use the money to pay bills?

Making Connections

What goods or services have you and your family paid for this week? How do you know you got a good deal for your money?

Chicago Board of Trade and Chicago Mercantile Exchange

The price you pay for goods depends on the value of a product. Both the Chicago Board of Trade and the Chicago Mercantile Exchange are major centers of buying and selling products such as wheat, soybeans, and corn. These products are called "futures." Futures are promises to buy or sell at a set price in the future. The price partly determines how much you, the consumer, will pay for a product.

This is how it works. A farmer is growing corn. Many factors will affect the supply and demand for the corn, which causes the price to rise and fall. These factors include new products, weather, and the products of other farmers. The farmer will watch the prices of corn at the Chicago Board of Trade and when he sees a price he likes, he agrees to deliver his corn at that price in the future.

1 MEMORY MASTER

1. Give some examples of goods and services.
2. Compare and contrast a producer and a consumer.
3. If there is a lot of something, the price is usually _____.
4. What are some of the choices a consumer makes?

export
finance
global
import
insurance
processing
tourism

Making a Living Today

When Illinois first became a state, almost everyone farmed. That is how they earned money for their families. There were jobs on farms, in food packing plants, and shipping yards. Farming is still very important, but today people do many different kinds of jobs.

People in Illinois design, build, and sell homes and other buildings. They work in banks and insurance offices. They solve problems and run computers. They produce goods in factories. They sell products in department stores. They sell and repair cars. They write stories and take photographs for newspapers. These are some of the ways people earn a living.

Would you like to earn a living by taking photographs for books or by fixing cars?

Government Services

Many people also work for the government. They are police officers on the streets, gardeners in parks, teachers in schools, and helpers in museums. They are street cleaners, secretaries, and city planners. Most of these government workers provide services.

Finance and Insurance

Finance is a word that has to do with money. A lot of people work in banks. Banks are businesses that help people save and manage their money. They are safe places to keep savings. Banks pay you interest on the money you save. Banks also make loans. Adults can go to a bank to borrow money so they can buy a house, a car, or start a business.

Insurance companies also work with money, but in a different way. A person can buy insurance on a car, a house, or even on his or her health or life. It works like this: Each month the person pays some money to an insurance company. Then, if the car gets in an accident, the water pipes break and flood a house, or the person needs an operation, the insurance company will pay all or part of the bill. Insurance companies charge more for this service than they think they will ever have to pay out. This is the way insurance companies make money. Many Illinois people work with insurance.

Making Connections

Ask your parents what kinds of insurance they have.

Manufacturing for Good Health

One modern industry that works to fight disease has its roots in Illinois. Abbott Laboratories was started by Dr. Wallace Abbott in Chicago in 1888. The company produces drugs and medicines. It was one of the first companies to distribute penicillin that fights infections. The company makes other products such as Ensure liquid food products and Similac baby formula.

Out of Work! What does that mean? Sometimes adults want to work, but they can't get a job for some reason. Maybe they don't have enough education or training. Maybe they are too sick. Maybe the company they worked for closed down. Maybe they don't speak English yet. These workers who do not have a job are "unemployed."

Income and Education

You already know that people work at jobs to make money. Some workers earn more than other workers. Why? Jobs that pay the most money often require the most education and many years of training. Jobs that pay the lowest wages usually do not require as much education. This is why a scientist, a doctor, and a banker would earn more than a clerk in a store or a person who cleans in a hotel.

However, some jobs don't fit these rules. For instance, sometimes a person who buys and sells homes, runs his own business, or works laying hot tar on roads can earn a high income without a college education. Why do you think this is possible?

Producing Food in Illinois

Illinois is a leader in agriculture, which means growing crops and raising animals for food. It is also a leader in *processing* farm goods into food products we use every day.

Workers in Illinois are very busy producing food. Did you know all these foods are produced in our state?

Soybeans are an important food crop, but they provide much more than food.

Soybeans: Decatur is called "the Soybean Capital of the World." Soybeans turn up in all kinds of products, such as soap, paper, and paint. Soybeans are also found in tofu, cereal, pizza, bread, cookies, and frozen dinners.

Popcorn: Popcorn was voted the official state snack of Illinois. Why shouldn't it be? There are 300 popcorn farms in the state. Eat it with salt and butter!

Corn: Illinois corn is fed to animals and canned or frozen for people. It is also made into tortillas, corn chips, and cold cereal. Corn is also used to make medicine, animal feed, paint, glue, plastic, rubber, and even baby diapers.

Making Connections

If you were to look up and down the aisles at a grocery store, how many products made with corn would you see? Read some labels on food products and find out!

Corn Syrup

An important product from corn is sweet corn syrup. It is used instead of sugar in many processed foods. You might find a bottle of clear corn syrup in your cupboard at home. It can be found in soda pop, chewing gum, cake mixes, salad dressing, and ketchup.

These sticky Illinois treats are all made with corn syrup:

Laffy Taffy
Tootsie Rolls
Charm's Blow Pops
Junior Mints
Madison Dots

Jelly Belly Candy
Pearson Carmels
Nestle Butterfingers
Nestle Baby Ruth

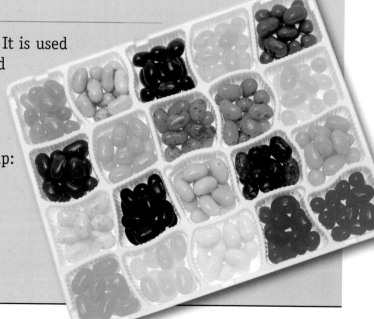

290

Food Processing

Food processing is one of our major industries. Thousands of workers earn a living producing food for people of the world.

One company, Archer Daniels Midland (ADM), is a *global* food processor. They produce enough food to feed 130 million people a day all over the world. ADM's products include vegetable oil, corn oil, soy products used in baby formula, corn syrup used in soft drinks and other sweets, wheat flour, and animal feed.

The following companies also produce food. They take food such as flour, corn, soybeans, and sugar and process them to make some of our favorite foods. Have you eaten any foods from these Illinois companies?

- Oreo cookies
- Jell-O desserts
- Capri Sun drinks
- Kool-Aid drink mixes
- Carl Budding lunch meat
- Azteca tortillas and chips
- La Preferida salsa, refried beans
- Good Chef soy sauce
- Classen pickles
- Eli's Cheesecake Company
- Connie's Pizza
- Kraft macaroni and chesse
- Libby's pumpkin pie
- Oscar Mayer bacon and lunch meat

Did you know that Jell-O and Eli's Cheesecake are produced right in your own state?

Lesson 2

Renewable Fuel from Corn and Soybeans

Illinois is the leading producer of ethanol. Ethanol is a liquid that can be used as fuel by itself or mixed with gasoline to fuel cars.

Ethanol is made from corn grown in Illinois. Since the corn can be replanted, it is a renewable source of fuel. Ethanol is also better for our environment. It causes less pollution. Cars do not need to use as much ethanol as gas to drive the same distance.

Illinois farmers also use another crop to produce a different kind of fuel. Soybean oil is used to make biodiesel, or diesel fuel. Trucks that use biodiesel fuel create less pollution. There is less wear on the truck engines. Biodiesel is a renewable source of energy that comes from the soil and the plants that grow on it.

Transportation Hub of the Nation

Thousands of men and women in our state work in the transportation industry. Transportation means moving goods and people from one place to another. This is very important for business. It allows people to ship their products and services to other places. Transportation also allows companies to ship and receive materials to make products. Good transportation helps Illinois' economy grow.

Illinois is a major hub of transportation for the United States. We have interstate highways, an important railroad system, and the busiest airport in the world. Lake Michigan and the Illinois and Mississippi Rivers are major transportation routes. This makes it easy for people and goods to move around the state. This also makes it easy to get from Illinois to anywhere in the world.

People Exchange Goods

Do you like bananas and pineapple? They are grown in places that have a warmer climate. Then they are shipped to Illinois. Look at the labels on your clothes. Were they made in other countries? Where are your favorite television shows produced? People all over the world exchange goods and services. It makes life better for everyone.

- *Imports* are things we bring INTO our state from other places.
- *Exports* are things we send OUT of the state.

Exports from Illinois are sent to over 200 countries. Our top exports include: machinery parts and equipment, chemical products, computers, electronics, and transportation equipment.

Pineapples and bananas are grown far away from Illinois. They are imported here for you to eat.

Nearly half of the goods created in the U.S. travel through Illinois.

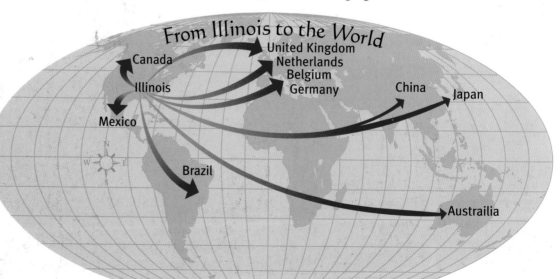

From Illinois to the World

Canada · United Kingdom · Netherlands · Belgium · Germany · China · Japan · Illinois · Mexico · Brazil · Austrailia

Study the map to see some of the places that use products made in Illinois.

Tourism Brings Visitors and Jobs

Tourism is another industry that provides jobs for people. Tourism brings money into the state. How? Tourists spend money on transportation, lodging, food, entertainment, and recreation. Tourism is big business in Illinois.

When people visit Illinois from other states and countries, they may eat at a restaurant in Peoria, explore the Cahokia Mounds, visit Lincoln's home in Springfield, or cheer at a baseball game in Chicago. Visitors also go horseback riding in Rockford, fishing on Cedar Lake in Shawnee National Forest, or canoeing in many parts of our state. Others visit Galesburg, the home of famous author Carl Sandburg, or enjoy a folk festival or a concert. This is all part of tourism.

People who visit places away from their homes are called "tourists." How can you be a tourist in your own state?

Making Connections

Where have you been in Illinois? What did you like about the place?

Local fans and tourists flock to the Chicago Cubs' games at Wrigley Field.

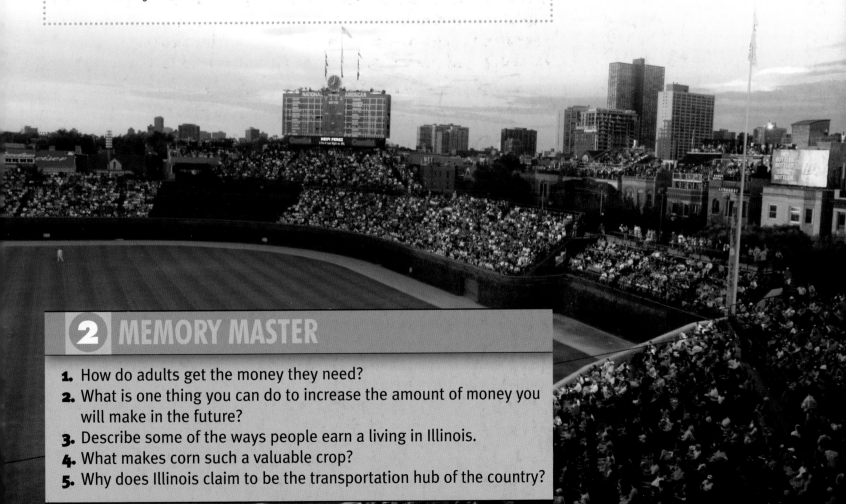

② MEMORY MASTER

1. How do adults get the money they need?
2. What is one thing you can do to increase the amount of money you will make in the future?
3. Describe some of the ways people earn a living in Illinois.
4. What makes corn such a valuable crop?
5. Why does Illinois claim to be the transportation hub of the country?

Chapter 12 Review

— Activity —

Collect Coins and Learn About Money

What is "numismatics"? It is a very big word for a very fun hobby—coin collecting. Many children and adults enjoy collecting coins. Maybe you have your own collection. Besides just the fun of collecting coins, you can also learn a lot about history, sports, architecture, inventions, and much more. Open your bank and see just who or what is on all those coins.

Visit **www.usmint.gov/kids** and go exploring. While you're there, read about smart ways to spend your money and ways you can save money.

— Activity —

Economic Sleuth

In a notebook, make a list of the vocabulary words from this chapter. Then go with your family or friends on a walk around a business area. Be on the lookout for examples of anything you've read about. Next to each word write down something you see that fits that word. For example, do you see someone buying an ice cream cone? Write that down next to the word "consumer." If the chocolate in that candy came from Germany, you could write that down next to "import."

How many words can you check off? Be creative and do some "cents-able" thinking!

Tourism Brochure

What do you like to do in Illinois? Maybe you enjoy visiting a science museum, going to a sporting arena, or camping with your family. Choose a place you like to visit. Then search the Internet, visit the library, or look through some souvenirs you may have, and gather information about the place. Plan a travel brochure to encourage tourists to visit.

Include important information to answer who, what, why, when, where, and how. Make sure to describe the place so that it sounds interesting or fun. Create your brochure on the computer. Add pictures and details to catch the reader's attention.

Where Do People Work?

Look at the pie chart to see where people in Illinois work.

Talk with your class about the jobs that are part of each industry. For example, people who work in hotels or hospitals are part of the service industry. What other service jobs can you think of?

People who drive taxi cabs and buses are part of the transportation industry. People who work for a telephone company or a cable television company are part of the communications industries.

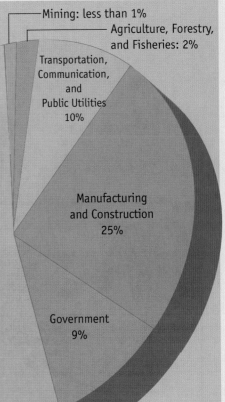

Mining: less than 1%

Agriculture, Forestry, and Fisheries: 2%

Transportation, Communication, and Public Utilities 10%

Manufacturing and Construction 25%

Services, including Tourism, Banking, Insurance, Retail Trade, and Medical 54%

Government 9%

Percent is the total value of goods and services produced in a year.
Source: U.S. Government Publications

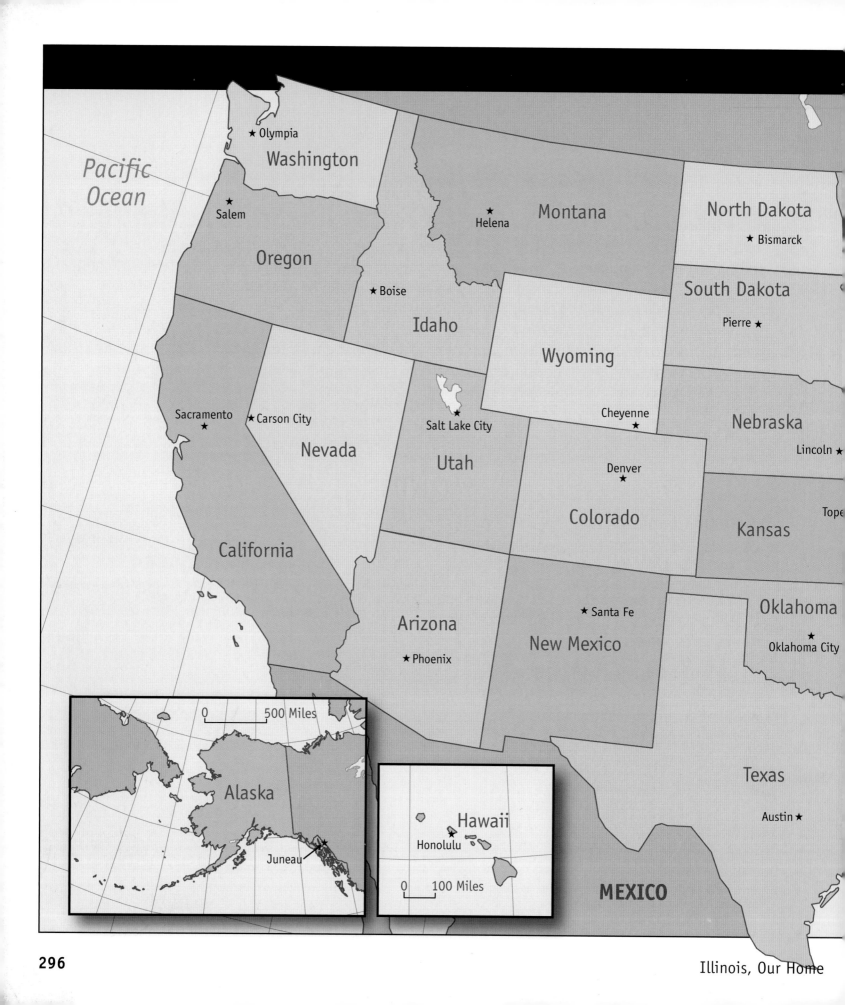

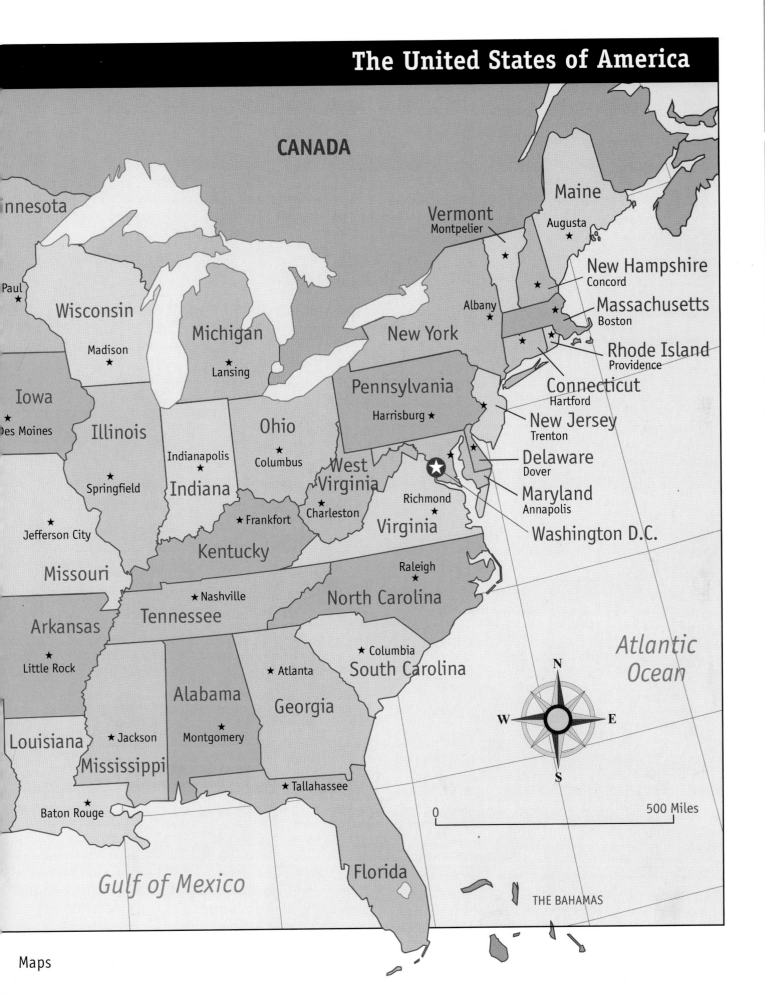

CANADA

innesota

Paul ★

Wisconsin

Madison ★

Iowa

Des Moines ★

Illinois

Springfield ★

Michigan

Lansing ★

Indianapolis ★

Indiana

Jefferson City ★

Missouri

Frankfort ★

Kentucky

Little Rock ★

Arkansas

Nashville ★

Tennessee

Louisiana

Jackson ★

Mississippi

Baton Rouge ★

Alabama

Montgomery ★

Columbus ★

Ohio

West Virginia

Charleston ★

Atlanta ★

Alabama

Georgia

Tallahassee ★

Florida

Gulf of Mexico

THE BAHAMAS

Vermont
Montpelier

Maine

Augusta ★

New Hampshire
Concord

Albany ★

Massachusetts
Boston

New York

Rhode Island
Providence

Connecticut
Hartford

Pennsylvania

Harrisburg ★

New Jersey
Trenton

Delaware
Dover

Maryland
Annapolis

Washington D.C.

Richmond ★

Virginia

Raleigh ★

North Carolina

Columbia ★

South Carolina

Atlantic Ocean

N
W   E
S

500 Miles

0

The World

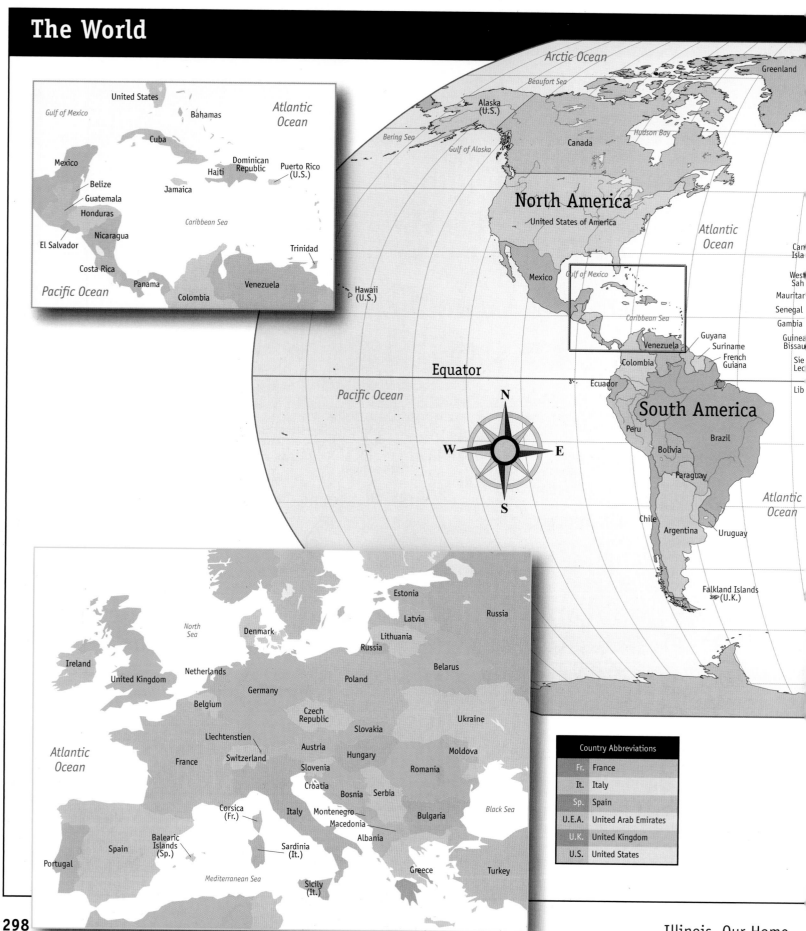

Inset map (Central America & Caribbean):

United States · Gulf of Mexico · Bahamas · Atlantic Ocean · Cuba · Mexico · Dominican Republic · Puerto Rico (U.S.) · Belize · Haiti · Guatemala · Jamaica · Honduras · Nicaragua · Caribbean Sea · El Salvador · Trinidad · Costa Rica · Panama · Venezuela · Colombia · Pacific Ocean

Main map (Americas):

Arctic Ocean · Greenland · Beaufort Sea · Alaska (U.S.) · Hudson Bay · Bering Sea · Gulf of Alaska · Canada · North America · United States of America · Atlantic Ocean · Mexico · Gulf of Mexico · Caribbean Sea · Venezuela · Guyana · Suriname · French Guiana · Colombia · Ecuador · Equator · Pacific Ocean · South America · Peru · Brazil · Bolivia · Paraguay · Chile · Argentina · Uruguay · Atlantic Ocean · Falkland Islands (U.K.) · Hawaii (U.S.)

Can Isla · West Sah · Mauritar · Senegal · Gambia · Guinea Bissau · Sie Leo · Lib

Compass: N · S · E · W

Inset map (Europe):

Estonia · Russia · Latvia · North Sea · Denmark · Lithuania · Russia · Belarus · Ireland · Netherlands · United Kingdom · Germany · Poland · Belgium · Czech Republic · Ukraine · Slovakia · Liechtenstien · Austria · Moldova · France · Switzerland · Hungary · Slovenia · Romania · Atlantic Ocean · Croatia · Bosnia · Serbia · Black Sea · Corsica (Fr.) · Italy · Montenegro · Bulgaria · Macedonia · Albania · Balearic Islands (Sp.) · Sardinia (It.) · Spain · Portugal · Mediterranean Sea · Greece · Turkey · Sicily (It.)

Country Abbreviations

Fr.	France
It.	Italy
Sp.	Spain
U.E.A.	United Arab Emirates
U.K.	United Kingdom
U.S.	United States

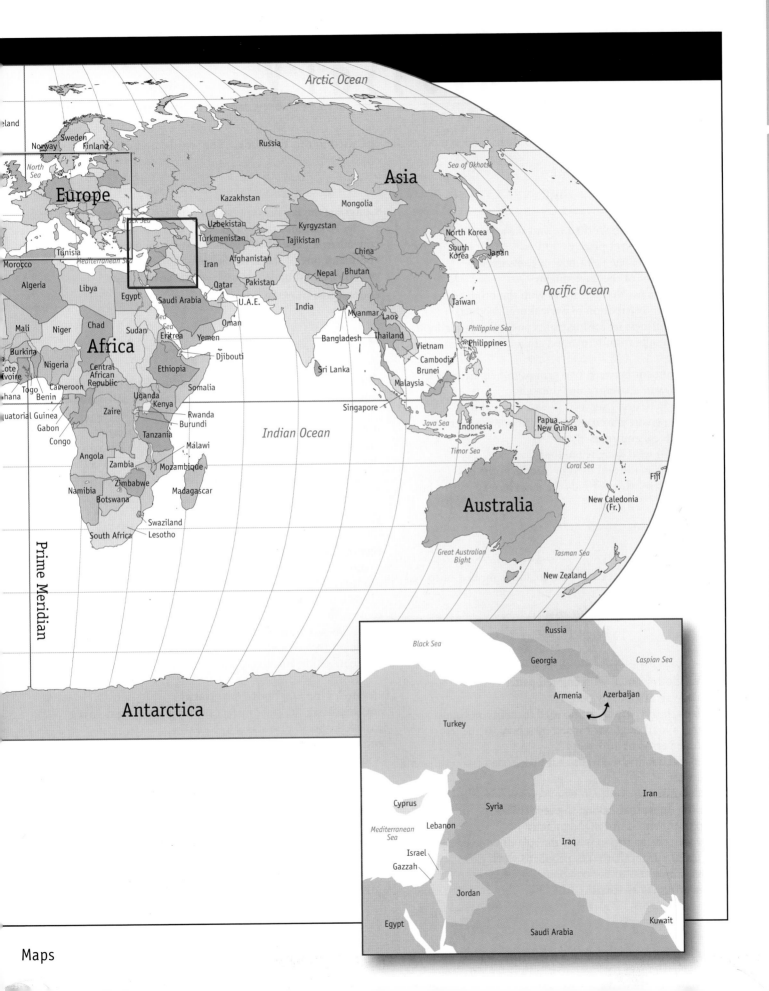

Glossary

The definitions given here are for the **Words to Understand** as they are used in this textbook. The words are highlighted in yellow where they first appear in the book.

A

abolitionist: a person who worked to end slavery

absolute location: an exact place or address

adapt: to adjust; to change to fit new circumstances

agency: a department of the government

agribusiness: a business that has to do with the production, processing, and distribution of agricultural products

agriculture: the business of raising plants and animals for food

alcohol: a drink made from fermented grain or fruit; rum, whisky, wine, or beer

alliance: an agreement between two groups to help each other

ally: a friend; in war, a country on your side

ambitious: eagerly desiring success, power, or wealth

archaeologist: a person who tries to learn about the past by studying artifacts and ruins

architect: a person who designs buildings

artifact: something made and used by people in the past

auction: a sale where whoever bids the most money gets to buy the item

B

barge: a large flat boat that carries cargo and is pushed or towed by another boat

barter: to trade what you have for what you want

C

calico: cotton cloth printed with colored patterns

canal: a waterway dug out by people

canvas: a thick, heavy woven fabric used for tents and sails

cargo: freight; a load of goods carried by a boat, plane, etc.

century: a time period of 100 years

character: moral quality; the traits that make one person different from another

chronological order: the order in which events happened

civil rights: the rights that belong to every citizen

civilian: a person who is not in the military

colony: a settlement or region under the rule of another country

commuter train: a train that takes people to work each day

competition: in business, other companies producing and selling the same products as you do

Congress: the lawmaking body of the United States consisting of the House and the Senate

consumer: a person who spends money on goods and services

continent: one of the seven large land masses of the earth

country: a land under the rule of one government

courageous: showing bravery

D

decade: a period of 10 years

delegate: a person chosen to speak or act for a group of people

depression: a time when there are not enough jobs and people are poor

descendents: the people who come after an ancestor

discrimination: prejudiced treatment of people who are different

document: an official written paper such as a birth certificate, will, passport, deed, etc.

E

economics: the study of how people make, sell, buy, and use goods and services

economy: the management of resources and the prosperity of a region or a country

ecosystem: a community of living things that interact and depend upon each other

edible: fit to be eaten as food

efficient: acting effectively with the least amount of time and effort

elevated: raised up above the ground

emancipation: the state or fact of being freed from slavery

enslaved: forced into slavery

entrepreneur: a person willing to take the risk of starting and running a business

environment: the air, water, minerals, and living things of a place

ethnic: relating to a minority race or group

executive branch: the branch of government that carries out the laws

exhibit: to display or show

export: to ship out of the country

expository: writing to explain

F

federal: a union of states under a central government
finance: having to do with money
frontier: the edge of settled territory

G

gangster: a member of a gang of criminals
generator: a machine that produces electricity
geography: the study of the earth and the people, plants, and animals living on it
glacier: a large, slow-moving mass of ice
global: having to do with the whole world
glossary: a list of words and their meanings
goods: products that are made, bought, and sold
governor: the top leader of state government

H

habitat: the natural environment of a living thing
hemisphere: half of the earth
historian: a person who studies the past
Holocaust: the mass killing of Jews and others in concentration camps during World War II
human feature: features made by people
humid: containing a large amount of moisture

I

immigrant: a person who moves into a country to live
immoral: not moral; not acting according to correct principles
import: to bring into a country
independence: freedom from the rule of another
index: a list of subjects and page numbers in the back of a book
infested: to have a great number of unwanted insects or animals
insurance: a promise to pay expenses in case of accident or illness
intersection: the place where two streets cross
interstate: between states

J-K-L

judicial: the branch of government that interprets laws and sets punishments
jury: a group of people who listen to a case and decide if a person is guilty or not
justice: fairness
legend: a story passed down from one generation to the next
legislators: people who are elected by citizens to make laws
liberty: freedom
linen: a cloth made from the flax plant
livestock: animals such as cows and pigs raised for food

logo: a printed design that identifies a business

M

massacre: the horrible, cruel killing of many people
memorize: to commit to memory
merchant: one who buys and sells goods; a store keeper
midway: halfway
military: the armed forces of a nation
mill: a building where machines grind grain into flour or saw logs into lumber; a building with machines for manufacturing
moderate climate: where there are not wide extremes

N

narrative: a fictional story
national: having to do with the whole nation
natural feature: a feature of the land that is made by nature
natural resources: useful resources provided by nature, such as water, soil, sand, gravel, minerals, grasses and trees
Northerner: during the Civil War, a person who lived in the North, or the Union

O-P-Q

oral history: history told out loud
ordinance: a rule made by a local government
permanent: lasting a very long time
pioneer: the first person to do something; one of the first settlers in a place
plantation: a very large farm in the South
portage: carrying furs from one place to the other
poverty: not having enough money for basic needs
prairie: the mostly flat land of the Midwest
precipitation: water that falls to the earth in the form of rain, snow, sleet, or hail
prejudice: an opinion made before the facts are known; a judgment made only on the basis of race or religion
primary source: a source that was made or written at the time
processing: changing basic food into other food products
proclamation: an official announcement
products: items made to be bought and used
protest: to complain; to speak out against what is being done
public schools: schools provided by the government

R

ration: a fixed amount of food for a day or a week
rebellion: a fight against those in power
recite: to say out loud
recycle: to use again; to save to use again
reference books: books that contain information

refrigerated: cooled; trucks or train cars that keep foods cold

refuges: people who flee a country for safety

reject: to refuse or turn down

relative location: the location of a place in relation to other places or landmarks

relatives: people who are related to each other

republic: a state in which the people elect representatives to make the laws

reservation: a place set aside for Indians to live on

reservoir: man-make lake formed when river water backs up behind a dam

responsibility: reliability or dependability

revolution: when citizens fight to take over their government

riot: a noisy, violent disturbance caused by a group of angry people

rival: a person or group who competes with another person or group

S

scarcity: when there is not enough of something

score: a time period of 20 years

secede: to break away from a country

secondary source: information produced at a later time by using primary sources

segregation: the separation of groups by race

self-propelled: moved by its own engine, motor, etc.

service: in economics, the work done for others in exchange for money

settler: a person who builds a home and lives there

shaman: an Indian leader who heals the sick and gives spiritual advice

skyscraper: a very tall building

slaughter: to kill animals and prepare the meat for sale

slums: areas of very poor and run-down housing

sod: dirt held together with roots and grass

Southerner: during the Civil War, people who lived in the South and were part of the Confederacy

specialization: when workers become expert at one kind or part of a job

starve: to be extremely hungry, or to die from lack of food

steamboat: a boat run by steam

stockyard: a fenced place where cattle are held before they are slaughtered

strike: when workers stop working until at least part of their demands are met

submarine: a boat that moves underwater

supply and demand: a rule in economics that explains the relationship between price, production, availability, and demand of goods and services

surplus: left-over or extra

surrender: to give up, especially in time of war

surveyor: a person who measures and marks off the land

T

table of contents: in a book, a list of chapters and the pages they start on

tax: the money citizens must pay to a government

tenement: a run-down apartment building

territory: a region of land ruled by a national government; not a state

terrorist: a person who commits acts of violence against a country

tourism: the business of providing visitors with food, hotels, transportation, and entertainment

trade-off: the decision to give something up in order to buy something else

treaty: an official agreement between groups of people, usually to gain land or end a war

U-V-W

union: an alliance of workers to get better working conditions and higher pay

valid: legally effective or binding

volunteer: to agree to work without pay

voyageur: a man who transported furs from one place to another by boat

Index

Credits

The following abbreviations are used for sources where several images were obtained:

ALPL - Abraham Lincoln Presidential Library
CHS - Chicago Historical Society
DT - DreamsTime.com
GR - Gary Rasmussen
Granger - The Granger Collection, New York
ISHL - Illinois State Historical Library
iS - iStockPhoto.com
JB - Jon Burton
LOC - Library of Congress Prints and Photographs division
NA - Neal Anderson
NARA - National Archives
NWPA - North Wind Picture Archives
PTG - PhotosToGo.com
SS - ShutterStock.com
WHS - Wisconsin Historical Society

All other images are from Gibbs Smith, Publisher Archives, Photos.com or Clipart.com.

Prelims: iv SS/Madeleine Openshaw, v SS/APSchorr, vi-vii GR
Chapter One: 4 LOC, 10 (L) SS/Clara Natoli, (R) WVAS Ruth Yeager Collection, 11 (TR) NARA, 13 SS/John Austin, 15 (T) SS/B. Speckart, (BL) James P. Rowan, (BR) SS/Steve Broer. **Chapter Two:** 16-17 SS/Tony Campbell, 24 (L-R) SS/ Dan Bri_ki, SS/Steve Geer, SS/Steve Geer, SS/Jim Jurica, 26 NA, 27 SS/Olga Perevalova, 28 (L) SS/Peter Blazek, (R) SS/Matej Krajcovic, 29 (TL) iS/Steve Geer, (TR) iS/Jim Jurica, (CL) DT/Ed Baumgarten, (CR) SS/Stock, (BL) DT/Dave Sinn, (BR) James P. Rowan, 31 (TL) iS/Maya Moody, (TR) James P. Rowan, (BL) James P. Rowan, (BR) iS/Judy Foldetta, 32 (L) SS/Neil Webster, (R) SS/Zavodskov Anatoliy Nikolaevich, 32-33 SS/Tony Campbell, 33 (L) SS/Tomasz Szymandski, (C) iS/Steve Geer, (R) SS/Hway Kiong Lim, 34 SS/Jim Jurica, 35 GR, 37 (T) SS/C. Paquin, (background) SS/Karlis Ustups, (B) SS/Graham Taylor, 38 (T) SS/khwi, 39 (TL) SS/Sharon Meredith, (TR) SS/Jan van Broekhoven, (BL) SS/Mark Bond, (BR) SS/Darrell Young, 40 (TL) SS/Nicholas Sutcliffe, (BL) SS/Maigi, (R) SS/Ivars Zoinerovies, 41 JB, 42 SS/Jim Jurica, 43 SS/Jaimie Duplass. **Chapter Three:** 46-47 NA, 48 GR, 49 (T) SS/Michele Bagdon, (B) NA, 50 (T) Hopewell Culture National Historical Park NPS, (B) Werner Forman/CORBIS, 50-51 National Park Service, 51 Michigan Department of State Archives, 52 (TL) SS/Krysztof Niediedki, (CL) SS/Trout55, (CR) SS/Michael Ledray, (TR) SS/Elena Ray, (B) SS/Glen Jones, 53-55 Cahokia Mounds State Historic Site, paintings by Don Vanderbeek, 59 (T) GR, (B) University of Oklahoma Special Collections, 60 GR, 61 (T) LOC, (B) Courtesy Illinois State Museum, photographer: Robert E. Warren, 63 LOC, 64 LOC, 66 GR, 68 GR. **Chapter Four:** 70-71 Picture Collection, The Branch Libraries, The New York Public Library, Astor, Lenox and Tilden Foundations, 74 Bettmann/CORBIS, 76 Bettmann/CORBIS, 77 Granger, 78 Granger, 80-81 Corel Professional Photos, National Archives of Canada, 81 (T) GR, 82 David Wright, 83 (T) GR, (B) LOC, 84 ISHL, 86-87 NWPA, 88 Photography Collection, Miriam and Ira D. Wallach Division of Art, Prints and Photographs, The New York Public Library, Astor, Lenox and Tilden Foundations, 90 NWPA. **Chapter Five:** 92-93 Peter Harholdt/CORBIS, 96 LOC, 97 Susan Myers, 98 Stapleton Collection/CORBIS, 99 Bettmann/CORBIS, 101 GR, 102 LOC, 103 LOC, 105 Museum of the City of New York/CORBIS, 106 (R) NWPA, 107 (T) SS/Laura Stone, (L) LOC, (R) GR, 109 LOC, 110 (T) State Historical Society of Missouri, (B) GR, 112 Smithsonian Museum, 113 Bettmann/CORBIS. **Chapter Six:** 116-117 NWPA, 118 (R) GR, 119 LOC, 120 (T) NWPA, 122 Granger, 123 LOC, 126 Collection of U.S. House of Representatives, 127 ALPL, 128 Granger, 129 ISHL, 130 NWPA, 131 CHS, 133 ISHL, 134 ISHL, 135 (TL) DT/Baument, (TC) PTG/Terri Froelich, (TR) ISHL, (BR) ISHL, 137 Granger, 138 Minnesota Historical Society, Painting by Henry Lewis, 139 WHS, 140 LOC, 141 GR. **Chapter Seven:** 142-143 ISHL, 144 NWPA, 146 JB, 147 ALPL, 148 (T) LOC, (B) CORBIS, 149 C&O Canal Museum, 150 (T) NWPA, (B) GR, 151 CHS, 154 CORBIS, 155 Bettmann/CORBIS, 156 WHS, 157 (T) WHS, 158 (L) Granger, (R) Bettmann/CORBIS, 159 LOC, 160 LOC, 161 (T) Glen Hopkinson, (B) NARA, 162 Bishop Hill State Historic Site, 163 (TR) SS/Joy Fera, (B) SS/Leon Ritter. **Chapter Eight:** 166-167 LOC, 168 JB, 169 (T) NWPA, (B) LOC, 170 (R) NWPA, 171 LOC, 172 (B) NWPA, 173 NWPA, 174 NWPA, 175 LOC, 177 Granger, 178 LOC, 179 (T) LOC, (B) NWPA, 180 LOC, 181 (T) Bettmann/CORBIS, (B) LOC, 182-183 LOC, 184 (T) SS/Jim Parkin, 186 (T) ISHL, (B) LOC, 187 (R) ISHL, 188 (T) National Park Service, (B) NARA, 190 SS/Jeremy R. Smith, 191 LOC. **Chapter Nine:** 194-195 Granger, 196 (L) NWPA, (R) WHS, 197 LOC, 198 (L) SS/Joy Brown, (R) LOC, 199 Chicago Public Library, 200 US Postal Service, Image provided by The Friends of the Lakeview Post Office Mural, 201 LOC, 202 JB, 203 (L) Bettmann/CORBIS, (R) SS/Simon Detjen Schmidt, 204 (T) WHS, (BL) SS/Leslie Stodden, (BR) LOC, 205 Bettmann/CORBIS, 207 (T) Lee Maxwell's Washing Machine Museum www.oldewash.com, (B) PTG/Ewing Galloway, 208 (L) SS/R. Gino Santa Maria, (R) Bettmann/CORBIS, 209 (L) E.O. Hoppe/CORBIS, (R) SS/Timothy Gray, 210 LOC, 211 ISHL, 212 LOC, 213 NWPA, 214 CHS, 215 LOC, 216 LOC, 217 CHS, 218 (T) LOC, (B) Bettmann/CORBIS, 219 (L) ISHL, (R) GR, 220 LOC, 222-223 SS/Costin Cojocaru, 223 SS/Madeleine Openshaw, 224 Granger, 225 (T) CHS, (B) LOC, 226 (T) LOC, CHS, 227 (L) Angelo Homak/CORBIS, (R) SS/Melissa Bouyounan, 228 LOC, 229 LOC. **Chapter Ten:** 232-233 Gideon Mendel/CORBIS, 234 (L) Bettmann/CORBIS, (R) LOC, 235 ISHL, 236 (L) Underwood & Underwood/CORBIS, (C) CHS, (R) LOC, 237 Bettmann/CORBIS, 238 PTG/Ewing Galloway, 239 Underwood & Underwood/CORBIS, 241 (L) FDR Presidential Library, (TR) LOC, 242 (T) Bettmann/CORBIS, (B) NARA, 243 H. Armstrong Roberts/CORBIS, 244 Courtesy of Vivian G. Harsh Research Collection, Carter G. Woodson Regional Library, Chicago Public Library, 245 (T, C) LOC, (B) Bettmann/CORBIS, 246 Chicago Daily Defender, 247 LOC, 248 (L) Chicago Daily Defender, (R) General Research & Reference Division, Schomburg Center for Research in Black Culture, The New York Public Library, Astor, Lenox and Tilden Foundations, 249 Bettmann/CORBIS, 250 (T, BR) LOC, (BL) Bettmann/CORBIS, 251 (L) NARA, (R) LOC, 252 (L) The Herald Dispatch, (R) U.S. Air Force Photo/Master Sgt. Scott Wagers, 253 iS/Bonnie Jacobs, 254 iS/Daniela Andreea Spyropoulos. **Chapter Eleven:** 256-257 Layne Kennedy/CORBIS, 258 (L) SS/Keith Muratori, (R) iS/Ronnie Comeau, 295 (T) SS/Robert F. Balazik, (B) SS/Natalia Bratslavsky, 266-267 JB, 262 LOC, 263 (T) LOC, (B) NARA, 264 JB, 265 (T) FEMA/Win Henderson, (B) FEMA/Ed Edahl, 266-267 JB, 269 White House/Susan Sterner, 270 JB, 271 ALPL, 273 James P. Rowan, 274-275 Bettmann/CORBIS. **Chapter Twelve:** 278-279 Ralf-Finn Hestoft/CORBIS, 280 SS/GeoM, 281 (T) SS/Mats, (B) SS/Marcin Balcerzak, 282-283 JB, 284 Bettmann/CORBIS, 286 SS/Brian McEntire, 287 Alan Schein Photography/CORBIS, 288 (L) SS/Svetlana Larina, (R) SS/William Casey, 289 SS/Magdalena Kucova, 290 (L) iS/Suzannah Skelton, (R) SS/WizData, Inc., 291 (L) Courtesy of Eli's Cheesecake, (C) iS/Marco Pat, (R) Kim Komenich/San Francisco Chronicle/CORBIS, 292 (T) SS/A&O Maksymenko, (B) SS/Marka Wariatka, 293 SS/Chad Bontrager, 294 SS/Travis Klein.